Inside Modernism

Inside Modernism

Relativity Theory, Cubism, Narrative

Thomas Vargish and Delo E. Mook

Yale University Press
New Haven and London

Set in Goudy by Print Line, New Delhi
Printed in Hong Kong through Worldprint

Library of Congress Cataloging-in-Publication Data
Vargish, Thomas.
    Inside Modernism: relativity theory, cubism, narrative/by Thomas Vargish and Delo E. Mook.
    Includes bibliographical references and index.
    ISBN 0–300–07613–4 (cloth: alk. paper)
    1. Modernism (Aesthetics)   I. Mook, Delo E., 1942–
II. Title.
BH301.M54V37   1999
700′.4112—dc21   98–54162
                                                                          CIP

A catalogue record for this book is available from the British Library

10 9 8 7 6 5 4 3 2 1

For kind permission to reprint extracts from *The Great Wall of China* (1974) and *The Penal Colony: Stories and Short Pieces* (1976), both by Franz Kafka, the authors and publishers gratefully acknowledge Random House, Inc.

To
Elizabeth Deeds Ermarth
and
Kathryn Hiltner Mook

Contents

Plates

Preface

This book has two aims: to offer a revised definition of Modernism and to propose a coherent method for defining periods of intellectual and cultural history. An element of this method is to acknowledge at the outset that although we have adhered to strict scholarly standards throughout we do not claim that our definition of Modernism is in any sense final. We do not intend it to be final, or irrefutable, or literally conclusive. We want our definition of Modernism to be suggestive and persuasive. Like all works of cultural and intellectual history, our definition is a construction. It differs from other constructions that attempt to define Modernism by the greater range of its sources, its freedom from conventional intellectual boundaries, the immediacy of its illustrations, and perhaps by its quality of concrete, hands-on analysis.

Although we enter this disclaimer against trying to provide an absolute or empirically verifiable structure to Modernism, we believe that our definition of the period has a very broad application. The values we identify as constituting Modernism can be shown to characterize in some significant degree *all* manifestations of advanced intellectual activity during this period, including those not analyzed in this book. By examining certain radical and analogous events in three areas of rapid development – in physics, in the visual arts, and in literature – we propose a new and more complete definition than has yet been published. We thus address our discussion to readers interested in a wide variety of creative and scholarly disciplines and encourage them to relate what they find here to their areas of specialization. With this in mind, we have taken pains to limit the use of jargon and to define in general language what specialized terminology we do use. If we have succeeded, readers interested in diverse areas of cultural history should be able to follow the argument everywhere.

But where are these readers? Who exactly is interested in a broad historical definition of Modernism? There are two preliminary problems with interdisciplinary studies: one is method and the other is marketing. They go together. In the book that launched Dickens's career in 1837, the ambitious editor of the *Eatanswill Gazette* boasts to Mr. Pickwick of the talents of his "critic" as demonstrated in a "copious review of a work on Chinese metaphysics":

> "He read up for the subject, at my desire, in the Encyclopedia Britannica."
>
> "Indeed!" said Mr. Pickwick; "I was not aware that that valuable work contained any information respecting Chinese metaphysics."
>
> "He read, sir," rejoined Pott, laying his hand on Mr. Pickwick's knee, and looking round with a smile of intellectual superiority, "he read for metaphysics under the letter M, and for China under the letter C, and combined his information, sir!"[1]

If we ignore a certain cultural implausibility in the subject itself, we can see that Pott and his staff critic have arrived at a very low-budget shortcut to the appearance of a learned article. Mr Pickwick affects some embarrassment at his ignorance of it.

Since Dickens's time, the Eatanswill method has been adopted by some practitioners of what has come to be called "interdisciplinary studies," and some deplorable absurdities have resulted – the most familiar ones based on misunderstandings by humanists of the actual implications of twentieth-century scientific theory, especially Relativity Theory, but also misunderstandings of the methods and aims of the humanities and social sciences on the part of natural scientists. Nevertheless the absurdity and ignorance of some interdisciplinary work has been more than balanced by excellent and perceptive analyses by other writers, many of whom receive acknowledgment in the following chapters. In any case, no one would claim that interdisciplinary studies hold a monopoly on academic absurdity and ignorance. More damaging to the present and future of interdisciplinary studies is the continued and probably still growing hegemony of established departments and programs, both in the United States and in Europe. The traditional disciplinary resistance to innovation has hardened during the recent decades of budgetary cutbacks, a financial desiccation dangerous to the organizational status quo and to those dependent on it. Under these conditions new intellectual ventures are perceived as threatening unless they fit into the established system. Organizational calcification encourages intellectual thrombosis.

For example, despite the positive rhetoric of agencies like the National Sciences Foundation and National Endowment for the Humanities, and despite programs putatively earmarked for (say) studies of science and art, it is in practice very difficult to win a grant for an authentically interdisciplinary project. Partly this is due to the tendency of such bodies to celebrate their grant-giving function even when they have pathetically little money to disburse. But there is also again a structural problem. If experts trained in one area see the point of the project, those in the other areas of the proposed study find its aims less articulate. Any single proposal that requires work in traditionally unassociated disciplines finds it hard to earn more than a B+ from any single

---

1   Charles Dickens, *The Posthumous Papers of the Pickwick Club*, p. 734 (Chapter 51).

review committee, and as everyone knows B+ does not get the money. Thus, in addition to bucking the naturally conservative nature of committee decisions applications for grants in interdisciplinary studies get judged on the basis of methodologies and aims alien to the projects in question. And if a part of the project is to establish a fresh methodology or even to clarify an existing one the application may be denied not on lack of merit but simply because the means for judging its value do not yet exist. The situation has ironies richly evocative of those Kafka protagonists who request validation on grounds that the validating bureaucracy does not acknowledge.

The same ironic comedy may be played out at the level of publication. If despite the shortage of support the project is completed (as would never happen in Kafka) and submitted for publication, the problem of audience arises. Who will read it? Or, to put the question in terms of academic *realpolitik*, who will feel they ought to read it? If the project (like the present study) deals with (say) physics, painting, and fiction then physicists or art historians or literature scholars can dismiss the work as being two-thirds out of their area of specialization or the field for which they hold academic responsibility. And how does a publisher find editors and readers who can take on the decision-making process? We can document the case of such an interdisciplinary work being proposed to a distinguished academic publisher. The director of this university press (which had already enjoyed a long and prosperous relation to the authors of the new project) wrote that he duly showed the proposal to his art history editor, his literature editor, and his physics editor. As none of these editors could speak with enthusiasm for the proposed book, he was unable to go further with it. He had in fact looked up art under A, physics under P, fiction under F and failed to find means for judging the result. The *Eatanswill Gazette*, in its opportunistic simplicity, was more advanced.

This book offers itself on two major premisses – that much serious cultural history must be interdisciplinary and that for such history to see daylight some publishers and some readers must be prepared to take chances. Our subject, Modernism, is all about taking such chances. If physicists, artists, and writers at the beginning of the twentieth century had not been willing to take chances with their proposed audiences Modernism would not have come into being and readers would be spared problematic studies like this one. Taking chances, however, does not mean indulging in free speculation or drawing murky analogies among various disciplines without rigorous semantic and scholarly standards. Nor does it mean jettisoning past scholarship and its achievement. When Picasso painted *Les Demoiselles d'Avignon* or Einstein set out the Special Theory they were able to draw on a history of achievement in the plastic arts and in the natural sciences of great depth and continuing power. Their achievements demonstrate not only a fierce intellectual courage in departing from aspects of those traditions but also a discriminating under-standing of and respect for them.

One final problem in finding an audience has to do with the superficiality of general education in the natural sciences and with the inherently counter-intuitive nature of Relativity Theory. This problem, however, we anticipated by writing and publishing *Inside Relativity* (Princeton University Press, 1987). This extensive explanation of Einstein's theories for non-scientists was a spinoff of the present project: we needed to be able to cite a lucid, correct, complete source of information for readers who want the kind of familiar direct contact with the physics that they might already have or could acquire with the painting and fiction. We refer to *Inside Relativity* freely throughout, but no reader will need to consult it in order to follow our argument in the present work.

We are grateful to our home institutions, the University of Maryland Baltimore County and Dartmouth College, for providing travel and research support. Much of this went toward the necessary and happy task of viewing in the original the paintings we discuss in the following chapters. We wish to acknowledge fully the immense opportunities offered by the numerous public collections of modernist art and sculpture, but most especially those at the Museum of Modern Art in New York, the Musée Picasso and the Musée National d'Art Moderne, Centre Georges Pompidou, in Paris, and the Kunstmuseum in Basel.

John Nicoll, Managing Director of Yale University Press in London, gave wise and patient counsel as we steered this project toward publication, and Candida Brazil as Managing Editor helped us solve the sometimes unprecedented technical and stylistic difficulties.

Finally we offer our special thanks to Elizabeth Deeds Ermarth, Saintsbury Professor of English Literature at the University of Edinburgh, for her continuing intellectual support of the project and her careful criticism of our manuscript during the several epochs of its composition.

Chapter 1 Defining Modernism

> "Like" and "like" and "like" – but what is the thing that
> lies beneath the semblance of the thing?
>
> Virginia Woolf, *The Waves*

Chronological Focus

Modernism as an aesthetic, as an ethos, and as a mode of perception has been defined many times. We will avoid taking the space that would be absorbed by an attempt to position our definition with respect to the numerous previous studies. In any case, the various attempts to conceptualize Modernism have been set forth recently and with distinction.[1] Specialists will soon judge whether we have anything to add to the study of the period and non-specialists will not miss detailed discussion of the relation of this to previous scholarship. The considerable body of existing scholarly and critical works forms the background for this one, though they are cited only when we find their influence on our findings specific and direct.

We try as well to avoid entering the lists of specialized controversy, even when our work touches on it. For example, it is a question of considerable interest and of even greater disputation to what degree French art during the nineteenth century progressively abandoned or devalued the subject matter of painting in the interest of raising attention to manner or treatment. We do not take a scholarly position on this controversy – which becomes highly involved aesthetically and epistemologically. It is enough for the broader canvas of our cultural history that certain artists began to treat the subject of their paintings, the objects painted, in ways that revealed a change in values and that we can support this change by reference to their paintings and in many cases by what they or their contemporaries said about their paintings. Similarly, it may or may not be the case that Kafka owes the ironic neo-allegorical quality of his writing to certain narrative traditions found in Judaism. The question is important, but not to this book. What is important to this book is whether Kafka's narrative techniques support certain values we identify as

---

1. Especially by Astradur Eysteinsson in *The Concept of Modernism*, which includes a definitive bibliography; and earlier in such collections of historical essays as the valuable *Modernism*, edited by Malcolm Bradbury and James McFarlane.

defining Modernism and whether we can demonstrate that they do. The fact that such techniques may have their origin in ancient narrative practice is entirely compatible with our attention to them in defining Modernism. Similarly, the riddle of whether Einstein made use of the Michelson–Morley experiment for his paper on Special Relativity certainly has considerable importance for the history of science, but we do not solve it here.[2]

We begin our definition with chronological parameters. In the analysis of Modernism the chronological definition of the period can pose problems for scholars as well as for general readers. The *Modern* period has variously been identified as everything following the medieval period, or as initiated by the Renaissance, or as enabled by the French Revolution, or as imposed by industrialism. Much can be said for calling each of these historical developments "modern," and from the study of each development valuable conceptions of modernity have emerged. But for the purposes of this study we follow a more constrained practice of historians of art and literature: the historical period we term "Modernism" falls between the 1880s and World War II. In this chronological frame, we examine Modernism as a culture made up of specialized but comparable phenomena at the forefront of intellectual change – a culture acutely aware of its own innovation. In the definition that emerges, Modernism succeeds high nineteenth-century intellectual conventions that we regard as late Realism and precedes (and itself helps to define) a distinguishable Postmodernism. Our Modernism is thus a period with clearly set historical limits, and one that has come to an end. Our chronology has the value of being specific and in general use by specialists in the diverse fields most engaged here. It marks widely acknowledged scientific, aesthetic, and intellectual revolutions and it locates the threshold of that dramatic revision of values and modes of perception we are now experiencing.

In distinguishing Modernism from nineteenth-century Realism we do not claim that a value or technique or event must be entirely new and unique. Successful students of intellectual and cultural history quickly learn to avoid attaching their generalizations too rigorously to specific dates. A value of Modernism is not a characteristic because it never appeared before (and thus had to be invented by modernists) but because it becomes a dominant theme or quality of the period in ways that distinguish it there from earlier appearances. It is equally true that certain characteristics of a period or movement will outlast the general outlines of the period or movement, and that movements will continue with considerable momentum to overlap other movements. We see examples of these phenomena in the chapters that follow. In our practice of cultural history, the fact that a work or a value appears to be an anachronism means, if it means anything, that it violates the historical preconceptions of

2. At various points we cite authorities who have taken positions on controversies of various kinds – aesthetic, political, philosophical. The scope of our study, however, means that we are not interested in (though we may be aware of) position-taking on most points limited to a specialization. We cite authorities only to illustrate or to help validate our own explicit arguments. For similar reasons we choose quotations for their clarity rather than their theoretical currency.

the observer. As Ortega put it in a study of modernist art, "It would be tedious to warn at the foot of each page that each of the features here pointed out as essential to modern art must be understood as existing in the form of a predominant propensity, not of an absolute property." But at the same time we also share his premiss that "it is amazing how compact a unity every historical epoch presents throughout its various manifestations."[3]

Finally, to attack briefly the question of cultural as opposed to intellectual history as it bears on this study, we need to make clear that the phenomena that define Modernism for us are exclusively made up of advanced intellectual and artistic activity on the very front lines of cultural development. Should we call this "intellectual history" or "cultural history"? Intellectual history still suggests the development of ideas by means of direct conscious influence of one thinker on another, or else by clots of philosophical or scientific activity that are again highly articulate and self-aware. The interdisciplinary values that emerge for us as defining Modernism meet the requirement of being contemporaneous but rarely that of conscious influence or even of systematic articulation in a common disciplinary vocabulary. We therefore prefer the term "cultural history," even though our study is limited to the upper and outer reaches of culture and the events we discuss have little direct relation to the daily lives of the great mass of humankind during the period. We regard what we are doing as cultural history although the culture analyzed is not popular culture. Of course by now these developments have directly or indirectly influenced the lives of everyone on earth, especially through Relativity Theory but also with the altered nature of space and time as manifested in art and literature.

Cultural Diagnostics and Values

We define Modernism through a selective comparative analysis of physics, painting, and fiction. These fields are so different in their language, their objects of attention, and their means of valorizing achievement that their selection requires some explanation here. In part it is precisely their disciplinary "conceptual distance" from each other that makes comparison valuable.[4] A central premiss of our study is that part of the confusion surrounding the

---

3. José Ortega Y Gasset, *The Dehumanization of Art*, pp. 37n., 4.
4. "Conceptual distance" is a formulation used by Stephen Kern in his pioneering work, *The Culture of Time and Space*: "In the process of integrating such an array of sources, I use a working principle of *conceptual distance*. Thus, there is greater conceptual distance between the thinking of an architect and that of a philosopher on a given subject than there is between the thinking of two philosophers, and I assume that any generalization about the thinking of an age is the more persuasive the greater the conceptual distance between the sources on which it is based. However the distance must not be too great or the juxtaposition becomes forced" (p.7; as in all quotations throughout this book, italics are the original author's, not ours). We differ from Kern in finding that so long as common values can be clearly articulated the apparent distance between fields – which often has little epistemological basis – can be regarded as secondary: as long as the generalizations can be well supported and articulated no juxtaposition need be dismissed as "forced."

definition of Modernism (within each field as well as among fields) is due to the fact that Modernism was inherently subdisciplinary or transdisciplinary in its operation and to define it, to identify it, and to understand it requires a multidisciplinary approach. If it can be shown that modernist physics, painting, and fiction all share in a high degree a recognizable, definable value then that value may be considered a constituent of Modernism, and not merely field-specific to a particular activity.

In order to arrive at such a comprehensive description of Modernism we choose from the wide range of possibilities three *cultural diagnostics*; that is, advanced intellectual activities that serve to reveal the underlying *values* of the period. By cultural diagnostic we mean any human activity or production that may be analyzed in order to abstract the historically defining values. Our diagnostics in this study include Relativity Theory, Cubism, and certain modernist narrative. In selecting these three manifestations of Modernism we do not aim at disclosing direct causal linkages among them. It is not part of our endeavor to discover whether Einstein influenced Kafka when they were in Prague at the same time or how seriously Proust took Poincaré. It proves important in interdisciplinary studies to distinguish the kind of work that aims at finding direct, causal influences from the quite different goals and methods employed here.

We can clarify this by taking one well-researched example. In discussing cubist art and Relativity Theory in physics there is a spectrum of statements that can be made relating these two creative efforts: such statements might range from "There is a provable causal connection between the creation of Relativity Theory and the development of Cubism" to "There is no connection of any sort between relativity and Cubism." We know of no published claim of the first sort, although art historian Paul Laporte seems to have been accused of making one.[5] In fact a careful reading of Laporte's papers shows his actual claim to be closely allied to those we will make, but it is our hope not to be misunderstood as he was. It is a fact that the claim of a causal connection between Cubism and Relativity Theory is not substantiated by any documented evidence; furthermore, Linda Henderson formulates an entirely convincing argument that such a connection did not exist.[6] It does not follow, however, that "Cubism has nothing to do with the Theory of Relativity and that is the end of the matter," as J. A. Richardson claimed.[7] Cultural history requires a larger view of relationships if it is to explain anything of value. In the words of Gérard Mermoz, "if we are to further our understanding

---

5. Papers relating to this matter are Paul M. Laporte, "Cubism and Relativity with a Letter of Albert Einstein," "Cubism and Science," and "The Space-Time Concept in the Work of Picasso." See also the letter by Paul M. Laporte in reply to that of L. Wynn Chamberlain and George DeWitt Herring, Jr. in *The Magazine of Art*; Linda Dalrymple Henderson, "A New Facet of Cubism: 'The Fourth Dimension' and 'Non-Euclidean Geometry' Reinterpreted," and *The Fourth Dimension and Non-Euclidean Geometry in Modern Art*, especially Appendix A, pp. 353–365.
6. Henderson, *The Fourth Dimension and Non-Euclidean Geometry in Modern Art*.
7. J.A. Richardson, *Modern Art and Scientific Thought*, p. 112.

of the epistemological status of the arts and sciences in a general theory of discourse, the search for influences . . . must be replaced by a study of structural correlations," and succeeding writers have discussed the relation of causality to structure in historical periods at considerable length.[8] Causal linkages, where they actually exist, are to us less interesting and more superficial than the common values that find contemporaneous expression in disparate fields. It is our belief that by studying examples of simultaneous efflorescence of these values in different modes of expression we will hone tools to use in defining cultural identity and in understanding its changes.[9]

The choice of our cultural diagnostics – Relativity Theory, Cubism, and certain selected modernist narratives – is of course a calculated one. These three developments of advanced intellectual culture are almost perfectly contemporaneous. They possess conceptual distance from each other. They cross national boundaries.[10] They develop rapidly, causing what have been termed "revolutions" in their respective disciplines. Individually they possess widely

8. Gérard Mermoz, "On the Synchronism between Artistic and Scientific Ideas and Practices, " p. 135. In her justly influential study *The Cosmic Web: Scientific Field Models and Literary Strategies in the Twentieth Century*, N. Katherine Hayles puts her own field model of cultural history like this: "That Saussure's proposals are remarkably similar in spirit to those occurring about the same time in physics and mathematics does not require that Saussure knew of Einstein's 1905 paper or read *Principia Mathematica*. Indeed, to suppose that such parallels require direct lines of influence is to be wedded to the very notions of causality that a field model renders obsolete. A more accurate and appropriate model for such parallel developments would be a field notion of culture, a societal matrix which consists (in Whitehead's phrase) of a 'climate of opinion' that makes some questions interesting to pursue and renders other uninteresting or irrelevant. Such a field theory of culture has yet to be definitively articulated, and is beyond the scope of this study. But it is already possible to see some of the elements it would include. It would, for example, define more fully how a 'climate of opinion' is established, and demonstrate that it is this climate, rather than direct borrowing or transmission, that is the underlying force guiding intellectual inquiry. This climate would be, of course, as capable of influencing scientific inquiry as it is of guiding any other conceptualization. Such a history would insist that we not be misled by a causal perspective into thinking of correspondences between disciplines as one-way exchanges, for example, by asserting that the change in scientific paradigms *caused* a shift in literary form. In a field model, the interactions are always mutual: the cultural matrix guides individual inquiry at the same time that the inquiry helps to form, or transform, the matrix" (pp. 22–23). We find this description of a climate of opinion highly valuable, in part because it manages to avoid the unfashionable term "Zeitgeist"; but as a formulation to describe a determining ethos, "climate of opinion" is perhaps a little fragile and perhaps implies conscious attitudes and programs. Astradur Eysteinsson points out that "For a more recent attempt to draw strict limits to modernism as a decisive moment in modern literary history, we can look to Douwe W. Fokkema's *Literary History, Modernism, and Postmodernism*. Fokkema argues, much as I have done above, that literary history must direct its attention to the system of conventions that regulates the organization of a text, or in other words to the code that helps produce a certain kind of text at a certain historical juncture" (quoted in Eysteinsson, *The Concept of Modernism*, p. 70).
9. Although we avoid making the extravagant structuralist claim of discovering the ultimate codes that determine reality, we do borrow from structuralist methodology. We clarify our relation to this methodology toward the end of the present chapter.
10. "While everyone seems to agree that as a phenomenon modernism is radically 'international' (although admittedly in the limited sense of that word), constantly cutting across national boundaries, this quality is certainly not reflected in the majority of critical studies of modernism. Such studies are mostly restricted to the very national categories modernism is calling into question, or they are confined to the (only slightly wider) Anglo-American sphere" (Eysteinsson, *The Concept of Modernism*, p. 89).

recognized intrinsic interest giving rise to a substantial body of scholarship and analysis that, while largely field-specific, provides specialized confirmation for our generalizations. And most importantly the three diagnostics are epistemologically synergistic: Relativity is a theory of the measurement of space and time; Cubism revolutionized the treatment of space in visual representation; and modernist fiction explores with remarkable concentration the possibilities of a new temporality in narrative.

In this study, a *value* is an underlying but identifiable characteristic common to the three cultural diagnostics, an impulse or logic capable of generating similarities among the cultural diagnostics. We have identified several such defining characteristics or values: epistemic trauma, contextualization (as a shift away from absolute or normative standards), observation (as replacing "reality" as the subject for representation and analysis), the concept of the "field," a particular kind of abstraction, and reflexivity. Such a bald list necessarily appears eccentric and perhaps formidable, but these values receive careful definition and specific illustration in the chapters that follow. We demonstrate that each characteristic (or value) is functionally common to Relativity Theory, Cubism, and modernist narrative. A play of values emerges that constitutes an original definition of Modernism more comprehensive and accurate than preceding definitions because it is not based on a single discipline with a limited historical and national vocabulary.

This use of "value" stretches and enlarges the term. We considered other possibilities, such as "common characteristic" (which we sometimes employ), "co-operant" (redolent of jargon), and "homology" (a strong candidate but potentially misleading because of its highly specific use in the study of biological evolution).[11] The fact that we lack a single common term for characteristics that are not field-specific and that express the broadest possible preconceptions, prejudices, affirmations, desires, aversions, and fears of a particular culture

---

11. As Stephen Jay Gould defines it, a homology in evolutionary theory bears strong affinities to our term "value": "Similarities come in many forms: some are guides to genealogical inferences; others are pitfalls and dangers. As a basic distinction, we must rigidly separate similarities due to simple inheritance of features present in common ancestors, from similarities arising by separate evolution for the same function. The first kind of similarity, called homology, is the proper guide to descent. I have the same number of neck vertebrae as a giraffe, a mole, and a bat, not (obviously) because we all use our heads in the same way, but because seven is the ancestral number in mammals, and has been retained by descent in nearly all modern groups (sloths and their relatives excepted). The second kind of similarity, called analogy, is the most treacherous obstacle to the search for genealogy. The wings of birds, bats, and pterosaurs share some basic aerodynamic features, but each evolved independently; for no common ancestor of any pair had wings. Distinguishing homology from analogy is the basic activity of genealogical inference. We use a simple rule: rigidly exclude analogies and base genealogies on homology alone. Bats are mammals, not birds" (Gould, *Wonderful Life*, p. 213). Gould's definition of homology offers a remarkably precise comparison with what we mean by "value," including his caution about misleading analogies. We do indeed look for similarities that are more than analogies, that have some dynamic relationship to a common ancestor, a common stem, source, logic. But at this point our hopes for colonizing the word "homology" break down, as our term "value" provides greater depth by denoting *both* a formal and an ancestral commonality. A distinction that works precisely in evolutionary theory fails to survive transference to cultural history.

at a particular period suggests the very considerable resistance interdisciplinary studies meet with up to the present moment. Although "value" can be misinterpreted at the popular level – what, for example, are termed "national values" or "family values" we regard as fuzzy complexes of attitudes perhaps underpinned by what we would call "values" – it can work for us in cultural history. A value is pervasive, almost ubiquitous at a certain level of culture during a certain period. It is subject to identification but not limited to a particular discipline. It has an enabling and a limiting force in the culture. At any given historical period the interplay, the dynamic of values, serves as the broadest and clearest source of identification, running through all the diagnostics of the culture but not subject to the parochialism of a single activity or event.

Probably the greatest source of resistance to our method comes from the sometimes voiced and sometimes latent deeply grounded cultural assumption that the natural sciences operate at a different, more demanding, more "real" epistemological level than the arts. As one of our colleagues (a biologist) put it: "I don't really think science has much to do with culture." Of course philosophers and historians of science have long abandoned such primitive assertions of positive independence, but lingering prejudices remain. These make it advisable for us to state our own position: we believe that scientific theories and models, such as Relativity Theory, are cultural products or constructs, permitted and driven by the values that shape other products and constructs; that such theories and models are fully accessible to methods of description and analysis regularly applied to historical events and works of art and literature. In this study, Relativity Theory gets the same treatment as Cubism and modernist narrative; if it earns a degree of privilege then that privilege derives from its immense resonance throughout the period and not from any claim to have discovered truth about the cosmos.[12] Another way of saying this is to acknowledge that we treat the Special and General Theories of Relativity as important modernist works of art, the most important for our purposes because they contain and express with the highest intensity the values that for us define Modernism.

For the sake of those not versed in physics we feel the need to observe that Relativity Theory can easily be confused with certain forms of cultural

12. We do not treat at length the various epistemological claims of the natural sciences in relation to other cultural manifestations. That is the province of the philosophy of science and this is an historical definition of Modernism. We do discuss Relativity's sphere of analysis, what Einstein called its "truth content," in our Chapter 6 (on Reflexivity). Excessive claims to unique and privileged relation to truth and history are not of course limited to scientists. For example, Wylie Sypher in *Rococo to Cubism in Art and Literature* seems at pains to show (unhistorically) Relativity following the lead of Cubism and even cinema: "The theory of relativity that evolves through F. H. Bradley, Whitehead, Einstein, and modern mathematics is only the scientific expression of 'the new landscape' of the twentieth century, a landscape revealed for the first time in cubist painting and the cinema" (p. 266). Einstein's paper on the Special Theory preceded Picasso's *Les Demoiselles d'Avignon* by two years and Whitehead's treatment of Relativity of course followed Einstein's.

and ethical *relativism*, to which it is only very indirectly related. When we refer to Relativity Theory we mean Einstein's papers on the Special and General Theory and certain developments among physicists and mathematicians, the actual physics and not its application in philosophy or ethics (endeavors that too often lead to embarrassments and absurdities). The physics, like the painting and the fiction, is discussed in terms accessible to non-specialists and even to those destitute of mathematics. We discuss the relation between cultural relativism and Relativity in connection with E. M. Forster's *A Passage to India* in our third chapter.

Another possible objection to our method attaches to the selection of modernist narrative fiction chosen to be our third cultural diagnostic. Relativity Theory as primarily the work of a single scientist (accepted and explained by a small group of contemporaries) and Cubism as the product of a small interactive group of painters living most of the time in Paris both have a well-established coherence and identity. The selection of modernist fiction, however, will appear much more arbitrary, diffuse, loosely defined. It stands out from the other two diagnostics and produces an ungainly asymmetry. We would have found it convenient if a single school of writers, such as those associated with Imagism or Vorticism, had shown the international breadth and consistency of purpose to extend the values we were examining into the modernist representation of time. That we did not find such a school in part derives from the historical fact that writers in the modernist period did not tend to work together with the reciprocity and single-mindedness of physicists or painters – or at least no group of fiction writers (those primarily interested in narrative temporality) together produced a common effort equal in importance and richness.

We meet this difficulty by selecting a number of writers considered modernist by literary historians and avant-garde by their contemporaries, and whose work best illustrates the values of Modernism as we have outlined them. This method may seem somewhat self-serving and there is a sense in which it is. It can give the impression that the narratives selected are selected because they very clearly share the values extracted from the diagnostics of Relativity and Cubism. Such indeed is the case: there are no random samples of modernist narrative analyzed here. But this in itself is not a departure from our method: as we explained earlier, our selection of Relativity Theory and Cubism was itself carefully calculated to yield the values most resonant with our analysis.

Our definition of Modernism is inclusive rather than exclusive. We believe that we identify here the dominant aesthetic and intellectual values of the time. We do not say that nothing else was happening. In any case, as with our selection of Relativity Theory and Cubism, the modernist narratives we examine are illustrative rather than conclusive. The persuasiveness of our argument depends on the persistence and pervasiveness of our identified characteristics throughout the culture and across its disciplinary boundaries.

Crossing these boundaries has presented us with considerable problems of terminology. Because most concise language is field-specific, technical terminology or jargon, we have taken pains to arrive at language that works throughout Modernism – in physics, art, fiction; and indeed in psychology, anthropology, linguistics, mathematics, and philosophy. In our description of values that are not field-specific we have had to employ language that is equally accessible across disciplines, and we do not doubt that the accessibility of certain characteristics to this kind of more general (but still precise) language has affected our definition. In other words, the fact that a value common to Relativity Theory, to Cubism, and to modernist narrative lends itself to expression in language not specific to those fields may favor that value in a study of this kind. But to admit this is to acknowledge what has become an accepted, even celebrated premiss of modernist and postmodernist theory: that there is a sense in which language determines thought, determines even the identity of things and the structure of the cosmos. Given our aims, we could only have chosen values that can be described by a language that crosses disciplinary boundaries. They are the values of our Modernism. Values that remain peculiar to specific disciplines are not values of Modernism in our sense but characteristics of cubist painting or of postclassical physics or of (say) Conrad or Faulkner.

Status of the Definition

As should be evident, we are concerned to suggest a working method for interdisciplinary study of cultural history and to avoid grandiose claims for its application or aggrandizing claims for our own originality. One question that has yet to receive adequate treatment is whether or not the analysis of three cultural diagnostics can be adequate to define a period as complex as Modernism. We have explained why we chose Relativity Theory, Cubism, and fiction and we know that investigation of other cultural diagnostics would certainly also have elicited a modernist dynamic of values. Our research suggests that other diagnostics would have yielded much the same dynamic, much the same values. Some readers would doubtless have preferred studies of psychoanalysis, or linguistics, or phenomenology, or structural anthropology, or twelve-tone music – and in fact Freud, Saussure, Husserl, Lévi-Strauss, and Schönberg all receive passing acknowledgment in what follows. We were doubtless influenced in our selection by our areas of specialization and by what we enjoyed analyzing. We urge readers who would have preferred to find the values of Modernism in other manifestations to go to it. We believe their results will resemble ours: if a value is central to Relativity Theory, to Cubism, and to modernist fiction it will not be alien to other advanced intellectual activity contemporary with these diagnostics.

More important to us than the limitations of specialization and preference are those of depth and complexity. If a study like this one is to succeed, it must engage readers in some specificity, some sense of hands-on play with the values derived. We need the space and the time to notice the influence of Cézanne's late hatchings of color, of Einstein's characteristic laconicism, of Proust's peculiar accounting of loss and gain in time. We want to take our readers *inside* the values and the play of values. What does it mean to shift one's attention from a presumed external reality, the world, to focus on one's observation or measurement of the world? What happened to the way we perceive when we began to shift our ideas of things away from normative standards for objects and events "in themselves" toward the apprehension of objects and events as inextricable from their context? What exactly is modernist reflexivity and how does it generate meaning? These are hard questions of cultural history and analysis; they can be answered, but only if we limit the scope of our discussion.

Our final reason for limiting our diagnostics was the scholarly standard we set for ourselves. So much generalization and off-the-wall speculation has been applied to some of the matters discussed here (the relation of Relativity to Cubism, for example), there were so many openings for self-indulgent assertion, for sloppy or misleading terminology, that we felt the need to be uncompromising in our own methods of verification and substantiation. Of course we expect some of our readers to disagree with certain of our generaliza-tions, but not because of weaknesses in our physics or carelessness in our analysis of paintings or novels. This is why we have examined the originals of all art works discussed: no one can make safe statements about the treatment of space in painting by using reproductions, at least not the treatment of space in early Cubism. We have checked our fiction in the original languages (though quotations are in English): if time is a function of language in fiction (as much current theory insists), then one had better check the time in the original language. We have also checked Einstein's theories in his own papers and not depended on the numerous subsequent explanations, including our own *Inside Relativity*. All this took time and takes space here. To add other diagnostics would have been to decrease the intensity of analysis by diluting our findings with more generalized information.

In cultural history and in interdisciplinary studies mistakes are inevitable: the terrain is often uncharted so that what appears straightforward and plain may be quite the reverse; on the other hand favorable opportunities often disguise themselves as difficulties. One strong example is enough to illustrate both the advances and the pitfalls of comparing disciplines. In *The Modern Theme* (1923), the Spanish philosopher José Ortega y Gasset expounds what he calls "The Doctrine of the Point of View." He imagines two men observing a landscape from discrete viewpoints. Each gives a somewhat different descrip-tion of what he sees. The observers account for these differences by the different positions from which they view the landscape. They do not accuse each other of falsehood: each view is accurate. Nor do they conclude that both views are illusory:

> Such a conclusion would involve belief in the existence of a third landscape, an authentic one, not subject to the same conditions as the other two. Well, an archetypal landscape of this kind does not and cannot exist. Cosmic reality is

such that it can only be seen in a single definite perspective. Perspective is one of the component parts of reality. Far from being a disturbance of its fabric, it is its organizing element.

And he goes on to insist that "all knowledge is knowledge from a definite point of view." There can exist, in Ortega's modernist philosophical analysis of the modern mind, no reality independent of point of view. No reality "possesses in itself, independently of the point of view from which it is observed, a physiognomy of its own." Instead, "reality happens to be, like a landscape, possessed of an infinite number of perspectives, all equally veracious and authentic."[13]

As a modernist intellectual, Ortega is well aware of the similarity of this doctrine of "perspectivity," which he was expounding in his university lectures as early as 1913, and the implications of Einstein's Relativity theories. He refers with understandable pride to the "impressive confirmation" of his doctrine in "the work of Einstein,"[14] especially the inference in the Special Theory that differing measurements of space or time can coexist as correct, that such measurements must be affected by the relative position, the reference frame, of the observer. He is also well aware that the similarities between his doctrine of perspectivity and Special Relativity are due neither to direct influence nor to accident but to some underlying force much larger and less easily formulated. This he terms the "route" followed by "the spirit of man."

So far so good. We have drawn a strong analogy between Ortega's work and Einstein's. Here, however, we must stop: Ortega tends to emphasize an epistemological radicalism in his own thinking that Einstein does not share but that Ortega wants him to share: "In the physics of Einstein our knowledge is absolute; it is reality that is relative."[15] Ortega argues that reality itself is a meaningless conception unless it is a reality made up of points of view. While this bears exciting and significant similarities to the perspectives of the various observers permitted by Relativity Theory, the fact is that Einstein never surrendered his faith in a reality independent of observation – however partial our ability to perceive it might be. For Einstein, the universe was always out there, always existent, always available in its imperturbable integrity for human beings to measure. In the Special Theory, his "principle of relativity" itself implies a reality independent of human apprehension: "the laws of physics must be of such a nature that they apply to systems of reference in any kind of motion."[16] And in his autobiographical notes he speaks of "co-ordination-possibility to the totality of experience."[17]

Our point here is that similarities in the cultural diagnostics need to be treated with caution, and claims of a common value require careful substantiation.

---

13. Ortega, *The Modern Theme*, pp. 89–90, 91–92.
14. Ibid., p. 92n.
15. Ibid., p. 138.
16. See Delo Mook and Thomas Vargish, *Inside Relativity*, pp. 139, 65–67, 170–171.
17. See Philipp G. Frank, "Einstein, Mach and Logical Positivism," and Albert Einstein, "Autobiographical Notes," both in Paul Arthur Schilpp, *Albert Einstein: Philosopher-Scientist*, I, 275, 13.

Plurality of measurement in Special Relativity and perspectivity in Ortega's epistemology look very similar. But there is an immense difference between saying that reality is itself made up of perspectives and that reality can yield differing measurements dependent upon the position of the observer in the field. This difference does in the end both reveal and determine values (in our sense of the word). Einstein and Ortega both go beyond Realism in their advocacy of coexisting, differing but correct plural perspectives. They share in the value shift from reality to observation that we examine in our fourth chapter. This agreement tells us something about Modernism, but not what Ortega thought it told us. Reality in itself is not perspectival for Einstein, and in this he agrees with the great majority of modernist painters and writers, even the most radical. In our Modernism, Einstein is the more representative modernist.

A final question, perhaps the most important, remains: when we have extracted the defining values from our cultural diagnostics – when, that is, we have defined Modernism – what do we have? If this method, which clearly owes something to Structuralism, were entirely structuralist in its claims then we would say that what we have extracted *is* the underlying code by which Modernism moved and functioned, the operational, driving *reality* of Modernism. As Roland Barthes observed, Structuralism has as its major strength the ability to "reconstruct an 'object' in such a way as to manifest thereby the rules of functioning."[18] Saussure, Piaget, Lévi-Strauss, and their allies and colleagues (including such hard-to-place figures as Chomsky in linguistics) seem to believe that such codes exist and can be discovered. They appear to say, and at points do say, that these codes are as real as the laws of Newtonian physics, descriptions of a reality independent of observation, descriptions of the dynamics of such reality. Such codes are not thought to be dependent on historical eventuality (diachronic) but are imagined as always currently functional (synchronic). In Structuralism the codes can thus lay claim to be real in their own right. In practice such universal systems of underlying directives have proved to be vastly difficult if not impossible to find. Structuralists have been much more successful in imagining what such systems might be like than in actually discovering or piecing together the systems themselves. In one very important sense, then, Structuralism harks back to the radical Positivism and scientific optimism of the nineteenth century, to the period that preceded Modernism. Despite its real share in the values of Modernism, it offers a kind of terminus or graveyard for the scientific hubris of the nineteenth century.

For these reasons, and despite the strong claims we make for the nearly ubiquitous presence of our defining values of Modernism, we do not see them

18. Barthes is quoted by Robert Con Davis and Ronald Schleifer in *Contemporary Literary Criticism*, p. 46. This collection of carefully introduced essays is an excellent introduction to postmodern theory, especially literary theory. Probably the "marker event" in the development of the postmodern critique of Structuralism is Jacques Derrida's 1966 lecture, "Structure, Sign and Play in the Discourse of the Human Sciences," published in *Writing and Difference*.

as the underlying or "deep" structure of the period. Instead, the values we define and discuss in the following pages are cultural products of a particular period and thus subject to historical change.[19] In fact, that is precisely their function: to characterize a particular class of activity at a particular historical moment, as distinct from other moments. Our values are thus time-bound, historically empowered. Our definition of Modernism is particular, specific, with the values at every point giving rise to concrete, observable, nameable objects: paintings, novels, models of the universe.

19. Our definition of Modernism contains certain affinities with what Richard Rorty terms a "conversation," meaning a kind of knowledge: "If we see knowing not as having an essence, to be described by scientists or philosophers, but rather as a right, by current standards, to believe, then we are well on the way to seeing *conversation* as the ultimate context within which knowledge is to be understood. Our focus shifts from the relation between human beings and the objects of their inquiry to the relation between alternative standards of justification, and from there to the actual changes in those standards which make up intellectual history" (*Philosophy and the Mirror of Nature*, pp. 389–390). We would choose, rather, to call our account a "persuasion," as being somewhat more focused and directed.

Chapter 2 Epistemic Trauma

> From a certain point there is no longer any turning
> back. That is the point that must be reached.
>
> Franz Kafka

A distinctive kind of difficulty is a distinguishing intellectual and aesthetic
value of Modernism. We term this characteristic "epistemic trauma." This
formulation, perhaps because it borrows authority from modernist psychological
and philosophical discourse, seems to suggest the precise nature of modernist
difficulty; and in identifying this quality we need precision. All historical
generalizations are liable to criticism, and this characteristic of difficulty seems
especially vulnerable to semantic slippage and historical revision. To say that
epistemic trauma is a value of Modernism does not mean that the physics,
art, and literature which preceded this era contain no daring, surprise, or
alienation. Such qualities have been evident in Western intellectual life for
as long as we have records of it. But the epistemic trauma that pervades
Modernism – a kind of primary or initial difficulty, strangeness, opacity; a
violation of common sense, of our laboriously achieved intuitions of reality;
an immediate, counter-intuitive refusal to provide the reassuring conclusiveness
of the past – seems to us its keynote.

This traumatic otherness stems in part from a conscious refusal by modernist
artists and other thinkers to give their audiences the kind of spatial and
temporal orientation that art and literature had been providing since the
Renaissance and that had reached a high finish in the mid-nineteenth century
– when novelists took pains to provide their "dear Reader" with temporal
and spatial coordinates and when the subject matter of most paintings was
generally accessible.[1] In surprising and historically sudden contrast to this
traditional solicitude, the cutting-edge artistic culture contemporary with

---

1. "Modern art," wrote Ortega Y Gasset in 1925, "will always have the masses against it. It is essentially
   unpopular; moreover, it is antipopular" (*The Dehumanization of Art*, p. 5).Ortega observed that
   the products of nineteenth-century art "far from representing a normal type of art, may be said
   to mark a maximum aberration in the history of taste. All great periods of art have been careful
   not to let the work revolve about human contents. The imperative of unmitigated realism that
   dominated the artistic sensibility of the last century must be put down as a freak in aesthetic
   evolution" (ibid., p. 25).

Einstein's theories offers everywhere this quality of trauma. In the painting of Picasso and Braque, in the music of Stravinsky and Schönberg, in the fiction of Kafka and Faulkner, in the poetry of Yeats and Eliot, the immediate difficulty, the epistemic trauma, is a given of the modernist aesthetic.

The *kind* of difficulty we find in the artistic culture of the time resembles the kind of difficulty Relativity Theory presented to the scientific establishment. It comes not so much from developments and complications of traditional techniques (what might be called a *baroque* difficulty), but more often from what is left out. We miss those qualities or techniques on which we had customarily relied for meaning, such as perspective in painting, tonality in music, temporal sequence in narrative, unvarying temporal and spatial reference frames in physics. Modernist difficulty is thus at least in part a form of simplification by abstracting and *streamlining* – a process we will examine when we take up the aesthetics of Relativity Theory in Chapters 5 and 6.[2] In terms of our present historical point, we observe that for many physicists, the initial difficulty of the Special Theory lay in the fact that Einstein found the nineteenth-century hypothesis of a luminiferous ether "superfluous," thus radically liberating physics from a laborious but comfortably familiar hypothesis.[3] General Relativity was to do without gravity as a Newtonian force, once again streamlining and making stranger, more alien, the established geometric models of the universe.

In any historical period, such liberation, the elimination of conventional techniques and concerns, is probably felt as a difficulty at first and the characteristic reaction to the new phenomena may be a feeling of bereavement and outrage. The traditional guidelines disappear along with the traditional complexities, those organizing ideas and devices that provided keys and coordinates of meaning. Relativity Theory, like modernist art and literature, appears to have grown over the years somewhat easier to penetrate. Nevertheless, we are left with the fact that Relativity's difficulty, like the avant-garde elitist difficulties characteristic of the art and literature, remains a barrier to its understanding and to its perceived assimilation into the general culture. Although we may see this assimilation taking place at a level beneath or beyond general recognition, the explicit stated theory (like much of the art and the literature) remains itself obscure to the majority of educated people in a way that in their times Newton's laws of motion or Darwin's theory of evolution did not.

It is true that modernist writers and artists were often committed to being avant-garde, to adopting a posture of caprice and difficulty as part of their social and aesthetic "statement." European cultural historians sometimes treat

2. *The Oxford English Dictionary* attributes the first use of "Streamline" to James Clerk Maxwell in 1873, who used it to describe a "Current-line or a Stream-line" (and of course this usage by none other than Maxwell, whose work helped to inspire Einstein's formulation of Special Relativity, is interesting in itself). The word comes into use in hydrodynamics around 1885–1906, or during early Modernism as we date the period. For Maxwell's relation to Relativity Theory see Delo Mook and Thomas Vargish, *Inside Relativity*, Appendix D, and pp. 18–19 below.

3. In Einstein's popular book co-authored with (and, in fact, largely written by) Leopold Infeld the ether is termed the "Enfant Terrible" of physics (*The Evolution of Physics*, p. 164).

the imperative to be in the avant-garde as synonymous with "Modernism."[4] In this they differ from their scientific contemporaries (and we will discuss the significance of this difference in a later section). In the work of artists and writers of the first rank, the difficulty is justifiable on aesthetic or substantive grounds. Charles Altieri has observed that the agenda of modernist writers was in part at least to create an object, make a gesture, that would resist co-option, something that can always resist the political imperative by means of the independent energy it generates.[5] Whatever the causes, there can be no doubt that the culture of Modernism permits an obscurity and an apparent arbitrariness of expression that would have been unacceptable in the first half of the nineteenth century and which doesn't always wear well today. Its prestige rises and falls with our appreciation of Modernism – and this includes modernist physics. Although Einstein and most of his contemporary physicists may have escaped a great deal of the obscurantist posturing, they lost contact with the mainstream of the educated public at least as thoroughly as did modernist painters, composers, and writers.

Nor can Relativity Theory's counter-intuitive quality be explained solely by the fact that the effects described by the model are ignored in daily life. Neither Newtonian gravity nor Darwinian natural selection was *recognized* until Newton and Darwin offered their models of the natural world. After Newton and after Darwin, educated people could understand aspects of natural phenomena as *explained* by the new models. But Relativity has proved more resistant to assimilation. For example, the phenomenon of magnetism, familiar since antiquity, could be demonstrated: whenever an observer is in motion with respect to an electric field she experiences a magnetic field as well. In other words, electricity and magnetism, two phenomena previously considered to be utterly different, were simplified by Relativity's unification of them into one force, now called by physicists the electromagnetic force. Despite this, electricity and magnetism are still understood by most people as different things, and even most contemporary introductory physics texts treat them as related but separate forces. This reluctance to accept their unity, even by textbook authors, is at least partly due to the perceived difficulty of Relativity Theory.

Relativity Theory

Although Special (1905) and General (1915) Relativity captured the attention of the scientific community and were received with widespread attention and pockets of enthusiasm, many physicists took some time to be convinced. To

---

4. See Astradur Eysteinsson's lucid discussion of this relationship in *The Concept of Modernism*, pp. 143–178.
5. Charles Altieri, "Defining Modernism: The Ideal of the Modern," Modern Language Association Special Session, Washington, DC, December 28, 1984. See also his *Painterly Abstraction in Modernist American Poetry*.

appreciate this initial and rather sustained opposition to Einstein's theories it is necessary to understand what late nineteenth-century physicists believed to be the outstanding problems in the new area of physics known as electro-dynamics, the study of objects moving under the influence of electrical and magnetic forces.[6]

Light's wavelike behavior is the central experimental fact dominating late nineteenth-century electrodynamics. This is due primarily to the work of Thomas Young between 1801 and 1817.[7] Given Young's demonstrations of the wave character of light, physicists needed to determine the nature of the medium carrying those waves, and wave media are best understood by a careful analysis of the properties of the waves themselves. For our present account, two wave properties recognized by the middle of the nineteenth century are important: the *kind* of wave motion represented by light and the *speed* of light.

Newtonian studies of mechanical waves showed that media can propagate wave disturbances in a number of distinct ways. For example, there are waves of the sort that travel across the surface of water, so-called "transverse" waves, meaning that the displacement of the water particles that comprise the wave disturbance takes place "transverse" to, or perpendicular to, the direction of propagation of the wave along the water surface. Waves in violin or piano strings are also of this sort. Transverse waves can only exist in situations where the wave medium has some measure of "rigidity," meaning that it will resist deformation and tend to return to some equilibrium shape as the wave disturbance moves by. Furthermore the speed with which the transverse waves propagate in a medium depends on the degree of rigidity: the more rigid the material (the more strongly it resists deformation) the greater the velocity of wave propagation in the material. Young's work had shown that light waves are transverse.

But "longitudinal" waves in media are also possible; these waves depend on the compressibility of a medium instead of its rigidity, and the wave motion takes place along the direction of propagation instead of perpendicular to it. Sound waves are the most common example of longitudinal waves. The motion of the air particles carrying sound waves cannot be observed easily and so the longitudinal character of the waves is less familiar than the more readily visible up-and-down, transverse motion of water waves. It is rather hard to find common visible analogies for longitudinal compression waves but they can be devised. For example, if you stretch a child's "Slinky" spring toy horizontally and then compress a few of its coils and release them you will observe a longitudinal compressional wave move along the stretched spring. A less contrived though perhaps less appealing analogy for longitudinal wave motion

6. Electrodynamics, electromagnetic forces, and Maxwell's equations are all discussed for the non-scientist in Mook and Vargish, *Inside Relativity*, pp. 48–52 and Appendix D.
7. The history of theories of light is discussed in detail in Sir Edmund Whittaker, *A History of the Theories of Aether and Electricity*. See in connection with the confirmation of light's wave properties, I, pp. 101–114.

is provided by the legs of a walking centipede. Some of the legs seem "bunched up" together and others seem "spread apart" on each side of its long body. As the centipede moves the pattern of "bunched" legs moves along the side of its body.

Longitudinal and transverse waves, though distinct kinds of disturbance, can coexist in the same medium provided that the medium is both rigid and compressible. For example, certain regions of the earth's interior are both rigid and compressible and so can carry transverse and longitudinal seismic waves. By analyzing the amplitudes and speeds of these waves during an earthquake it is possible to infer the mechanical properties of the interior of the earth. Similarly, by studying the character of light waves physicists hoped to infer the properties of the light medium.

That light is transverse with no evident longitudinal aspect suggested that the medium carrying light is rigid and incompressible. The degree of rigidity could be estimated from the speed of the light waves. Experiments designed to measure the speed of light can be traced back at least as far as Galileo in the 1630s, but the first reliable estimate was made by Olaf Roemer in 1675.[8] Since then the speed of light has been regularly measured with increasing accuracy and by the middle of the nineteenth century the value was known with great precision. The high speed of light indicated that its medium must be extremely rigid, more rigid even than the hardest steel. This conclusion had to be reconciled with the fact that light was carried by its medium throughout the observable universe, through which comets, planets, and stars seemed to move freely. How light's medium could be so rigid and yet permit free motion of material bodies seemed, to say the least, problematic.

Beyond dictating high rigidity, the value of the speed of light plays another key role in our understanding of the light medium. In the 1860s James Clerk Maxwell published a set of four equations that still comprise the basis for analyzing electrical and magnetic phenomena. When he combined these equations using the rules of calculus he discovered that they predict the existence of propagating transverse waves of electrical and magnetic disturbances. The propagation speed of Maxwell's waves depends on two measurable numbers characteristic of the medium bearing the electromagnetic disturbances. These numbers (called the permittivity and the permeability of the medium) measure the intensity of electric and magnetic forces transmitted by the medium, and experimentally determined values were available to Maxwell for a variety of materials as well as for a vacuum. When these measured quantities were used in Maxwell's theoretical formula for the speed of electromagnetic waves he found a value the same as the measured speed of light. "We can scarcely avoid the inference that light consists in the transverse undulations of the same medium which is the cause of electric and magnetic phenomena," he said.[9] So optical phenomena became theoretically unified with electromagnetism.

8. Ibid., p. 22.
9. Ibid., p.254.

But a central problem remained, and this was the identification of the medium responsible for transmitting electromagnetic disturbances (including light) through the vacuum of space. In addition the theoretical description of electromagnetic phenomena had to coexist with Newton's mechanics. It therefore became necessary to combine Newton's theory with Maxwell's in the science of electrodynamics in order to understand how electromagnetic waves and other manifestations of electrical and magnetic forces could interact with matter. In other words, a *medium* had to be found, a medium responsible for bearing electromagnetic forces and for carrying electromagnetic waves. This medium was the problematic "luminiferous ether," an entirely hypothetical substance permeating all of space, which had to have an extremely high degree of rigidity while, at the same time, permitting objects to move through it freely.

Despite the ether's entirely theoretical status, "ether physics" had become a lively field of research by the end of the nineteenth century. The greatest theoretical physicists invested their time and talent in pursuing the properties of the ether and the models that would permit these properties to be understood. This ether was of course very different from the "aether" of medieval cosmology – that quintessential or "fifth element" which occupied the supralunary region and cradled the changeless spheres in their perpetual circular motion about the central earth. But the "luminiferous ether" was quite as real to many physicists before 1900 as the "aether" had been to their intellectual forebears of the Middle Ages. In its own way the post-medieval ether was as necessary to the empirical Newtonian universe of the nineteenth century as the quintessential element had been to the theocentric cosmologists of the Middle Ages. Both substances were constituted according to the physics of their times and functioned in support of their contemporary epistemology, embodying their culture's dominant values.

In less academic language, we can say that the existence of both ethers had been a matter of "common sense." The loss of the nineteenth-century ether as a necessary hypothesis marked the loss of the intuitive, commonsense vision of the physical world. In the natural sciences, the advent of Special Relativity not only changed the structure of the universe as we perceive it but (as we will show) altered irretrievably the *way* in which we perceive it. What it meant to know something about the physical world was changed. Relativity thus participated in what we call the *epistemic trauma* that we see as a defining characteristic, a value, of Modernism.

Einstein's delivery of his theory was characteristically demure and laconic – characteristic not only of his professional style but of modernist discourse in general. The 1905 paper on Special Relativity addressed the problems inherent in the hypothesis of a luminiferous ether and in the necessity of reconciling the discoveries in electromagnetism with Newtonian mechanics, but not by following the mainstream approaches. Ignoring the ether and setting aside both Newtonian mechanics and Maxwell's equations for subsequent treatment, Einstein opened with a careful analysis of the processes of temporal and then spatial measurement in physics. The relevance of these matters of ether physics was simply not understood by many physicists. Furthermore, the conclusions of Einstein's analysis of measurements required a complete revision of Newtonian physics and therefore stood in opposition to the assumptions and direction of the mainstream research program in electrodynamics and ether physics. As historian of science Arthur I. Miller has put it, "Einstein's relativity paper looked insignificant alongside the papers of Abraham, Lorentz, and Poincaré, which used the most au courant methods of mathematical physics."[10]

Just as critics contemporary with the development of Cubism questioned whether it was a forward or a retrograde step (or even if it were "art" at all) so Einstein's peers failed to appreciate the "Einsteinian approach" to Relativity. William F. Magie, during his presidential address to the American Physical Society on December 28, 1911 put his objections like this:

> The principle of relativity . . . professes to be able to abandon the hypothesis of an ether. . . . Indeed the principle asserts our inability even to determine any one frame of reference that can be distinguished from another, or, what means the same thing, to detect any relative motion of the earth and the ether, and so to ascribe to the ether any sort of motion; from which it is concluded that the philosophical course is to abandon the concept of the ether altogether. In my opinion the abandonment of the hypothesis of an ether at the present time is a great and serious retrograde step in the development of speculative physics. . . . How are [the supporters of the theory of Relativity] going to explain the plain facts of optics?[11]

Magie then goes on to express his sense of epistemic trauma with reference to Relativity's implications for Newtonian space: "A description of phenomena in terms of four dimensions in space would be unsatisfactory to me, as an explanation, because by no stretch of my imagination can I make myself believe in the reality of a fourth dimension." Since Einstein's theory, as mathematically cast by Minkowski, used *time* as a fourth dimension,[12] one wonders just how carefully Magie had read Einstein's or Minkowski's papers. In any case he next expresses the traumatic effect of the relativity of time:

> The description of phenomena in terms of a time which is a function of the velocity of the body on which I reside will be, I fear, equally unsatisfactory to me, because, try I ever so hard, I can not make myself realize that such a time is conceivable. . . . I feel that the principle of relativity does not speak the final word in the discussion about the structure of the universe. The formulas which flow from it may be in complete accord with all discovered truth, but they are

10. Arthur I. Miller, *Imagery in Scientific Thought*, p. 117.
11. William F. Magie, "The Primary Concepts of Physics," p. 290; this speech was brought to our attention in L. Pearce Williams *Relativity Theory: Its Origins and Impact on Scientific Thought*.
12. See, for example, Mook and Vargish, *Inside Relativity*, pp. 86–96 and references cited there.

expressed in terms which themselves are out of harmony with my ultimate notions about space and time.[13]

Magie's frustration was echoed in popular accounts of Relativity. For example an editorial from the *New York Times* of January 28, 1928 asserts:

Not even the old and much simpler physics was comprehensible to the man in the street. To understand the new physics is apparently given only to the highest flight of mathematicians. Countless textbooks on Relativity have made a brave try at explaining and have succeeded at most in conveying a vague sense of analogy or metaphor, dimly perceptible while one follows the argument painfully word by word and lost when one lifts his mind from the text. . . . The situation is all the harder on the public because physics has become unintelligible precisely in an age when the citizen is supposed to be under the moral obligation to try to understand everything.[14]

The difficulty with Relativity expressed by physicists and by non-scientists proved useful to Nazi propagandists: "The most important example of the dangerous influence of Jewish circles on the study of nature has been provided by Herr Einstein with his mathematically botched-up theories consisting of some ancient knowledge and a few arbitrary additions. . . . Even scientists who have otherwise done solid work cannot escape the reproach that they have allowed the Theory of Relativity to get a foothold in Germany because they did not see, or did not want to see, how wrong it is, quite apart from the field of science itself, to regard this Jew as a good German."[15] Or, again: "Modern physics is an instrument of Jewry for the destruction of Nordic science. True physics is the creation of the German spirit. . . . In fact, all European science is the fruit of Aryan, or, better, German thought."[16]

In an obliquely hostile approach to Einstein's work on Relativity Theory in his two-volume *History of the Theories of Aether and Electricity* (1910), the eminent British mathematical physicist Sir Edmund Whittaker entitled his chapter on Relativity "The Relativity Theory of Poincaré and Lorentz." He summarizes Einstein's contribution this way: "In the same volume of the *Annalen der Physik* as his paper on the Brownian motion, Einstein published a paper which set forth the relativity theory of Poincaré and Lorentz with some amplifications, and which attracted much attention."[17]

In justice to this early resistance we need to point out that even today Relativity Theory retains to a remarkable degree its persistently counter-intuitive quality for scientists as well as non-scientists. This quality is a source of its great attractiveness, what we might call its intellectual athleticism, but

---

13. Magie, "The Primary Concepts of Physics," p. 293.
14. *New York Times*, January 28, 1928, p. 14.
15. This is taken from a newspaper article by Philip Lenard, himself a Nobel prize-winner in physics. Quoted in Ronald W. Clark, *Einstein: The Life and Times*, p. 471.
16. Herr Tomaschek, Director of the Institute of Physics at Dresden, quoted in ibid., p.525.
17. Whittaker, *A History of the Theories of Aether and Electricity*, II, p. 40.

it blocks the reception, understanding, and non-technical uses of the ideas. There has been much discussion about what constitutes a scientific revolution,[18] but if we take Newton's *Principia* (1687) and Darwin's *Origin of Species* (1859) as marker events in the history of scientific thought and compare their reception with the response to Einstein's publication of the Special (1905) and General (1915) Theories, we notice a portentous difference. Although each of these theoretical constructs demonstrably belongs to its own time,[19] the intellectual content of Einstein's theories remains much less accessible to thinking people, even after eighty years of testing and acceptance.[20] That fact provides one justification for books like the present one, but beyond this the very *difficulty* of Relativity helps to set it in its cultural context. The difficulty is itself an aspect of the epistemic trauma.

An underlying cause of the peculiar strangeness or alienation from common sense that nearly everyone experiences when first confronted with Relativity Theory – a cause that also helps to characterize it as a phenomenon of Modernism – lies in its apparent proposal to alter fundamental constituents of consciousness itself: space (the medium of images) and time (in which language functions).[21] This is the source of the anxiety William Magie so candidly expressed in his 1911 address. Our question here does not address the familiar alternatives of whether space and time may actually be the ultimate biological or psychological constituents of consciousness or alternatively whether we think in terms of realistic Newtonian space and time because we are products of a cultural epoch that constructs and supports them. Instead we are concerned with the tendency in Modernism to subvert what *seem* in our time and place to be the media of our awareness of ourselves and our context.

In the sections to come we will discuss the tendency in the plastic arts and in literature to subvert realist time and space. Here we wish to observe that a major traumatic effect of Relativity Theory lies in its tendency to assert that time and space are not as we assumed they were. Time is not uniform inalterable duration but dependent upon relative motion. Straight lines are not the shortest distance between two points. In fact physicists employing Relativity Theory no longer even speak of the separation of points in space but of the distinction of events in four-dimensional spacetime. This development seems threatening because it introduces an unfamiliar degree of mutability into what we take to be the primary media in which we think and express our thoughts.

18. See, for example, Thomas S. Kuhn, *The Structure of Scientific Revolutions*; and I. Bernard Cohen, *Revolutions in Science*.
19. As Silvan Schweber has said, "Natural Selection has become a paradigm for the demonstration of the influences of external factors on the formulation of scientific theories" ("Darwin and the Political Economists: Divergence of Character," p. 195).
20. See, for example, the extensive discussion of experimental verifications of Einstein's Relativity Theory in Clifford M. Will, *Was Einstein Right: Putting General Relativity to the Test* and the study of Relativity Theory's reception by Stanley Goldberg, *Understanding Relativity*.
21. We refer here to the temporal elements and aspects of language; the extent to which it appears to function in and require uniform sequential time.

We can illustrate this with a notorious example from Special Relativity. In carefully analyzing the process of time measurement for two observers who are moving at a constant speed with respect to one another, Einstein was led to appalling alternatives: either the speed of light must differ for these two observers or the rate at which their clocks tick (that is the rate at which objective, physical time passes) must be different. Einstein bravely went with the available physical evidence and assumed a constant speed for light; he chose to let the passage of time depend on a clock's state of motion; even the rate of "biological" clocks (as measured by the aging of an organism) depends upon the clock's state of motion with respect to an observer. In the General Theory this mutability of time was extended to clocks experiencing a gravitational force. And the length that is measured for an object similarly depends upon its state of motion with respect to an observer and its proximity to any gravitational field.[22]

It is important to recognize that in Relativity Theory the necessary disagreement among observers concerning such measurements is not caused by psychological differences between individuals. Relativity Theory holds that the measurements vary according to the physical contexts of observers and not according to their inner peculiarities (with which it has nothing to do). Of course the relativity of "subjective" impressions of time and space has long been known and is in fact a comfortable assumption of most people's ideas of how the world works. It is a cliché of courtroom drama, among many other forms, that spatial (figurative/identifying) and temporal (sequential/causal) perceptions and memories will differ with each witness. But precisely *because* of our acceptance of the "subjective" elements in consciousness, the assumption of an "objective" (external or "real") time and space has remained almost a psychological necessity for most of us: it is, as the eighteenth-century philosopher David Hume observed with some irony, a premiss of almost unqualified importance, carrying too great a value to be left to reasoning and speculation.[23] We could accept the well-established unreliability of our individual perceptions because as Newtonians, realists, and empiricists we had uniform, verifiable standards against which to measure degrees of distortion and thus, like the nineteenth-century ether, render the universe more apprehensible.

These external standards were deeply reassuring. We could rest in the assumption that homogeneous, consistent, "objective," measurement of space and time permitted (by rendering ultimately correctable) our individual distortion of them. Our individual minds could twist space and elide or distend time but we could always find true measures in Newton's external universe. Because we assumed it was there, we could feel that absolute duration was the true medium of our consciousness, the time in which we really live,

---

22. See Mook and Vargish, *Inside Relativity*, pp. 72–78, 110–111, 111–113, and 152–162.
23. And thus, of course, to be maintained beyond the reach of philosophers. See J. M. Cameron, *The Night Battle*, pp. 220–221.

despite the superficial subjective distortions our individual minds habitually impose upon it. It was the practically unquestioned *basso continuo* of our psychic life. It may be this confidence in the unshakeable uniformity of external standards that permitted us such freedom in exploring subjective phenomena: if we have a world of scientific, empirical objectivity to refer back to, then we can permit ourselves to venture deep into the varieties and vicissitudes of individual consciousness and unconsciousness. The *control* (to employ the operative methodological term) would always be accessible.[24]

It is of course true that Relativity Theory asserts that a measurable external time exists, and that measurable lengths and masses exist as well. But Relativity Theory also says that these external standards can be neither uniform nor absolute. Measured rates, spatial dimensions, and masses depend upon the speed or acceleration of the observers with respect to the object they are observing or upon the presence of mass nearby. Time and space are neither uniform nor homogeneous because their measurement depends upon the physical context of the observer.

This variousness or perspectivity has appeared to some writers to be closer to our felt experience than absolute Newtonian reference frames and possibly therefore a more humanly indulgent model.[25] At the level of intellectual play this may be so, but for most people brought in contact with Relativity Theory the effect is not to make them more confident in the analysis of their own subjectivity. Like our inner world, the external world is now no longer uniform and therefore dependable, but has become deformable, varying. The homogeneous, "objective" empirical standards against which our internal time and space can be tested are gone, and with their disappearance the *ways* in which we think about the world have altered. It is the process of this alteration that produces the epistemic trauma evoked by Relativity Theory. And as we will show later in this chapter, modernist art and literature are characterized by the same kind of shock.

Finally, it is important to remember that Relativity Theory did not by itself erode the prestige of absolute or homogeneous time and space. Einstein's physical models were manifestations and expressions of a revolution in thought and feeling taking place throughout Western culture, the revolution called Modernism. This seems a proper place to repeat the principal methodological premiss of our argument. In pointing to a value of Modernism, such as epistemic trauma, in the diverse fields of literature, art, and physics, it is not our intention to suggest a direct causal linkage between these creative fields. As we noted earlier, there is good reason to doubt any such causal linkage between Cubism in art and Relativity in physics. But in our view this absence of causal connection makes a value like epistemic trauma all the more interesting because it suggests

---

24. Freud's long adherence to an external, verifiable, empirical reality serves as an example here, and is nowhere so evident as in *The Future of an Illusion* (1927). It bears as well on his controversial decision to regard his early patients' accounts of sexual abuse as primarily psychological rather than empirical/historical phenomena.
25. For example see Strother B. Purdy, *The Hole in the Fabric*, p. 74.

an underlying dynamic of values bearing the development of several contemporary but not necessarily intercommunicating creative expressions of modernist culture. In the pursuit of our current value of "epistemic trauma," we turn to its most important aesthetic expression in our perception of the visible world, that of Cubism.

Cubism

In Western art before Modernism the principal visual model for representing the world was that of optical similitude or perspective, pioneered in fifteenth-century Florence by the architect Brunelleschi and such painters as Masaccio and Piero della Francesca and rationalized by Alberti in *De Pittura* (1436).[26] This model valorized the space of single-point perspective, space which dominated visual representation from the early Renaissance to the late nineteenth century. Such space is sometimes called "classical" by art historians and sometimes "realist" or "realistic," whether or not the subjects represented could be considered classical or realistic.[27] As the cubists and other modernist artists were fond of pointing out, in giving painters a technique for representing depth from a two-dimensional plane (as if the painting were a window into three-dimensional space), single-point perspective was not realistic but actually "illusionist," a species of *trompe-l'oeil*. "Classical perspective" assumes a neutral, homogeneous space in which objects exist independently and are represented according to certain rules, the presumed *laws* of linear perspective. This model of spatial representation employs the same geometric principles as Newtonian space – it is also neutral, homogeneous, and in all ways a suitable medium for Newton's laws of motion, his mechanical worldview.

The fundamental goal of the practitioners of linear perspective was the rendering of three-dimensional objects on a two-dimensional surface: paint was applied to the canvas to reflect light rays to the observer's eye in a manner identical to the light reflected by an actual three-dimensional subject. An underlying premise in linear perspective is that light travels in straight lines. This premise is combined with the premises of Euclidean geometry to formulate rules for the geometric construction of a perspective rendering of a scene as if observed through a window. One draws lines representing light rays going from representative points on the subject through the hypothetical

---

26. Throughout this chapter we are heavily indebted to Elizabeth Deeds Ermarth's definition of Realism and its development; see her *Realism and Consensus in the English Novel*, especially pp. 13–19, 26–35, and 39–40.
27. We would like to call this space the space of Realism, but a dominant convention of art history (and to a considerably lesser degree of literary history) holds that Realism is an aesthetic and social phenomenon of the nineteenth century. This conception of Realism is based largely on content or subject matter rather than on methods of representation and audience expectation, which would be of more value in serious cultural history. But in accordance with the disclaimer in our introduction we are unwilling to bog down our study of Modernism in largely semantic controversy that is at present the realm of specialists within individual disciplines.

window pane (the picture plane) and to the pupil of the viewer's eye. The artist adds paint to the canvas to reflect light that will travel to the eye as would rays from the imagined "real" object or model. This method of rendering perspective, premised on the validity of Euclidean geometry, may properly be termed "linear" for two reasons. First, the geometric constructions used by artists to determine the placement of the paint involve drawing straight lines, corresponding to the straight-line character assumed for the trajectory of light.[28] Second, the adjective "linear" is appropriate because the artist uses what mathematicians call "linear functions" to determine the distances between dabs of paint on the canvas. For example, suppose the subject to be rendered on canvas is a long rectangular supper prepared for thirteen diners. The front and rear edges of the table will be represented by two parallel lines on the canvas, and the ratio of the lengths of those two painted lines will be the same as the ratio of the distances between the canvas and the front and back edges of the actual table. A mathematician would say that there is a "linear" relationship between the distance of a portion of a subject from the canvas plane and the length of the painted line on the canvas representing that portion. In this context the word "linear" means a direct proportionality.[29]

These linear/Euclidean techniques proved in practice to be vastly effective. Nevertheless, there remained an inherently problematic aspect to single-point perspective. The purpose of this artistic technique is the creation of a painted, optical analogue to the act of seeing a three-dimensional subject. But actual subjects are normally seen with two eyes, each of which receives light rays from a slightly different direction. The brain receives these two independent images and uses them to provide us with a psychological impression of a three-dimensional view. The canvas only represents one of these two necessary images. We have all learned (through what we term below a "consensus") to interpret this "single-eye" view as an adequate approximation to the "two-eye" view of an actual subject.

Einstein's theories involved a massive derogation of Euclidean geometry in the physical sciences at the same historical moment that Cubism was rejecting the premises and assumptions of single-point perspective. According to the General Theory, whenever mass is proximate to an observer space is inherently non-Euclidean, with the consequence that the paths followed by light rays are curved. A physically accurate rendering of a subject on a flat canvas would involve using a non-linear perspective. According to the new rules of perspective positions of dabs of paint on the canvas would be determined by drawing curved lines corresponding to the curved path followed by the light rays. The relation between the length of a line on the canvas and the

28. Readers who recall their encounter with plane geometry in high school will find many of these rules familiar as methods of "constructing" geometric entities with ruler and compass.

29. The technology of the camera obscura was devised to make the geometric constructions easier for an artist by projecting an image of a subject on to the working surface of the artist's medium in such a way that the distance between any two points on a subject is directly proportional to ("linearly related to") the distance of the points from the surface.

distance from the canvas to the portion of the subject being represented by that painted line would no longer be one of direct proportion because of the spacetime curvature. In an extreme situation the more distant of the two parallel edges of the supper table might appear larger on the canvas than the nearer edge and the entire shape of the table would no longer appear at all "rectangular."

The fact that spacetime is, in general, non-Euclidean means that the "laws" of linear perspective are generally invalid from a physical point of view and that linear perspective does not represent the "real" world. It is a close enough approximation in most terrestrial situations, however, because the departures from linearity are ordinarily so minute that they are impossible to measure. Nevertheless, from the vantage point of modernist physics we must recognize that linear perspective is, at best, an approximation and a convention accepted by means of an extensive tacit cultural consensus. As Elizabeth Ermarth has shown, it is precisely such consensus that makes Realism as a representational convention possible.[30]

In the visual arts as in physics the break from Euclidean space – the perspectival space of optical verisimilitude – was traumatic. A foremost student of Cubism, Edward F. Fry, has recently characterized the cubist departure from "classical" space, and in doing so has given us a brief indication of what that space had meant in the history of Western painting:

> The Cubist treatment of space and time is directly but reflexively related to the classical tradition. In that tradition, all aspects of a subject are presented in such a way as to concentrate and unify the underlying idea, be it the depiction of a myth or allegory or of a pregnant moment that summarizes past, present, and future in a single pictorial image. Such ideas or moments were in turn represented in an illusionistic space mediated by the conventions of one-point perspective, in which space is understood to be measurable and continuous in all of its depicted extensions. These conventions of mediated time and space are so fundamental a part of Western representation that they are often accepted, at least unconsciously, as natural rather than cultural phenomena. Cubism unveils these mediated conventions and re-presents them reflexively.

Cubist space, Fry goes on to say, is "at once a denial and an affirmation of classical space, effected from within the tradition of perspectival illusionism itself. The affirmation is in the receding steps from plane to plane, comparable to the evenly measurable space of one-point perspective; the denial is in the disruption and scrambling of that recession."[31]

---

30. Ermarth, *Realism and Consensus in the English Novel*, pp. ix–x, and *passim*.
31. Edward F. Fry, "Picasso, Cubism, and Reflexivity," p. 298. In 1949 Paul Laporte described this development of perspectival space and Cubism's departure from it. But he, like certain other art historians, added an intermediate stage of depth perception based on the treatment of light: "The shift from the perceptual approach of impressionism to the conceptual approach of cubism may be interpreted on more than one level of the general historical development. The perceptual approach in painting got under way with Cimabue and Giotto, in the thirteenth century. Byzantine

In creating this new conception of spatial representation the cubists owed a good deal to the innovations of nineteenth-century painting, just as Einstein owed key elements in Special Relativity to the work of nineteenth-century predecessors like Maxwell.[32] As Fry puts it, "The evolution of painting, and of cubism in particular, shared with science the common characteristic of drawing upon late nineteenth-century achievements, but in so doing, of intensifying and transforming them."[33]

The history of nineteenth-century painting, especially of French painting, has been said to show a progressive devaluation of non-visual elements and an eventual triumph of the representation of the effects of composition, light, and color over them. In other words, the religious, historical, or symbolic meaning that the subject of a painting – or indeed any object represented in the painting – once possessed became less important than the quality of the representation and finally less important than the approximation of the act of visual perception of the original subject by means of the representation. What ultimately became important in pre-modernist painting was not the representation of the object but the representation of *the way the object may be perceived "in nature"* (as independent of established artistic conventions). The subject thus retained what importance was left to it largely because of its visual characteristics and not because of its spiritual, historical, political or even its symbolic status (as it had in previous realistic painting from the Italian Renaissance through Neoclassicism). This change in emphasis becomes clearly visible in the landscape painting popular in the mid-nineteenth century, especially in the work of such painters as Corot and Millet; it has its celebrated classical location in conventional art history in the painting and statements of purpose by Courbet; and it achieved a kind of final apotheosis in the work of the great impressionists.

Whether or not we now see this as the way values changed in the history of painting (always an embattled terrain), it became the accepted account for most early twentieth-century critics and painters. Fernand Léger, one of the great cubists, summarized the advances of Impressionism like this:

art, which was basically conceptual, is being replaced by slowly increasing observations, and by a steadily accumulating knowledge about the visual appearance of nature. By the first half of the seventeenth century a consistent interpretation of nature is completed which is not any longer based upon the application of mathematical perspective but on the varying intensities of light. The perfection of this mode of interpretation is found in the work of Velázquez and Hals. The second wave of the perceptual art of the post-medieval world started with Delacroix and culminated in the impressionists of the eighteen-seventies. Color is now no longer taken as an incidental quality of light, but as an integral part of it" ("Cubism and Science," p. 247). The distinction emphasizes a departure from strict rules of perspective, but in Velázquez and Hals, as in the impressionists, the space is still illusionist, homogeneous, "deep" space.

32. See Mook and Vargish, *Inside Relativity*, pp. 48–50, 260–285.
33. Edward F. Fry, *Cubism*, p. 9. See also Clement Greenberg, *Art and Culture*, p. 98: "Cubism was more than a certain response to a certain historical moment. It was also the outcome of previous events in painting and an understanding of these is necessary to an understanding of Cubism as an event in itself."

The Impressionists were the first to reject *the absolute value of the subject* and instead to consider *its relative value only*.

That is the historical link which explains modern artistic evolution as a whole. The impressionists are the great originators of the present movement – they are its primitives, in the sense that, trying to free themselves from the imitative aspect, they considered painting in its colour only, almost entirely neglecting form and line.[34]

Léger's generalization indicates the debt cubists felt to Impressionism. The impressionists achieved not the final liberation of the treatment (the effects of light and color) from the subject (their subjects, like those of the cubists, fall on the whole into catagorizable patterns) but the primacy of treatment over subject. The impressionists were interested not primarily in the extra-visual implications of what we see but in *how* what we see appears to us. Thus the subject can be Madame Monet in a hat and garden, a cathedral façade at various times of day, or water-lilies. What matters is the way the color and light strike the eye of the observer – or, rather, what matters is the painter's attempt to represent the way light and color strike the eye of the observer *in nature*. The impressionists thus achieved a large measure of independence not merely from the hierarchy of significant subjects but also from the established conventions for representing these subjects, the traditional codes of representation in painting.

But this is not yet Modernism. The impressionists are firmly anchored in the nineteenth century by their commitment to imitate or reproduce the perceptive interaction between an observer and a stable, perceptible natural order. The primacy given to this almost unquestioned order and the assumption that we can perceive it directly characterizes almost all nineteenth-century painting (as it does nineteenth-century literature) before the 1880s. The ultimate adherence to a perceptible external reality and to the human ability to perceive it is signaled in impressionist painting (as in almost all Western painting since the Renaissance) by its adherence to the laws of single-point, "linear" perspective. Whatever advances Monet and Renoir and their colleagues made in the representation of the effects of light and however these advances affected the composition of their paintings, they did not reject or abandon the laws of perspective. The formal agreement among viewpoints that constructs neutral, homogeneous space, held for the impressionists. George Heard Hamilton formulates the liminal historical position of Impressionism in this way: "Impressionism . . . is thus not only the end point reached by Renaissance realism (as is seen in the persistence of Albertian perspective concepts), but it is the last pictorial realization of a Newtonian timeless space."[35] And when

---

34. Fernand Léger, "The Origins of Painting and its Representational Value" (1913), in Fry, *Cubism*, p. 122.
35. George Heard Hamilton, "Cézanne, Bergson and the Image of Time," p. 5. But for an exemplary discussion of the relation of Impressionism and early Modernism to contemporary developments in physics, see Alex Keller, "Continuity and Discontinuity in Early Twentieth-Century Physics and Early Twentieth-Century Painting," pp. 97–106.

at last we begin to see a general impatience with the assumption that external reality is stable and neutrally perceptible, the form this impatience takes in Western art appears in an attempt to push the rules of perspective to their limits, to distend and ultimately to violate them. We can see this impatience in the work of Van Gogh, Gauguin, and – most clearly – Cézanne, artists now characterized as post-impressionist.

Less often credited with such developments is Degas, who nevertheless in certain works contemporary with Cézanne's departures from classical Realism suggests or at least hints at violations of the laws of perspective. His pastel *Le Tub* (1886) (Plate 1), the clearest example we can find, shows a nude woman crouching in a shallow round tub in the left three-quarters of the picture. The right-hand quarter is occupied by a shelf which cuts obliquely down the picture surface. This shelf is not represented as being vertical (in which case it couldn't be a shelf): there are things standing on it. But its angle suggests that it may be canted upward somewhat more toward the vertical (i.e. up toward the picture plane itself) than the plane of the floor and the bottom of the tub (the perspective that accommodates the nude figure) would allow. That is, the shelf may be seen more from above. As if to emphasize his conscious assertion of this apparent deviation or subversion, Degas has placed the woman's water pitchers on the shelf at angles still more difficult to justify, in unmistakable violation of "realistic" perspective and "realistic" physics. We have the sense that the perspective is not single, that the shelved objects and the nude, at least, require more than one viewpoint. Finally, to cap the whole *jeu d'esprit*, a hairbrush lies on the shelf with its handle protruding off into the bather's space – a space which, as the handle enters, seems to cause it to twist or bend a little to accommodate the tentative shift in perspective. Although it is well known that Degas was fond of "shooting" his scenes from odd viewpoints and thereby justifying all sorts of play with perspective (all sorts of *tours de force*), we can see that *Le Tub* seems to strain the rules to their limits and beyond. Degas may be said to *manipulate* the rules, to cheat on them, but perhaps not to confront them with any kind of theoretical rejection (such as representing what would be logical impossibilities in realist space).[36]

---

36. This distortion in a work by Degas provides a small example of things happening before they are usually said to have happened. Students of cultural history do well to avoid attaching their generalizations too rigorously to specific dates. As we observed in our introductory chapter, a characteristic of Modernism is not a characteristic because it has never appeared before (and thus had to be invented by modernists) but because it becomes a dominant theme or quality of the period in ways that distinguish it from earlier appearances. It is equally true that certain characteristics of a period or movement will outlast the general outlines of the period or movement. And that movements will continue with considerable momentum to overlap other movements. For example, "The historical fact is that the reaction against Impressionism came in the 1880s before some of its most original possibilities had been realized. The painting of series of chromatic variations of a single motif (the Haystacks, the Cathedral) dates from the 1890s; and the Water Lilies, with their remarkable spatial forms, related in some ways to contemporary abstract art, belong to the twentieth century" (Meyer Schapiro, "Nature of Abstract Art," p. 82).

It is with Cézanne that the Newtonian, illusionist space of Realism consistently begins to give way. As early as 1880, Cézanne allowed himself to suggest discontinuities in the premised realistic space of his compositions and often to show dislocations in the objects represented.[37] For example, in *Fruits, serviette et boite à lait* (c. 1880) (Plate 2), the rear edge of the table seems to have suffered some kind of incision or fold, though the implied location of this departure is covered by a cloth. Obviously the left rear edge of the table cannot be represented by a straight line, but consists on the left of a kind of jog forward and then a short diagonal back again. Most viewers don't mind this implausibility (as it would be considered in the parameters of realist space) because the composition appears to gain in the decisiveness of its focus and in the play of its rich formal relationships. Admirers of Cézanne's work rejoice in his distortion of single-point perspective in the interest of aesthetic integrity, in the interest of what for him was its necessary truth to nature. And here in fact Cézanne goes farther: the wall in the background, the left half of the background wallpaper between the glass and the blue milk jug, surges forward into the incision or fold of the table surface, and this effect does not depend entirely on the irregularity of the rear table edge but is heightened by a slight enlargement and darkening of the diamonds in the pattern of the wallpaper when compared with those on the right. What we see is literally a curved space.

Still more complicated examples of this desertion of classical perspective may be seen in *Nature morte au panier* (1888–90) (Plate 3). Here Cézanne implies a dislocation or discontinuity in the point (or, rather, what now become the *points*) of view. Specifically the edge of the table top nearest the viewer is discontinuous (although the point of discontinuity is characteristically hidden again by folds of white cloth). In addition the table top itself is represented from two different viewpoints: the left end is seen more from above than is the right, and the whole collection of fruit and pottery is perched to suit the inspired composition rather than the laws of perspective or even of gravity. The tilt of the floor and the furniture in the background also support Cézanne's organic but studied formal organization rather than the rules of realistic space. For a viewer of this painting, the angles of the objects and the pitch of the planes on which they rest (the table, the mantelpiece, the floor) logically

37. These effects – like all treatment of depth in serious painting – are much clearer and more impressive when viewed in the original work. Reproductions tend to blur or dampen them. In any case, such subversions of classical perspective in Cézanne's work have often been commented upon. Paul M. Laporte gives a particularly clear example of Cézanne's violation of the laws of single-point perspective in "The Space-Time Concept in the Work of Picasso," p. 27. Stephen Kern gives others in *The Culture of Time and Space*, p. 141. We are here emphasizing Cézanne's innovative power for the sake of outlining his influence on Cubism. It is generally agreed, however, that neither his intentions nor his techniques would have led him into Cubism itself. See also, for some disagreement about priorities, Clement Greenberg's essay "Cézanne" (1951) in which he argues that the artist "was making the first pondered and conscious attempt to save the key principle of Western painting – its concern for an ample and literal rendition of stereometric space – from the effects of Impressionistic color" (*Art and Culture*, pp. 51–52). See List of Illustrations for dates and locations of all art works discussed in this book.

imply at least *three* perspectives, three points of viewing and thus *logically* violate the rules of realist perspective. The result is a taut and continuously interesting unity of form. Cézanne's paintings offer satisfaction in the tension between their aesthetic integrity and the subtle violence of the challenges they pose to traditional representation. It is not their meticulous realism that we admire, but (as he called it) a "truth to nature" that requires a revision of realist logic and realist technique.

Thus in Cézanne's work we can see formal composition more and more frequently bending and finally breaking the rules of single-point perspective. Picasso and Braque did in fact see this. Braque's landscapes from the autumn of 1907 to that of 1909 show with particular clarity a transformation of Cézanne's formal innovations into the development – in conjunction of course with Picasso – of analytical Cubism. Cézanne's departures from the strict logic of single-point perspective, along with his somewhat sudden and immense prestige in the world of French art (especially after the major exhibitions of 1907) gave to early Cubism a necessary legitimacy and authorized its more radical and programmatic departures.

It was in Picasso's revolutionary masterpiece, *Les Demoiselles d'Avignon* (1907) (Plate 4), that we find the conscious beginnings of a new treatment of space combined with a direct and violent denial of the rules of perspective. In the words of Edward Fry, "what makes *Les Demoiselles d'Avignon* a truly revolutionary work of art is that in it Picasso broke away from the two central characteristics of European painting since the Renaissance: the classical norm for the human figure, and the spatial illusionism of one-point perspective."[38] It may be said that Picasso did this in a single gesture. The faces and bodies of all five of the women violate the classical norm for the human figure (though of course varying degrees of deviation from that norm are quite common in a good deal of earlier painting, including work by Michelangelo and El Greco among many others). But Picasso did not merely exaggerate certain characteristics of the human form: he presented more than one perspective of it in a single image or representational "instant." For example, the nude in the lower right quadrant of the canvas has a "folded" nose. The face seems frontal but the nose is in profile. In addition, although she appears to be facing us, her left leg is in profile and we are offered a nearly unobstructed view of both buttocks. From the standpoint of single-point perspective she is not merely exaggerated or twisted: she has actually been disassembled and represented in sections. Her fellow nudes lead up to this outrage in stages from left to right, culminating in a group attack not only on the formal privilege usually accorded the human, especially female, figure but on the space in which it is customarily represented.[39]

38. Fry, *Cubism*, p. 13.
39. An ancient but famous example of such multiple-point perspective in rendering the human form extends back to early dynastic Egypt where important people and anthropomorphized images of deities were typically drawn with both feet and head in profile but their torsos from the front so that both arms are visible. It is notable that the figure on the left side of *Les Demoiselles d'Avignon*

The initial effect of this painting on Picasso's contemporaries appears to have been disturbing, and not just to them but to Picasso himself. If this challenge to pictorial space as they had understood it were valid, into what space did painting now move? What techniques of representation would be adequate to deal with the challenge? Herschel Chipp tells us that "The cubist movement was a revolution in the visual arts so sweeping that the means by which images could be formalized in a painting changed more during the years from 1907 to 1914 than they had since the Renaissance."[40] The new ground was broken so rapidly that within five years such cubist painters as Albert Gleizes and Jean Metzinger felt themselves irreversibly separated from their realist predecessors. Here is a passage from their 1912 book, *Du Cubisme*, and what is interesting is their treatment of the aesthetic past:

> To estimate the significance of Cubism we must go back to Gustave Courbet [1819–77].... He inaugurated a realistic impulse which runs through all modern efforts. Yet he remains the slave of the worst visual conventions. Unaware of the fact that in order to display a true relation we must be ready to sacrifice a thousand apparent truths, he accepted, without the slightest intellectual control, all that his retina presented to him. He did not suspect that the visible world can become the real world only by the operation of the intellect; and that the objects which most forcibly impress us are not always those whose existence is richest in plastic truths.[41]

The tone here suggests a kind of distanced scorn, of alienated superiority, of intellectual rarification. It is a characteristic attitude of early Modernism, an attitude that has affirmed intellectual difficulty and epistemic trauma, one that sees no aesthetic viability without them.

The "operation of the intellect" that Gleizes and Metzinger refer to is central to the "plastic truth" of Cubism. What exactly constitutes this operation has been the object of much critical speculation, but the chief initial difficulty for artists in 1907 and for audiences since then is not so hard to uncover: it lies in the uncertainty concerning what is being represented. It is often hard to tell what these pictures are about – even experts sometimes rely on the artist's title to identify the subject of a painting (and sometimes even experts are mistaken or misled). The techniques of representation are counter-

---

is striking just such an "Egyptian" pose, with one fist clenched as Pharaoh's is often seen to be in ancient Egyptian paintings, reliefs, and statuary.

40. Herschel B. Chipp, *Theories of Modern Art*, p. 193.
41. Ibid., pp. 207–208. There is a good deal of debate about whether these authors "really understood" the Cubism of Picasso and Braque. We lack the space to enter into such controversy. It may be that Gleizes and Metzinger grasped the fundamental departures of Cubism but were unable to take them as far aesthetically as Picasso and Braque, Léger and Gris. The Italian futurist Umberto Boccioni excluded Picasso and Braque from the cubist school, of which he sometimes spoke with contempt. Nevertheless, *Du Cubisme* remains an important modernist document. What people thought they were doing in their own time is at least as important in cultural history as what we now think they were doing.

intuitive for people whose visual perception and aesthetic expectation are still guided by the principles of perspectival, Newtonian space.

The techniques are counter-intuitive because the space of the painting does not obey the laws of single-point perspective and denies the correlative insistence on the integrity and independence of objects.[42] Cubism requires us to adjust our habitual expectations of painting to understand that what we are looking at is an artist's conception and arrangement of reality, or, more accurately, the artist's *presentation* of that conception and arrangement.[43] When we look at a cubist picture we are not gazing at a representation of reality itself as classical realist art suggests in its use of single-point perspective and illusionist space. A cubist painting requires us to recognize that our confusion about what is implied in this new method of representation is the result of misplaced expectations, not only the expectation that the artist will represent reality to us as it has traditionally been represented (and as most cameras are designed to represent it) but expectations about our own ability to identify and organize our world. If we achieve this realization – that our traditional, realist assumptions are themselves arbitrary, as arbitrary as the cubist techniques before us – then the visual trauma and the consequent effort of recovery that characterize the experience are justified.

This justification of the modernist use of epistemic trauma as an aesthetic principle does not rationalize away or even mitigate the experience of trauma. On the contrary, if this analysis is correct the trauma is essential to the success of the work of art, to its realization by an observer. The challenge of Cubism, like the challenge of Relativity Theory, appears to be nothing less than a challenge to the functioning of our consciousness because our sensation of consciousness is almost coincident with those assumptions about the nature of the physical world bound up with classical and realist aesthetics and associated by many people with psychological health and social order. What Cubism suggests – implicitly and by means of its techniques rather than explicitly and pedantically – is that reality has many faces and not just the single one of single-point perspective.

To illustrate this, let's take Herbert Read's description of a cubist masterpiece (Plate 5):

42. Modernist revision and rejection of the assumption that objects may be considered "in themselves" are discussed in our third and fourth chapters.
43. Like other critics of art and literature, Edward Fry terms these acts of conception and presentation the artist's *mediation*. He points out that neoclassicists and realists share this act of mediation with the cubists, that David, Delacroix, Manet, and Picasso enjoy a common heritage of "classical, mediated representation." Fry asserts that "for our understanding of Cubism, the most important aspect of this heritage is its densely mediated relationships between thought and experience" ("Picasso, Cubism, and Reflexivity," p. 196). We cite this passage here to suggest that while we are in the process of paralleling the revolutionary aspects of Relativity and Cubism, there is in Cubism as in Relativity Theory a conservative element that has to do with their ultimate commitment to the existence and primacy of external reality, to what Picasso, Matisse, and other modernists respected as the "object." We will be discussing this commitment to "reality" in sections to come, especially in Chapters 5 and 6.

Picasso's *Aficionado* (Kunstmuseum, Basle), painted in 1912, is "abstracted" in the sense that the fragments or facets into which it is divided have a direct reference to the subject. One may discover not only elements derived from the features (nose, eyes) and clothing (hat) of the bullfight fan who was the point of departure, but also fragments of typography (Nimes, where presumably the bullfight took place, and the word TORERO from a poster announcing the bullfight). That is to say, although the composition is derived from reality, there is no immediate perceptual image to be represented – rather a group of visual elements associated with a memory-image. These associated elements may indeed, as Picasso always insisted, be derived from visual experience; but the important distinction is that the painting becomes a free association of images (a construct of the visual *imagination*) and not the representation of a subject controlled by the laws of perspective.[44]

Those laws of perspective were laws we all agreed on, or thought we had.[45] It was a consensus initiated in fifteenth-century Florence and confirmed in the succeeding four and a half centuries. But what compact do we have with Picasso? Is he the person to dictate our visual reality to us? What has become of our consensus that spatial reality can only be represented by obeying laws of perspective?

Some such resistance seems to be behind much of the difficulty people have with twentieth-century painting generally, and especially with Cubism. This kind of defensiveness – even though it may be an understandable response to modernist epistemic trauma – can distract us from the strong values that modernist art manifests. Understood in terms of its own claims, most modernist painting is actually more modest and less dictatorial than the art that preceded it. Unlike Realism, Cubism (for example) does not require us to assume that any particular painting conforms to universal guidelines for the representation of visual reality. Cubism does not pretend to represent the single possible visual conception from a given perspective. Instead each cubist painting proposes to engage the viewer in a specific conception of a contained visual reality – in what Herbert Read called "a construct of the visual *imagination*." A cubist work presents itself not as the only valid representation of a given reality, but as one legitimate representation of it.[46] A cubist work of art does

44. Herbert Read, *A Concise History of Modern Painting*, pp. 95–96.
45. See Ermarth, *Realism and Consensus in the English Novel*, pp. 1–64. Once such agreement or consensus has been reached it is propagated by being *taught* to following generations. One is taught to "see" paintings (that is, one is taught to interpret the artistic conventions agreed upon by consensus) as one is taught to read fiction or indeed to order the phenomena of the natural world. Different cultures develop different artistic conventions, conventions that support the particular culture's dominant values. This is precisely why, for example, "oriental" landscapes are identifiably "oriental" to eyes trained in the Western conventions.
46. The same statement could be made in Relativity Theory for the measurements of the time and location of an event by any inertial observer: such measurement is not the only true representation of a given event but is a legitimate representation of it. The significant difference between measurements in Relativity and paintings in Cubism is that in Relativity Theory the measurements are not themselves seen as constructs of the imagination – that is the province of the theory.

not say, "If you stood here where I specify at the moment I dictate you would see exactly what you see represented in this picture." Only Realism gets that dogmatic. Instead the cubist work says, "I represent this plastic reality, this visual conception. My representation is imaginative. It has a right, a right not to demand your passive agreement but to invite your imaginative participation." In saying this the cubist work of art carries the traumatic implication that the assurances of optical verisimilitude and of the laws of perspective were in every sense illusory. Their bankruptcy is what has made this new representation possible and necessary. And it follows that there no longer exists a general consensus on the way the world looks and on the ways in which it may be represented.

The primary modernist difficulty, in Cubism as in Special Relativity, is the difficulty of letting go, of giving up. Picasso's *Aficionado* is not a realist painting of a fan attending a bullfight, not a photograph in paint, but a witty, zephyrous rendering of the conceptual reality of a fan at a bullfight – with his head full of the imagined reality of bullfight spectatorship, its hype and gear. On his head is the right hat for going to a bullfight, and the right moustache wandering off to the left of the excessively serious mouth. The eyes of the aficionado, at least three of them, scan simultaneously the three hundred and sixty degrees of the arena visible from a good seat. Once the viewer of the painting gives up his conservative desire to have his expectations met (the desire, perhaps, of an aficionado of realist art) and instead engages with Picasso on this field of visual conception and wit – taut in its breezy geometry, rich in its suggestiveness of the event – he too can get hooked on trauma. Like those scientists who embraced the first papers on Relativity Theory, who gave up their ether and their force of gravity and their Newtonian laws of physical reality, such viewers can enter into the difficult dialogue of a visible universe without prescribed measurements.

Narrative

We would have found it exceedingly convenient if during this period a number of novelists had organized themselves or could be organized into a single clearly labeled school or group analogous to the cubists in painting.[47] But although loose associations of modernist fiction writers can be found working at the same time in Paris, especially, and Prague, for example,[48] they don't seem to have developed that conscious similarity of means and ends which characterized Picasso, Braque, Gris, Léger, Metzinger, Gleizes and the other

Our point is that both Cubism and Relativity limit their epistemological claims much more severely than do the practices they are supplanting.

47. See our explanation for our selection of modernist writers, including our decision not to examine a single "school" of poetry such as Imagism or Vorticism, in Chapter 1, p. 8.
48. See "A Geography of Modernism," Chapter 3 of *Modernism*, ed. Bradbury and McFarlane, pp. 95–190, which contains valuable essays on "The Cities of Modernism."

cubists. In cultural history, however, advantages are often disguised as difficulties. Despite the absence of clearly defined schools, the themes and techniques of the most widely studied modernist narratives sustain and develop our values of Modernism as pervasively as do Relativity and Cubism. Our definition depends far less on the tracing of individual and group influence than on the pervasiveness and persistence of identifiable characteristics across disciplinary and other traditional boundaries. In this context, the very geographical diffusion of modernist writers and their comparative independence from each other support our definition. What is at stake is the integrity of an historical period, not the footnoting of influences.

And the dates are right. Between the publication of Einstein's paper on Special Relativity in 1905 and his full explanation of the General Theory in 1915 literary Modernism may be said to have arrived. This ten-year period includes among other milestones Kafka's *The Trial* and "The Metamorphosis," Joyce's *Dubliners*, Proust's *Swann's Way*, and Conrad's *The Secret Agent*.

The initial reaction to modernist writing was one of epistemic trauma, our first defining value of Modernism. Readers experienced the same kind of difficulty that was associated with Relativity and Cubism: an initial difficulty, a confrontational difficulty. As we observed earlier, this is not the kind of difficulty that derives from an increased complication or sophistication of techniques already in use, what we have called a "baroque" difficulty, but a bewilderment at something left out, at being given *incomplete information*, inadequate data to understand the phenomena before us. When Einstein observed in his 1905 paper "On the Electrodynamics of Moving Bodies" (Special Relativity) that "the introduction of a 'luminiferous ether' will prove to be superfluous,"[49] he made a gesture that was characteristically modernist both in its intellectual abruptness and in its laconicism. After all, it had been largely the hypothesis of a luminiferous ether that had given the current physical model of the cosmos coherence for his scientific contemporaries. Viewers of cubist painting experienced a similar shock of bereavement in the loss of realist perspective. The same kind of difficulty met readers of modernist fiction.[50]

What did readers of serious fiction expect when they picked up a novel in, say, 1900? As with our thumbnail sketch of single-point perspective in painting, what follows is highly abbreviated and therefore vulnerable to scholarly

---

49. See Albert Einstein et al., *The Principle of Relativity*, p. 38; and Mook and Vargish, *Inside Relativity*, pp. 69–70.

50. And generally still meets them. As Astradur Eysteinsson puts it, a scholar like Jonathan Culler may be able to argue in a work aimed at the academic study of literature that "'The Waste Land or *Ulysses* once seemed strange and now seems intelligible,' whereas we know that for a great majority of readers in any society *Ulysses* is still a very strange book indeed" (*The Concept of Modernism*, p. 82). The is perhaps a good place to remind our own readers that what we call "epistemic trauma" applied to the great majority of early readers of modernist literature, including academics, and that most general readers still experience such trauma when confronted with this literature. Academics are to a degree immunized to such a reaction by their immersion in literary history—but such numbness is eccentric, an accident of professional engagement.

exception. But (as with the reaction to Relativity Theory and to Cubism) the traumatic effects of modernist narrative cannot be understood without some such general picture of traditional expectations.

In general, then, we can say that the overwhelmingly dominant novelistic conventions since the first half of the eighteenth century had been realist conventions. Although these conventions had been subject to criticism, parody, and even abuse within the novel itself since the inception of the form with Cervantes's Don Quixote (1605/1615), and especially by the eighteenth-century English writer Laurence Sterne, these conventions tightened into an apparently unassailable tradition during the nineteenth century in much the same way that Realism in painting came to dominate that art. The extent of this triumph of the realist novel in nineteenth-century Europe and America can be suggested by naming its greatest practitioners: Hugo, Balzac, Stendhal, and Flaubert in France; Turgenev, Gogol, Dostoevsky, and Tolstoy in Russia; Austen, the Brontës, Dickens, and George Eliot in England; Hawthorne, Melville, and Twain in America. The list indicates a greatness of form, an aesthetic and intellectual achievement comparable to Renaissance painting in the fifteenth and sixteenth centuries. It was this aesthetic fortress, as firmly based on its own ground as Newtonian mechanics in the natural sciences, that modernist writers attacked.

The great realistic novels of the nineteenth century adhered to certain aesthetic conventions that supported and were supported by the values of the culture that provided their context. Much has been said concerning this relationship.[51] As we did with Cubism, we generalize our discussion here by taking little notice of distinctions that could be made between technical achievements and by emphasizing what for our present purpose are the more important similarities. For example, a primary practical assumption that held for both painting and fiction was that the business of art is to mirror reality, especially to reflect the unity and integrity of the world. For this reason the image of the novel as a mirror – a device for reflecting natural, social, and psychological circumstance – is probably its dominant descriptive metaphor throughout the nineteenth century. Stendhal tells us, "a novel is a mirror journeying down the high road."[52]

The simple attraction of this analogy has caught the attention of many critics and readers. But with regard to their own work, the major realist novelists were highly conscious of the inadequacy of the mirror metaphor, and Stendhal's comment contains consciously subversive ironies. Dickens and Flaubert, great realists, also understood that simple reflection might produce journalism but would not create art, and in fact was not adequate to an

51. See, for example, on this general subject Robert Alter, Partial Magic; Erich Auerbach, Mimesis; Elizabeth Ermarth, Realism and Consensus in the English Novel; George Levine, The Realistic Imagination; Georg Lukács, The Theory of the Novel and Studies in European Realism, J. P. Stern, On Realism; Thomas Vargish, The Providential Aesthetic in Victorian Fiction; Ian Watt, The Rise of the Novel, among many other historical studies.
52. Stendhal, Scarlet and Black, p. 365.

accurate representation of the world and its ways. Great realistic fiction is no more simple mirroring than is the painting of Corot or Degas. But the great realists went far beyond simple mirroring precisely in the interest of a more accurate representation of the world *as it works*, of an objective world that can only be represented through an understanding of its underlying dynamics as well as of its appearances.

Readers of nineteenth-century fiction expected the narrating voice (called the "narrator" for short) to be essentially trustworthy, whether formally the first person "I" or the more distant third person. It is, after all, the narrating voice that provides the "perspective" of realist fiction. A realistic painting seems to say to the viewer, "If you were standing there when I was painted you would have seen this." The reliable narrator of most nineteenth-century fiction says essentially the same thing: "If you had been here when I was here, if you had experienced this, you would recognize it in my description."

In order for a representation to qualify as realistic, it does not matter whether the reality being painted or narrated is thought to be actual or imagined. The reality represented may have the status of an actual physical object like the façade of Rouen Cathedral or of a contemporary historical event such as the Dreyfus affair; or it may implicitly present itself as a product of the painter's or novelist's imagination like Courbet's *Painter's Studio* or Tolstoy's *Anna Karenina*. The techniques for using the media (paint or language) are the same, the assumptions governing the nature of the reality represented are similar, and the responsibilities generally accorded to the artist are those of a straightforward relation to the viewers or readers. Much subtle skill and energy went into the narrative voices of nineteenth-century fiction, especially from such masters of the art as Flaubert, Dostoevsky, and George Eliot, and the roughly termed "objective" narrator could show a range of perceptive power from near omniscience to obtuseness. Nevertheless, a fundamental understanding between the reader and the author was sustained: the narrator narrates the real world, an "objective" world that exists independent of the narrator's perception, whether that world be natural, social, or psychological.

The narrator can do this because in the realist aesthetic language has the power to describe these realities. That is how Realism values language. The conventions of realist narration assume no barrier between reality as represented and reality as it exists independent of representation. As in realistic painting, if the use of the medium is weak (the use of perspective, light, color; of diction, syntax, rhythm) then the representation will be inexact or unconvincing. The fault will lie in weaknesses in the way the medium has been employed, not in epistemological or aesthetic problems inherent in the act of representation. And the power of language to represent reality adequately depends upon the stability of the reality represented. Elizabeth Deeds Ermarth has shown that Realism in the novel has its basis in a "consensus," a consensus that constructs time as a neutral, homogeneous medium for representation in much the same way that Renaissance painting based the convention of single-point perspective on a construction of space as neutral and homogeneous, "empty."[53]

Our way of putting this is to say that the realistic conventions of fiction before Modernism premise Newtonian conceptions of space and time.[54] If an author assumes the pervasiveness of media like Newtonian space and time – objective, independent of Perception, "without relation to anything external" (as Newton described them)[55] – then the fictional text always reserves the possibility of complete knowledge of temporal and spatial coordinates. The author retains the power to tell the reader the location and moment of any event. And in almost all realist fiction before the 1880s readers are in fact given the temporal and spatial coordinates as if the fiction contained the media of time and space in exactly the same way that the real, material world was supposed to exhibit them. In Dickens's novel it takes David Copperfield five days to make the harrowing escape from London to Dover; in Tolstoy's *War and Peace*, while Prince André lies wounded at Semënovsk in August 1812, Natasha and her family are preparing to leave Moscow; in Stendhal's *The Red and the Black*, while Mathilde desperately tries to secure his pardon, Julien Sorel in the Besançon prison finds perfect happiness with Mme de Renal during the two months before he is executed. Readers of realistic fiction expect to be given these coordinates – coordinates that exist in novels *because* they are presumed to exist in the real world and novels were supposed to imitate the real world. Of course the coordinates are not always given in world historical time (as they are for André and Natasha in *War and Peace*) but in a time suited to the subject (when, for example, Jane Eyre was a girl at Lowood School). The times and places are nevertheless understood to have an existence outside the limits of human perception and measurement: they are grounded in the absolute scope of God's order and of Newton's cosmology. In realist novels, providing the coordinates seems the simplest of courtesies, a periodic narratorial task like chapter numbering. In fact the coordinates valorize and sustain the worldview of Realism, the dominant aesthetic and scientific worldview before Modernism.

In realist fiction, as in most Western painting from the Renaissance to the late nineteenth century, the worldview that valorizes "objective" time and space has its roots in and borrows much of its authority from an ancient habit of mind, one that antedates Newtonian mechanics by millennia. This is the *providential* habit of mind, a primary attitude and value of many different religions that sees God (or the gods) as the Creator of the universe and its Governor, whether as an immanent presence or as an absent watchmaker. This ancient and still powerful tradition becomes important at this point in

---

53. Ermarth, *Realism and Consensus in the English Novel*, pp. 38–64.
54. In our fourth chapter we deal with the tendency in Modernism to abandon the representation of reality in favor of the analysis of measurement, the abandonment (in physics) of Newtonian assumptions of absolute space and time in favor of relative measurements of space and time, and with parallel developments in art and literature.
55. Sir Isaac Newton, *Principia*, p. 6; Mook and Vargish, *Inside Relativity*, pp. 25–31.

our discussion of modernist fiction because the medium of narrative is time and because in Western cultures time has traditionally been implicated in the Judeo-Christian idea of Providence, of a being who controls and otherwise *comprehends* time. The word "providence" means the ability to see ahead, to secure the future by dispensing and sustaining the medium in which it will be found.[56]

Newton was conscious of his participation in the providential worldview when he developed his models of the physical universe and he supported it in his definitions of absolute and relative time and space in the *Principia* (1687). In Newtonian mechanics, as in other essentially realist developments, Providence not only became the controller of the temporal medium but its *regulator*. Time became not merely the medium of God's will (and subject to His emphases as in much ancient and medieval writing), but the evidence for His constancy, His "logos" or reason. In other words, Newton's time demonstrated the qualities that Newton's culture considered divine: "Absolute time . . . of itself, and from its own nature, flows equably without relation to anything external, and by another name is called duration." Newton distinguished this absolute time from what he termed the "relative time" that we use in all our human measurements. Relative time is "some sensible and external (whether accurate or unequable) measure of duration by the means of motion, which is commonly used instead of true time."[57] Although there is no way in Newtonian mechanics that human beings can employ absolute time (which must be the province of divine Providence), the more accurate your measurement of relative time the more it will approximate "absolute time," the more it will "flow equably without relation to anything external." This equable relative time, this scrupulous imitation of the absolute, is the "objective" time of classical physics and of realist fiction.[58]

The intimate relation between realist time and the providential habit of mind can be seen in many eighteenth- and nineteenth-century novels. The present-day assumption that accurate representations of realistic and of religious subject matter are somehow distinct is in general a very recent development in Western culture. It appears in the nineteenth century, perhaps most distinctly in painting in Courbet's flamboyant representations of "nature" and "life" and throughout the work of the impressionists. It appears equally in what seemed at the time a radical secularization of fiction in the novels of, for example, Flaubert and George Eliot. Renaissance painting treated religious subjects extensively and found no insurmountable contradiction between the new methods of treatment and religious faith: in fact for many painters – Masaccio, Fra Lippo Lippi, Raphael, Leonardo, for example – optical similitude was a technique for greater, more accurate expression of devotion. Similarly,

---

56. For a fuller definition of Providence and the function of the providential habit of mind in the novel, see Vargish, *The Providential Aesthetic in Victorian Fiction*, pp. 6-55.
57. Newton, *Principia*, p. 6; Mook and Vargish, *Inside Relativity*, p. 24–31.
58. See Watt, *The Rise of the Novel*, pp. 11–34, for the relation between this form and empirical habits of thought.

in the novels of Richardson, Charlotte Brontë, Dickens, Tolstoy, and Dostoevsky the plots contain explicit indications that the action is providential: the fulfilling of divine benevolence for characters who use their free will in the service of virtue and the dispensing of celestial punishment for those who do not. Because these novelists saw Providence as a determining part of their world, as the governing principle of reality itself, the representation of a providential decorum in their fiction is strictly realistic.

Even when realist writers had dissociated themselves from the religious tradition – as did Stendhal, Flaubert, and George Eliot – they employed the temporal convention of "objective" time just as those nineteenth-century painters who dropped devotional subjects continued to use single-point perspective, or realist space, and even sharpened and advanced certain of its techniques while they dissociated it from its traditional subject matter. The history of painting and of fiction shows that realist conventions can accommodate the representation of religious or secular subjects and probably all conceivable combinations. Everything depends upon the cultural assumptions about what is real and their individual application by the artist. Regarded from this point of view, Realism can best be understood as a method of representation – and not (as is so often assumed) as a category of experience in the world.

Nevertheless, the dissociation of realist methods of representation from their religious underpinnings had immense historical consequences. The nineteenth century saw the gradual drift of realistic space and time away from their origin as absolute space and time in the mind of God. This was an aspect of the evanescence of belief in the divine so often cited as the dominant theme of nineteenth-century cultural history. As religious faith and devotional practice became less common among the scientifically and aesthetically literate, as the painting and fiction dealt less (and less seriously) with religious themes, the traditional validation of "objective" assumptions was weakened. We could say that the valorizing assumptions of realist methods became *merely empirical*. It is one thing to believe that homogeneous, neutral, regular time (empirical time) exists because it represents our best approximation to the absolute time (Newton's "duration") of divine dispensation.[59] It is quite another to say that "objective," empirical time exists because that is the hypothetical medium in which our measurements function. A culture that on its intellectual cutting edge has ceased to validate its scientific models by ontological or teleological arguments has left those models exceedingly vulnerable. A culture that has ceased to justify its most dominant aesthetic conventions on grounds other than their own momentum will see those conventions change. Such a culture is ripe for creative *trauma*, like that provided by Relativity Theory, by Cubism, by modernist narrative.

It is thus possible to speculate, though not to prove, that what in 1905 enabled Einstein to hypothesize the relativity of temporal measurements was

---

59. See Mook and Vargish, *Inside Relativity*, pp. 30–31.

a general cultural decline in the prestige of the assumption of absolute time. Or, to put the converse of this speculation, what prevented natural scientists before Einstein from arriving at this conclusion was the authority of the assumption that absolute time exists, an authority derived from its initial association with providential time.[60] This is not to detract in any way from the importance of Einstein's breakthrough; it is only to suggest how it became possible. When time was fundamentally bound to providential habits of mind, habits that continue even now to outlast conscious religious conviction, it could not have been possible to think of it as relative to human measurement.

Cultural assumptions about the nature of time and space, the basic media of perception, can be consciously changed only by means of the greatest strokes of courage and genius. We have already observed this courage at work in science and in art. It took Einstein's relentless devotion to the logic of his argument and his evidence to bring it to physics. Picasso and Braque made the comparable final breakthrough in painting; and before them, during the last two decades of the nineteenth century, it took Cézanne's relentless search for a more precise representation of nature to interrupt the straight edge of a table or the angle of a surface in violation of the "laws" of perspective.

A remarkable parallel to Cézanne's achievement in breaking the ground for modernist painting can be found in the fiction of Henry James. Although his work lacks the laconic abruptness of much modernist narrative and is often grouped with that of the nineteenth-century realists, it was he who moved fictional narrative off its realist center.[61] He did this by using that technique of withdrawal, of aesthetic deprivation, that we have seen as characteristic of Modernism generally. In his later work, the range of ambiguity, the range of our possible interpretation of events, is vastly increased even over such masters of restraint as Flaubert or George Eliot. This is especially true of his representation of inner or psychological phenomena and its expression in social events. In his late work, James's readers are often left without the usual instructions, without the moral or psychological road maps that earlier realist narrators directly or indirectly supplied.[62] There is a sense, of course, in which this may now strike us as *more* realistic than the expectations of earlier narratives permitted. In James's work, we are left to interpret and judge characters as we might in "real life," as mysterious strangers who can

---

60. One is here reminded of Einstein's expressed intellectual indebtedness to the work of Ernst Mach (see for example Schilpp, *Albert Einstein*, p. 21), in particular his science of mechanics wherein he attacks the "Monstrous conceptions of absolute space and time" (Ernst Mach, *The Science of Mechanics*, p. xxviii; see also pp. 271–297). The cultural and scientific erosion of absolute time has been discussed by Kern, *The Culture of Time and Space*, pp. 18ff.

61. A proposition advanced in Ermarth's *Realism and Consensus in the English Novel*, pp. 257–273.

62. We lack the space to treat this departure with the discrimination necessary to satisfy specialists. Of course sophisticated technicians like Austen, or Flaubert, or Turgenev rarely tell their readers "what to think." But it is nevertheless true that the accumulation of events, the full development of the chief characters, the repetition of stylistic gestures all in the end direct readers toward a general ethical and aesthetic agreement. The resolutions of James's late novels are much more "open."

conceal as well as reveal what they are, and to whose intentions and agendas we have limited access.

We can go farther. Sometimes James's characters don't know what they themselves are or what drives them (as of course is also often the case in life outside of novels). Probably the most famous example of this in his fiction, and indeed in all fiction, is the narrator-governess in *The Turn of the Screw* (1898). She is often cited as an extreme example of the "unreliable narrator," a modernist critical formulation indicating that in various ways the events of the text and the attitudes of other characters raise doubts about the strict empirical accuracy of what the narrating voice tells us. As with dramatic monologues in poetry or in prose, like Browning's or Poe's, the narrator may be duplicitous or mad or oblivious of the real significance of the events narrated. In almost all nineteenth-century narrative, the limitations of such a narrator become clear to the reader, who is given the means to see beyond the sub-jectivities to the empirical fact.[63] Most important to Realism is the preservation of the assumption that the empirical fact (whether a material circumstance, a social event, or a state of mind) exists external to and independent of the narrator and the narration. We may have trouble finding out what it really looks like but we assume that the real world is there, the world of our premised "objective" time and space.

But the governess in *The Turn of the Screw* cannot with certainty be identified as unreliable. It may be her *world* that, according to the premises of Realism, turns out to be unreliable. In this story, as in most of James's fiction, the realistic assumptions of a common, external time and space exist. But here it is *either* the nature of that reality which is doubtful, *or* the ability of the governess to narrate it unambiguously (in all its "real" ambiguity). The problem is that the reader is confronted with *two* fully plausible and equally suggestive explanations for certain most important events and thus with antithetical views of the reliability of the governess.

Her narrative (in the form of a private memoir) is "framed" or distanced by being read as a sort of entertainment to guests at a country house. The events the memoir narrates took place at least fifty years before the house party at which they are read; the host who reads the memoir is himself at least middle aged; the governess who wrote it is dead. In modest (or is it evasive?), flexible (or is it equivocal?) prose she tells us of her employment by a man-about-town to look after his orphaned nephew and niece at a large family estate called Bly – to which he, the owner, never goes. This is her first position as governess and she brings to it an eagerness approaching religious devotion. Both children are exquisitely charming and at first Bly seems to be Eden before the Fall. Then a letter arrives from Miles's school declaring

---

63. Such unreliable narrators play a less important part in the history of nineteenth-century Realism than the critical search for them suggests. They do, however, exist: Lockwood in Emily Brontë's *Wuthering Heights*, the employer in Melville's "Bartleby," the deranged tellers of several of Poe's stories, and most famously the madman or genius of Dostoevsky's *Notes from the Underground*, to name a few.

that he has been expelled but declining to give reasons. The governess begins to see apparitions which, with the help of the housekeeper Mrs Grose, she identifies as Quint, her employer's dead valet and as Miss Jessel, her deceased predecessor as the children's governess. In her increasingly direct efforts to "save" the children from the ghosts the narrator drives the little girl into an hysterical illness and Miles to his death from heart failure.

The question – to put it mildly – arises: is the governess insane or are evil spirits from the dead past attempting to possess the children for the forces of evil? The hypothesis that the governess is mad suits modern psychological theory very well.[64] According to this naturalist/psychological interpretation, the governess has fallen in love with or been sexually awakened by her employer but her repressive background as a parson's daughter leads her to deny the sexual feelings she experiences. These are heightened by the beauty of Bly and the "couple" suggested by the two beautiful children. Her repression leads to hysterical symptoms, most importantly the hallucination of the ghosts (again a male and a female, but now a demonic male and a "lost" lady). She identifies with the ghost of the former governess, thus admitting in "Freudian" disguise her otherwise inadmissible emotional condition. Finally, she devises a scheme for "saving" the children obviously patterned on her orthodox Christian model of the spiritual world. Thus in the naturalist/psychological interpretation everything works, down to "Freudian" (or given the extreme unlikelihood of direct influence, para- Freudian) sexual symbols and a language of unintentional (but significant) sexual innuendo. There is no event and no action that cannot be explained by this interpretation.

On the other hand, the evidence is equally solid for the "actual" existence of the ghosts – that is, their existence independent of the governess's apprehension of them. The corrupt valet, according to the housekeeper Mrs Grose, *was* a demonic womanizer; the former governess, Miss Jessel, became his minion; the children were enrolled in the sexual activity and heard and saw things that children shouldn't see.[65] The angelic goodness of the children (they do seem too good to be true) may be explained as duplicitous collaboration with the evil spirits. In the historical past that neither interpretation challenges, Quint *was* given complete control of the household at Bly and over the children and their governess. Is the unwillingness of the children ever to speak of this past the repression of abused innocents or the deceit of little devils? The appearance of the ghosts in shapes that correspond exactly to their historical identities *before the governess knew of these identities* can best

---

64. By 1898 when the story appeared, Sigmund Freud in Vienna had concluded a series of studies on the etiology of hysteria in which he postulated that hysterical symptoms were the result of repressed memories with "sexual content." James had probably not had the benefit of reading Freud's "The Aetiology of Hysteria" (1896) but he had been dealing with problematic sexual phenomena in fiction, especially in *What Maisie Knew* (1897).

65. Mrs Grose represents the common, reliable witness of everyday time and space, "common sense," realist time and space. She is authorized to give a mundane, factual account of past events, but she does not – to the governess's dismay – see the ghosts. By the end of the story, Mrs Grose commits herself (on weak evidence) to the governess's version of events.

be explained by postulating the existence of "real" ghosts.[66] Besides, the governess seems quite aware of her emotional condition, admitting that she was "swept away" by her employer and actually raising the question of her own sanity at points – a level of self-awareness unlikely in a hallucinating hysteric (at least in fiction). There is no event and no action that cannot be explained by this interpretation as well.

Both interpretations have received numerous defenses by scholars and critics of established reputation.[67] Some of these are passionate and others ingenious. But to take sides at all is to fall into the relativistic trap that James set for such thinkers back in 1898. What the story inescapably asserts is that *the governess may be mad* and that *the ghosts may be real*. That these two possibilities appear to contradict each other does not disqualify either one. In the world of this modernist narrative, as in the world of Relativity Theory, two contradictory measurements of the same reality can coexist as correct. Both interpretations of the governess (as hysteric and as savior) have equal rationality. Both views are therefore justified. There is no realist "objectifier" here, no superior reference frame against which the systems can be measured. In fact, the absence of any "objectifier," of any privileged point of view, is symbolized within the story itself by the inaccessibility of the owner/employer, the absent god of the tale.[68] There is no Providence for the reader to look to, no omniscient narrator, no empirical testing or verification. *The Turn of the Screw* marks the beginning of the end for the old Realism in fiction as surely as Cézanne's contemporary violations of perspective did for painting.[69]

Finally, the story implicitly but massively attacks precisely the mental rigidity that cannot tolerate the relativistic presence of two contradictory interpretations (measurements). At the end of the action the governess arranges to be alone with little Miles. She believes that if she forces him to "confess" his participation in the evil she can "save" him. This interpretation is the one

---

66. Or can it? Doesn't the governess lead Mrs Grose to descriptions that suit her emotional script of what happened, the script born of her own hysterical repressed sexuality? Or doesn't Mrs Grose lead the governess to a description (which immediately assumes the status of a memory in her hysterical mind) that corresponds to the historical events with Quint, Jessel, and the children? The passages of equivocal dialogue between Mrs Grose and the governess are superbly inconclusive. And then how do we explain the governess's ability to give a detailed description of Quint, etc. etc. ?

67. A handsome collection may be found in the Norton Critical Edition of *The Turn of the Screw*, ed. Robert Kimbrough, pp. 169–273.

68. The narrator tends to think of her employer as the being who could set everything to rights, if she were to violate the chief condition of her employment and contact him: "'He' of course was their uncle in Harley Street; and we lived in much profusion of theory that he might at any moment arrive to mingle in our circle. It was impossible to have given less encouragement than he had administered to such a doctrine, but if we had not had the doctrine to fall back upon we should have deprived each other of some of our finest exhibitions" (James, *The Turn of the Screw*, pp. 53–54).

69. We speak, of course, of serious, artistically advanced fiction. One can still today find nineteenth-century Realism alive and well in good and bad painting, in good and bad fiction, just as Newtonian cosmology is still taught in our schools as the best available model for certain types of reality. Currently we speak not of reality but of types of reality.

permitted by her Christian model of the cosmos. In the concluding scene, the dialogue alternates between the polarizing extremities, giving weight first to a primary thesis of the dialectic and then to its antithesis. With increasing violence the implication slams back and forth between the perceived alternatives: either the ghosts exist or the governess is mad ("for if he *were* innocent then what on earth was I?"). The governess bets everything on one exclusive interpretation of the events because mutually exclusive dualities are tied to the survival of absolutes in her culture, the culture of nineteenth-century Christianity. In so doing, she strains her small charge beyond his ability to endure: "His little heart, dispossessed, had stopped."[70]

There is an assertion here, one we can call relativistic. What kills little Miles and what has trapped so many clever critics is an outmoded adherence to the habit of mind addicted to some form of exclusive and singular reality. The critics and readers who take sides in the psychological-hysteric versus supernatural-ghost duality, a duality in which one reality is lethal to another, may not be nineteenth-century Christians and yet they too are wedded to belief in a single, privileged "reality." But what if the nature of reality itself is logically inconsistent or contradictory? What if multiple explanations of events can coexist in the same way that multiple measurements of the same physical phenomenon can coexist? Then the critics and other readers who take sides in the apparent duality are no more perceptive than the governess and probably not as courageous. She, at any rate, confronts the ghosts. *The Turn of the Screw* shows that what kills is our inability to relinquish absolute alternatives, our inability to accept the existence of simultaneous, logically exclusive interpretations. Who ordained that a table and a bowl of fruit can only be represented from one point of view at a time?

The kind of difficulty *The Turn of the Screw* presents is an extreme and therefore a vivid example of the difficulty presented to readers who were used to the conventional reassurances of a reliable narrator, a narrator who described an ultimately intelligible world to us, who told us what "really happened." We can see that the disappearance of this epistemological and aesthetic guidance from fiction substantially alters the relation of the reader to the text. In fact, this extreme narratorial opacity becomes in its different tonalities almost a universal characteristic of early Modernism.

Shortly after the turn of the century, contemporary with the Relativity Theory and the first cubist painting, the absence of the reliable and guiding narrator began to establish itself as a modernist convention in fiction. The narrating voice (or voices) of James Joyce's *Dubliners*, which he tried to publish as early as 1912, is (to put it mildly) noncommittal. The chief themes of the collection – the ironic and humiliating failure of romantic and heroic aspiration, isolation and alienation even from those who live closest to us, brutal and sordid compromise, exploitation, bankruptcy of religion and national pride – run through the individual stories with synergistic power. The writing is almost

---

70. James, *The Turn of the Screw*, pp. 87, 88.

preternaturally lucid, a rarefied clarity, but never does the narrator suggest how we are to take all this, what we are to make of it.[71] Even now these stories leave readers lonely and bewildered; their effect in 1914 must have been disorientation. The descriptive language is that of remorseless objectivity and the reality described has been emptied of affective and moral reference. We are left with impressions of a world, a Dublin, that has become meaningless. Readers who had grown up in the tradition of nineteenth-century Realism must have wondered why they were being presented with these grim vignettes. The narrator doesn't say.

We could multiply examples of this kind of narratorial withdrawal, but it will be a recurring preoccupation for us as we deal with other aspects of modernist narrative. These observations on *The Turn of the Screw* and *Dubliners* are sufficient to suggest that a double change was taking place between the end of the nineteenth century and World War I. While modernist writers still appeared to be in the business of representing reality, the quality of that reality had become increasingly equivocal, alien, unfriendly – "dense" as Camus was to call it.[72] Correspondingly, the narrative voice becomes withdrawn, noncommittal, "indifferent" (to use Joyce's term). Modernist narrative retains a key element of Realism in the sense that it proposes to represent a world (natural, social, or psychological) whose existence is presumed to rest independent of the narration. In this it has much in common with Relativity Theory, which also premises a physical reality independent of observation but asserts that measurements of it will differ. Cubism, and most other modernist painting, keeps its connection with the object but the means by which that object can be represented have undergone a radical detachment. Similarly in modernist narrative the world represented ceases to be the kind of common property that the providential/empirical world of nineteenth-century fiction assumed.

Nowhere are these developments more pronounced than in the writing of Franz Kafka. Kafka is the Einstein of modernist fiction. Not only can his work be appealed to whenever generalizations concerning Modernism in literature are in order, but it will often provide the earliest examples of modernist innovations. Certainly it illustrates that immediate, confrontational trauma that we have identified as a modernist value. There is a sympathetic cartoon in which a perplexed speaker says to a companion, "I forget: Is Kafkaesque a good thing or a bad thing?"[73] Like the cubist paintings with which they are precisely contemporary, Kafka's stories refuse to tell us explicitly what they are about.

71. Stephen Dedalus, in *A Portrait of the Artist as a Young Man*, gives a famous – though again ironic – prescription for artistic impersonality: "The artist, like the God of the creation, remains within or behind or beyond or above his handiwork, invisible, refined out of existence, indifferent, paring his fingernails" (p. 215).
72. Albert Camus, *The Myth of Sisyphus*, p. 11.
73. By William Hamilton, © 1998 The Cartoon Bank, a division of *The New Yorker Magazine*, http://www.cartoonbank.com/home.html.

The surreal stroke with which "The Metamorphosis" (written in [?]1912, published in 1915) begins has become a marker event, even for people who have never read the story: "As Gregor Samsa awoke one morning from uneasy dreams he found himself transformed in his bed into a gigantic insect."[74] It is hard to imagine a reader in 1915 who could avoid rereading that first sentence. The protagonist too finds his metamorphosis strange, but he does not go mad with the shock as we might expect; and the obliquity of his reaction heightens the trauma for the reader. Gregor finds his metamorphosis inconvenient – or rather worse than inconvenient, inefficient. Time is passing. He must get to work but he doesn't know how to roll over and get out of bed. He'll miss even the seven o'clock train! What will the chief clerk say? How will Gregor explain his lateness? And the chief clerk confirms these bizarre anxieties by preposterously arriving at the Samsa home, indignant, to find out why Gregor is late. Gregor emerges in his monstrous form to explain. The family is embarrassed. "Life" goes on.

In "The Metamorphosis" a reader is confronted with initial difficulties of the kind we have identified as valorized in Modernism. The *donnée* of the story, that such a transformation can be literally asserted and maintained, is carried out with meticulous attention to realistic detail, to the severe practical problems that result from being turned into an insect. Monstrous transformations are, we know, common in mythology where Io might be transformed into a heifer or Tiresias into a cricket, and in fairy tales where princes become toads. But myth and fairy tale do not insist on their fidelity to the mundane world as "The Metamorphosis" does. Fairy tales do not trouble us with descriptions of the dietary problems of the prince-toads. "The Metamorphosis" in its assault on nineteenth-century Realism nevertheless relies on the expectations raised by the reader's familiarity with realist conventions for its éclat.[75] In this story the experience of finding oneself turned into a beetle is treated with an economical exactitude that itself is part of the problem. The deadpan narrative voice proves as empty of aesthetic and moral guidance as the narrative voices of *Dubliners*. Is the story a grotesque joke, or is it a lacerating comment on the human condition?[76] Early readers of Kafka complained on the one hand that his writing suggested an obscure, though fascinating, allegory; and on the other that it seemed irritatingly elaborate.[77]

Kafka's writing does employ the techniques both of allegory and of nineteenth-century Realism. These are not incompatible: a sort of loose realist allegory may be found occasionally in Dickens and in Tolstoy, for example. The problem with Kafka is to discover what exactly is being allegorized. Allegory traditionally reveals itself by employing a symbolic structure or complex

---

74. Franz Kafka, "The Metamorphosis," *The Penal Colony*, p. 67.
75. In other words it develops a relation to realist narrative conventions not unlike that of Picasso's *Demoiselles d'Avignon* to realist representations of female nudes.
76. The answer, of course, is a relativistic one: it is a grotesque joke *and* it is a lacerating comment: the human condition may be seen as a grotesque joke, and this is a lacerating comment.
77. Ronald Gray, *Franz Kafka*, p. 5.

that is widely accessible to literate audiences in the general culture. Once
we discover the "real" meaning (which is often made explicit in the allegorical
text itself) the pleasure lies in decoding the symbols – in watching the pilgrim
Little Nell, for example, sustain her purity in her progress through a corrupt
world or in following Ivan Ilych to the light.[78] But Kafka's symbols (if they
are symbols) and his plots do not point toward unified, coherent, "real" meanings.

For example, if ever literary language proclaimed itself to be allegorical it
is that of Kafka's "In the Penal Colony" (begun in 1914 and published in
1919). First we have the machine itself. "The Officer" describes its ghastly
assemblage and function with the didactic exactitude reserved for apocalyptic
allegory. We have the "Bed," "Harrow," the "Designer." We have the rhythm
of the executions described in detail. Beyond the machine we have the "Old
Commandant" and the "New Commandant." We have the putatively neutral
observer. We have the condemned man. We even have an action in which
the judging officer is himself brutally extinguished by his own machine. The
terms employed, the personae, the action are all resonant of deeply structured
meaning in Judeo-Christian culture.

Too resonant for comfort, in fact. The problem for the reader is not that
the story is rich in symbolic meaning – so was a good deal of nineteenth-century
realist writing. The problem is that the story contains so many possible meanings
that *the* meaning, or any *primary* meaning is dissolved in the very multiplicity
of possibilities. In other words, the plurality of relative measurements (interpretations dependent on one's political or ethical or aesthetic point of view
– the movie of life that the reader brings to the story) obliterates the allegory
that certain of the symbols suggest. At first it seems that the story may be
saying that the old justice, eye-for-eye Old Testament punishment for guilt
as dictated by the "Old Commandant," is being superseded by a kind of
liberal humanitarianism administered by the "New Commandant," who will
institute Christian compassion and/or civil liberties. But as the ironies of the
story begin to compound, doubt is cast upon the authentic benevolence of
the new regime. At least under the old order one knew what one was guilty
of. Under the new dispensation suffering will be intolerable because it will
be absurd. Or so it appears: we learn of a prophecy (evocative of such prophecies
in Judaism, in Christianity, in the religions and legends of the world), that
the Old Commandant will return and reassert his authority over the colony.
The enlightened "neutral" observer from a constitutional republic uses a knotted
rope to keep the soldier and the prisoner from following him to his ship.
Clearly the story is rife with possible meanings, but there is no objective
narrator, no reliable guide of any kind to give one meaning priority. Kafka's
fictional universe has become relativistic. It asks us to accept the simultaneous
existence of multiple, occasionally contradictory meanings. This is its epistemic
trauma.

78. In Dickens, *The Old Curiosity Shop* (1840–1); and Tolstoy, *The Death of Ivan Ilych* (1886).

Chapter 3 From Normative to Contextual

Demand calls forth supply. . . . What decadence!

Fernand Léger

One way to defend oneself against the epistemic trauma of Modernism is to reject or dismiss its physics, art, or literature on the grounds of "distortion." Almost all modernist developments in these fields depart from or alter traditional representations of reality. From the point of view of the tradition these developments *are* distortions.[1] What is often missed, even in some specialized analyses, is that this classification stems not from the phenomena perceived but from the frame of perception. No equation, painting, or narrative is distorted of and in itself. It is the aesthetic-intellectual-cultural context against which such manifestations are seen that determines the qualifying frame of reference. We-the-perceivers view the object from within these cultural imperatives, from our way of seeing the world. The "distortion" thus arises from the challenge that the modernist work poses to one's *expectations* of what that work should be. The word "distortion" presumes an expected or "natural" or "right" way to execute the work – natural and right being defined in terms of the prevailing standards of analysis and representation.

For example, if a viewer in 1908 understands that she is about to see a painting called "Les Demoiselles d'Avignon" her expectation may be that she will see a recognizable or "natural" representation of some young women. She "knows," within a fairly broad but nevertheless limited range, what young women look like and thus how they may be represented. Such representation for a Western viewer in the late nineteenth or early twentieth century is one following the conventions of realist painting. And so while Picasso's painting *is* a painting, and while its stated subject may be young women, the viewer's expectations are disappointed, and the degree of departure of the work from the expectations may be measured as a degree of distortion.

For the same reasons, relativistic descriptions of phenomena in space and time have often been regarded as "distortions." Here the word presumes one

---

1. *"Distortion in painting and science"* is a section in Paul Laporte's essay of 1949 on "Cubism and Science," pp. 254–256.

"natural" or "right" set of geometrical rules, such as Euclid's, or one universal natural clock for time measurements. It presumes by extension a preconceived normative structure to the cosmos from which the relativistic effects depart. It often implies as well that there is one practical, commonsense way of looking at the world from which only abstruse scientists, depraved artists, or deranged writers would want to depart. It has been shown that the same kind of statement about the alienation of science from the general culture can be made about the alienation of modernist art, that it gives rise to the same kind of popular resistance.[2]

This popular resistance is directly related to the epistemic trauma we dis-cussed in the preceding chapter as a leading characteristic of Modernism generally, but it is of a particular kind with peculiar consequences of its own. The immediate logic of the popular rejection runs as follows: the perceived distortions (whether in physics, painting, or fiction) are being passed off as serious work but they really reflect the incompetence or bad faith of the scientist/painter/author. This is sometimes articulated as a version of "My little daughter could do better than that!" Such objections are in turn usually met with some justification of the intellectual or aesthetic complexity of the work, like "Your little daughter might have trouble with tensor calculus/cubist composition." The ground of the objection then typically shifts to a more sinister, quasi-political line: the distortions are not essential; the artist or scientist does not need the distortions to express what the art or science purports to convey. It follows that the distortions must arise from some other motive. The real agenda of the science or the art – such objections may continue – must be to create a false elite, or to deprive the common person of common sense or self-respect, or to undermine established values ("the American/German/French way of life").[3] Historically this political or cultural resistance surfaced as an objection to Relativity as a theory that distorts the harmony and proportion of nature, "natural harmony."[4] Similar objections to Cubism and modernist narrative included attacks on its elitist nature, class bias, and antagonism to either putatively democratic or socialist Realism.[5]

2. George Kubler commenting on "The New Reality in Art and Science," by E.M. Hafner, *Comparative Studies in Society and History*, 2, no. 4 (October 1969): 387.
3. Louis Vauxcelles, who with help from Matisse coined the term "Cubism," wrote a xenophobic review of that movement in 1912 as the work of foreigners and as barbarically subversive of French culture (Malcolm Bradbury and James McFarlane, *Modernism*, p. 167).
4. One most extreme manifestation was the Nazi claim that Relativity Theory was part of a Jewish scientific conspiracy to deprive German youth of their healthful and strengthening contact with "Nature." See Philipp Frank, *Einstein*, p. 252 and our Chapter 2, p. 21 above. Frank quotes from a lecture given to the German National Student Association in 1936: "Einstein's theories could only have been greeted so joyfully by a generation trained in materialistic modes of thought. On this account it would likewise have been unable to flourish in this way anywhere else but in the soil of Marxism, of which it is the scientific expression, just as this is true of cubism in the plastic arts and of the melodic and rhythmic barrenness of music in recent years" (p. 253).
5. Repressively in the former Soviet Union, especially under Stalin, but also well known in Western Europe and America as varying shades of popular opinion leading to what is sometimes called "economic censorship."

The initial rejection of Einstein's theories resembles the still widespread popular resistance to modernist art and literature. For example, William Magie, president of the American Physical Society, in an address of 1912 attacked Relativity Theory precisely because it is not easy to understand:

> A solution to be really serviceable must be intelligible to everybody, to the common man as well as to the trained scholar. All previous physical theories have been thus intelligible. Can we venture to believe that the new space and time introduced by the principle of relativity are either thus intelligible now or will become so hereafter? A theory becomes intelligible when it is expressed in terms . . . as they are understood by the whole race of man. When a physical law is expressed in terms of those concepts we feel that we have reason for it, we rest intellectually satisfied on the ultimate basis of immediate knowledge. Have we not a right to ask of those leaders of thought to whom we owe the development of the theory of relativity, that they recognize the limited and partial applicability of that theory and its inability to describe the universe in intelligible terms?[6]

History has been justly harsh on reactions like Magie's, but he makes a significant point very well: "All previous physical theories have been [widely] intelligible." Einstein's was not then and is not yet.

At this point, however, we need to identify one important historical difference between the scientific culture on the one hand and the artistic and literary culture on the other. Relativity Theory's initial difficulty (its effective elitism) did not arise from any felt need by its advocates to protect it from, say, "bourgeois philistinism," but rather out of its intrinsic modes of expression – the counter-intuitive "mathematical" logic of the Special Theory and the sophisticated mathematics of the General Theory that seemed inseparable from the theories themselves. The Physics Nobel Laureate Stephen Weinberg has addressed the necessity to make a distinction between recent work in the natural sciences and what can appear to be the more willful or arbitrary difficulties of contemporary art:

> Our theories are very esoteric – necessarily so, because we are forced to develop these theories using a language, the language of mathematics, that has not become part of the general equipment of the educated public. Physicists generally do not like the fact that our theories are so esoteric. On the other hand, I have occasionally heard artists talk proudly about their work being accessible only to a band of cognoscenti and justify this attitude by quoting the example of physical theories like general relativity that also can be understood only by initiates. Artists like physicists may not always be able to make themselves understood by the general public, but esotericism for its own sake is just silly.[7]

---

6. William F. Magie, "The Primary Concepts of Physics," p. 293.
7. Stephen Weinberg, *Dreams of a Final Theory*, p. 150. The question of whether the obscurity of mathematics in modern physics is a "forced" necessity is of course open to debate at a basic epistemological level.

Relativity Theory's "elitism" derived primarily from its inherent difficulty, its counter-intuitive qualities, whereas modernist art and literature very often had a specific social agenda: to assert (by shocking the expectations of the middle class) the superiority and independence of the medium – to avenge what artists often saw as the betrayal of art by a philistine social establishment. The conscious use of distortion by artists and writers was occasionally and in part an intentional attack on the established sensibilities and expectations of the viewer or reader. Such distortion could serve the avant-garde's assertion of its avant-garde status. This socially motivated assertion may be found in some cubist painting and in a good deal of Expressionism; it became the founding impulse and life of Dada.[8] Nevertheless, when modernist developments like Cubism, Fauvism, and their corresponding innovations in literary narrative are examined seriously we see that the major changes – even as the innovators themselves understood them – grew out of perceived needs in their aesthetic evolution and were not primarily designed to confront social conditions. In other words, the representational difficulties were as essential to the identity of their subject as mathematical language is to physics.

This did not prevent hangers-on and critics from attempting to enlist the new developments as allies of their own ideas of political necessity or, conversely and more conservatively, excoriating them as scapegoats. It is to such attempts that we largely owe the political associations that certain modernist developments evoke, in contradiction to the more specialized and modest desires of the scientists, artists, and writers who actually did the original work. Of course such exploitation of the original developments is itself significant – though it must be kept distinct.[9] Much has been written about the possible identity of the idea of the avant-garde with Modernism in literature and the arts, but for purposes of this study the avant-garde is a subcategory, a phenomenon, of Modernism. The inclusion of the physics in the definition of the period leads to such a clarification.

Finally, we can see a tendency in the avant-garde to distance itself from traditional, large themes in the general culture, to devise an aesthetic culture of its own, with a non-traditional language of color and form in art, of symbolism and narrative devices in literature, and of unfamiliar mathematics in physics. In Modernism the aesthetic discourse, in turning away from its traditional subjects, began to turn inward, to become self-referential (what in Chapter 6 we will call "reflexive"). Clement Greenberg has put it like this: "the avant-garde's specialization of itself, the fact that its best artists are artists' artists, its best poets, poets' poets, has estranged a great many of those who were

8. See, for example, Richard Sheppard, "German Expressionism," and Robert Short, "Dada and Surrealism" (in Bradbury and McFarlane, *Modernism*, pp. 274–310), where the social agenda of these movements is discussed.
9. See, for example, Eric Cahm, "Revolt, Conservatism and Reaction in Paris 1905–25," in Bradbury and McFarlane, *Modernism*, pp. 162–171. Or, in the words of Astradur Eysteinsson: "while the avant-garde movements are historical phenomena in their own right, they are also salient motors of modernism" (*The Concept of Modernism*, p. 178).

capable formerly of enjoying and appreciating ambitious art and literature, but who are now unwilling or unable to acquire an initiation into their craft secrets."[10] Such intentions and results give some credibility to the intuitive objections we noticed above.

The similarity in popular resistance to the perceived "distortions" in modernist physics, art, and literature is paralleled by a similarity in the usual defenses employed by advocates of the innovations in each field: that what appear to be distortions are in fact *more accurate* models or representations of reality than Newton's physics, realist art, or the "objective" narration of preceding centuries; that they are actually *closer* to nature, to the visual object, to society in its real agenda, to temporal experience of life seriously and fully understood.[11]

We all know that these defenses are granted very different levels of prestige in our culture. The physicist designs experiments to "measure" phenomena and to compare these measurements with predictions of physical theory. That these predictions are borne out by the agreement (usually within some "margin of error") with the measurements is taken as evidence for the validity (or even the "truth") of the theory.[12] At various times such tests have successfully defended the sun-centered universe, the reality of "caloric fluid" as the cause of heat, or an age for the earth of less than a few million years.[13] In contrast, the pronouncements of artists and critics are easily dismissed, sometimes because they "lack hard data" or because they only make "qualitative" statements. Nevertheless, philosophers of science have long recognized that the epistemological basis for many scientific statements can be questioned as well, a challenge which Relativity Theory and Quantum Theory helped to valorize during the period of Modernism.[14]

Relativity Theory

Despite the comparatively high credibility accorded science throughout Western culture during the period of Modernism,[15] certain consequences of

10. Clement Greenberg, *Art and Culture*, p. 8.
11. We note in passing that this is not a defense popular in Postmodernism, where adherence to "reality" is meaningless in the absence of an independent reality or in a dazzling plurality of realities.
12. See Delo Mook and Thomas Vargish, *Inside Relativity*, Chapter 1, especially pp. 21–23.
13. The caloric theory of heat is discussed by Hugh Callendar in the article "Heat", in *Encyclopaedia Britannica*, 11th edn, Handy Volume Issue (New York: Encyclopaedia Britannica Company, 1910), pp. 138–139. This age estimate of the earth and sun is discussed by Hermann Helmholtz, "On the Interactions of Natural Forces," pp. 211–247; an abridged version of the argument is given in Jefferson Hane Weaver, *The World of Physics*, I, 705–721. The geocentric model of the universe is discussed briefly in I. Bernard Cohen, *The Birth of a New Physics*, Chapter 3, and more extensively in Thomas Kuhn, *The Copernican Revolution*, Chapters 1–4.
14. We will have more to say about these developments in Chapters 5 and 6.
15. Though there was a well-known drop in the prestige of science and technology late in World War I and immediately afterward.

Relativity Theory were resisted on the grounds of "distortion." Until Einstein's theory the physicist's space *was* Euclidean space, and the physicist's time *was* uniform and absolute. Indeed the world was rendered "beautiful" through these uniformities of nature, and the body of "classical" physics was the medium for articulating this beauty. Einstein's Theory of Relativity challenged all of this.

For example, according to Relativity Theory if an object bearing a familiar geometric form, perhaps a circular compact disk bearing a digital recording of *Sacre du Printemps*, could be photographed or otherwise imaged as it moved at increasing speed past an observer it would gradually lose its resemblance to the idealized circular form familiar to us from millennia of geometric preconception.[16] The form of the circle, we say, is "distorted." More generally when Relativity Theory offers a model of the cosmos that lacks consistent distinction between matter and energy, acceleration and gravity, rest and motion, or even between simultaneous and consecutive events, we say that the spatial distortions represent changes in the rules of geometry and the temporal distortions represent changes in the rates at which clocks tick.

The distortions represent a disappointment of expectations, expectations based on the assumed validity of Euclidean geometry and Newtonian mechanics, a validity thought to be natural, a normative validity. Just as we have traditionally tended to assume that continuous unvaried homogeneous temporal duration and spatial dimension are the true media in which physical objects and events exist, so we have traditionally assumed that Euclid's geometry and Newtonian mechanics are accurate descriptions of space, time, and motion. Anything else is to be classified as a distortion.

But Einstein's Relativity Theory and its subsequent experimental confirmation demonstrates that Euclidean geometry does not apply in general to the world, and – worse still – that there is no single, uniform geometric system that can be applied universally. The presence of mass and energy,[17] according to Relativity Theory, actually causes the *rules* of geometry to change and so the observed non-uniform distribution of matter and energy in the universe means that the rules of geometry will differ from place to place. Furthermore Relativity Theory dictates that the *measurement* of time differs as the geometry changes. Thus the media of time and space undergo a profound redefinition, one that leads to the suggestion that it is most economical to consider space and time as two mathematical components of the single concept *spacetime*.[18]

For example, a classical physicist asked to describe the path of a speck of dust on the spinning compact disk of *Sacre du Printemps* would draw (literally with a pencil or more abstractly with an equation) a picture of a circle and describe the dust speck as a point moving with constant speed around that

16. Computer simulations of such hypothetical photographs are provided on pp. 129 and 130 in Mook and Vargish, *Inside Relativity*; see also pp. 117–136, 150–162, 153 n. 19.
17. Even though we here use the two classical words "mass" and "energy," Relativity has led to the recognition—by physicists, at least—that mass and energy are two aspects of a single entity.
18. See Mook and Vargish, *Inside Relativity* pp. 86–95.

circular path. A modern physicist would use spacetime in which the circle becomes a helix,[19] and the deviations from Euclidean geometry caused by the presence of the mass of the CD player and other nearby objects would cause the helix to be further "bent" along its axis like a child's "Slinky" spring caught in its motion between stairs. The classical physicist would say that the relativistic path is "distorted," meaning "warped from the Euclidean–Newtonian path" that pre-modernist physicists used to describe the event.

But the available physical evidence supports General Relativity as a substantially more accurate model of the cosmos than that put forth by Newton. This being the case, in what sense are the relativistic effects *distortions*? If the concept of distortion has any realist application at all, it is Newton's physics that distorts and Euclid's geometry becomes a reductive tool useful mainly in illustrating situations in small regions of space where slow speeds and low masses are involved. Einstein's theory *distorts* largely as the Copernican–Keplerian–Newtonian cosmological model did the highly intuitive medieval cosmology: by being less an idealization of an established preconception of the way things ought to be, by being less a projection of our replayed movie of the world.

But this is not to say that the Relativity revolution was of the same *kind* as the Newtonian. In the case of Newton's "revolution" we see that the revolutionary character emerged from a series of statements in the *Principia* that were largely consistent with the "common sense" of his time so that Newton's laws were "intuitive." Special Relativity was based on the highly counter-intuitive postulate affirming the constancy of the speed of light.[20] Though "true," insofar as it is predicted by Maxwell's theory and has withstood experimental confirmation, this postulate is nevertheless an aspect of nature that is new and distinct from well-known phenomena. It has not found a place in our common sense.

Despite its counter-intuitive quality, however, some physicists found the new approach to natural phenomena liberating rather than intimidating, clarifying rather than distorting. To Arthur Stanley Eddington, for example, the sacrifice of time-honored standards seemed a natural progression from Newtonian physics:

> It has been left to Einstein to carry forward the revolution begun by Copernicus – to free our conception of nature from the terrestrial bias imported into it by the limitations of our earthbound experience.

In response to critics like Magie, who felt that Relativity represented an unnecessary obfuscation of issues well explained by classical physics, Eddington wrote:

> It is sometimes complained that Einstein's conclusion that the frame of space

19. Ibid., pp. 93–95 and especially Figure 3.29.
20. Ibid., pp. 70–72.

and time is different for observers with different motions tends to make a mystery of a phenomenon which is not after all intrinsically strange. . . .[However] the consequence in physics of the discovery that a yard is not an absolute chunk of space, and that what is a yard for one observer may be eighteen inches for another observer, may be compared with the consequences in economics of the discovery that a pound sterling is not an absolute quantity of wealth, and in certain circumstances may "really" be seven and sixpence.[21]

Eddington was clearly undistracted by the epistemic trauma of Einstein's conclusions and was able to place them in a meaningful historical context. Just as certain intellectuals like Gertrude Stein were able to recognize the importance and validity of the cubist movement very early on, to comprehend its difficult language almost by assimilation and to articulate its virtues to others, so did Eddington champion the ideas of General Relativity and embrace the highly abstract mathematics necessary to articulate it fully. He quickly grasped the utility of four-dimensional spacetime as a mathematical concept and in 1922 brilliantly elucidated Einstein's original paper on the General Theory in what is still one of the standard texts.[22]

There was also in Eddington and other early enthusiasts of Relativity an aesthetic sense that Einstein's difficult and radical approach articulated a new sort of "beauty" in physical law. In 1909 the great German physicist Wilhelm Wien wrote:

The most important point in favor [of Special Relativity] is the inner logical consistency that makes it possible to lay the foundation for the entire body of physical appearances whereby all the older conceptions undergo a transformation.[23]

Like cubists and their supporters striving for a more "true" or "accurate" representation of visual reality in art, physicists like Eddington and Wien supported the modern turn represented by Einstein's theory as a closer approach to "beauty," "consistency," and even "universality," values that had accorded Newton's theories so much prestige.

There is yet another aspect to the "distortion" often found in Relativity Theory, one that has to do not with one's preconceptions of how natural phenomena should be represented but with received ideas, normative standards, for what constituted a physical theory itself. As Gerald Holton has said of Einstein, "His physics looked to [his fellow physicists] like alchemy."[24] Typically, an early twentieth-century theoretical paper might begin with observed phenomena, perhaps even a set of measurements. From this observational basis would develop a theoretical concept or framework with which to "explain"

21. A. S. Eddington, *The Theory of Relativity and its Influence on Scientific Thought*, pp. 3–6, 11–12.
22. A. S. Eddington, *The Mathematical Theory of Relativity*, pp. 43–76.
23. Quoted in Stanley Goldberg, *Understanding Relativity*, p. 200.
24. Gerald Holton and Yehuda Elkana (eds) *Albert Einstein: Historical and Cultural Perspectives*, p. xxi.

or "describe" the phenomena. Expression of this framework often culminated in a mathematical statement derived, perhaps, by combining other more "basic" mathematical statements from physical theory. While the rules of mathematical manipulation would guide this process and justify the conclusions (after the fashion of mathematical "proofs"), the exposition was never far from the phenomenon under study and mathematics *per se* was not part of the argument. Indeed the original (1905) Special Relativity paper begins with a discussion of phenomena – the relationships between electric and magnetic forces observed by Faraday – but then the text shifts to a highly abstract attack on the classical ideas of space and time, matters that would appear to have no bearing on electricity or magnetism. The attack itself is entirely "hypothetical," based on no direct experimental evidence that space and time need questioning.

Einstein's (1916) paper on General Relativity theory, on the other hand, opens with the admission that the original Special Theory was incomplete; after sketching what was needed to complete it and pointing out that such completion will involve a theory of gravitation, the discussion turns to a series of mathematical definitions and a statement of the goal of the theory in mathematical terms. This is followed by a purely mathematical exposition not of physics but of the branch of mathematics now called tensor calculus. It is little wonder that some of Einstein's colleagues reacted to such "distorted" expositions with dismay.[25]

In a novel with an historically resonant title, *Night Thoughts of a Classical Physicist*, historian of science Russell McCormmach presents the state of mind of a "classical" theoretical physicist caught in this period of confusion:

> Over his lifetime, physics had taken a turn toward increasingly advanced mathematical conceptions of nature. . . . In the past, mathematics and physics had a close relationship, but Einstein fused the two, and [the "classical" theoretical physicist] found it hard to see where the physics was.[26]

McCormmach's classical physicist has his "night thoughts" in the Germany of World War I. The collapse of classical physics in confrontation with the grotesquely distorted physics of Modernism seems to the classical physicist somehow central to and representative of the destruction of the old Germany and the fragmentation of traditional European intellectual culture. For him, the new intellectual order offers no place to live.

Einstein's approach to the construction of his Relativity Theory was indeed deeply confusing to many scientists at the time. Like much of the art and literature of the period, Relativity Theory seemed to show little respect for the traditional forms, the established "manners" of presentation. Writing in 1912, the physicist Louis More put it this way:

> In the past, as new phenomena were discovered, theories were advanced to

25. See Albert Einstein et al., *The Principle of Relativity*, pp. 109–164.
26. Russell McCormmach, *Night Thoughts of a Classical Physicist*, p. 64.

explain them in terms of [the] primary mechanical concepts [of space, time, and mass], and if discrepancies remained between the theory and the phenomena, the theory was abandoned or allowed to lie dormant, but the concepts were not questioned. This may be called the classic attitude; but a new scientific method . . . has been lately evolved by German physicists.

[Einstein] draws the conclusion that we must radically alter our concepts of space and time and abandon our concept of mass. . . .This relativity . . . depends on a mathematical formula purely abstract in source and character. This really amounts to saying that experience is not a criterion of truth and that we must rely on an inward sentiment of knowledge as revealed in subjective formulae.

Here the method behind the theory is perceived to be fundamentally flawed, a "distortion" of what a theoretical approach should be in physics, or, as More observed, "it is better to keep science in homely contact with our sensations at the expense of unity than to build a universe on a simplified scheme of abstract equations."[27]

Cubism

All major movements of modernist painting and sculpture have been criticized for their "distortions." In focusing on Cubism we do not wish to deprive other major schools – Fauvism, Futurism, Expressionism, for example – of this badge of courage. But as we observed in our introductory chapter, an inter-disciplinary study must be constrained in its choice of illustrations in order to focus the central themes.

Cubism serves very well to illustrate the shift in values. What some con-temporary viewers took to be its barbarous distortions (and what some viewers still object to) arise with rare clarity from the aesthetic motives of the effort. The perceived distortions are inseparable from what the cubists and their commentators saw as the movement's distinguishing innovations, advances leading to a liberation from artistic tradition and to an enlargement of the plastic arts. Although certain political or at least social drifts can be identified in early Cubism, the chief originality of the movement lay in its aesthetic departures. The great cubists – Picasso, Braque, Léger, and Gris – worked in the avant-garde because that is where they earned their place in relation to the aesthetic tradition, not (like certain of their hangers-on) with some an-tecedent political agenda. In cubist art, what viewers who want their painting to be "realistic" in its representation of objects see as perverse distortions are actually the hard-won achievements of a revolution in aesthetics.

27. Louis More, "The Theory of Relativity," pp. 379, 371. More ascribes this difference in aesthetic to a nationalistic difference: "Undoubtedly the German mind is prone to carry a theory to its logical conclusion, even if it leads to unfathomable depths. On the other hand, Anglo-Saxons are apt to demand a practical result, even at the expense of logic."

Herbert Read provides a well-known summary of the effect of this revolution on the visual arts:

The "focus" is no longer concentric, fixing the object in a spatial continuum which recedes to a culminating point on our horizon. The focus is in the picture-space itself, and to the organization of this picture-space all visual elements contribute as color and form, but not as the representation of an immediate perceptual image. There is only one "percept": this is the composition itself: any elements from nature, that is to say, visual images derived from the subject, are broken down so that they may serve as structural elements. The solid rock is quarried (broken up into cubes); the stones are then used to build an independent structure.

This is the moment of liberation from which the whole future of the plastic arts in the Western World was to radiate in all its diversity.[28]

Read's comment gives a sense of the momentousness of the departure from artistic tradition, a momentousness that helps to establish the strong historical parallel with Relativity Theory that we have been tracing.

Although they might agree with Read about the breakthrough and its approximate moment, many art historians would want the credit shared with movements and individuals preceding and paralleling Cubism. Impressionism, with its emphasis on color, on light, and on the techniques of representation, brought the viewer's attention to the picture surface in a way that earlier realists sought to avoid. Similar claims could be made for post-impressionist masters such as Gauguin and Van Gogh with their unorthodox freedom of color and form and their tendency to emphasize these at the expense of traditional realist "depth." Even more obvious departures were made by Matisse and other Fauves with their advanced treatment of space as integral to the objects represented.[29] To conventional apprehension, all these movements and artists were guilty of distortions from the established normative standards and techniques of Realism.

But for the earliest logical, persistent, courageous working out of a departure from realist conventions, with the risks and difficulties acknowledged in the work itself, we turn again to Cézanne. In art history, many aesthetic "paradoxes" are associated with his work. For our present purpose – the tracing in Cubism

28. Herbert Read, A Concise History of Modern Painting, p. 96.
29. "You must not tell me that in 'discovering' this [space whose dimensions are not limited by the objects represented], I have recreated the space separately from the object–I have never abandoned the object. The object is not of such interest by itself; it is the environment which creates it" (Henri Matisse, "Notes of a Painter" (1908) in Herschel B. Chipp, Theories of Modern Art, p. 142). Such observations clearly echo ideas related to the notion of a field as expressed in General Relativity, a point we will take up in Chapter 5. Paul Laporte makes a significant distinction between the "distortion" of Matisse and the fauves and that of the cubists: "The reason for the dissolution or distortion of the object in painting is not the same for the fauves as for the cubists. In Fauvism, the object is 'distorted' for the sake of subjective 'expression,' while in Cubism it is being distorted in the process of a search for new objective categories of representation. . . . The 'distortion' of the object by the cubists is not willed but, quite to the contrary, the result of a distinct process of perception" ("Cubism and Science," p. 254).

of the shift in *value* from realist prescription to the primacy of context – the Cézannean paradox that strikes us is his discovery that strict realist single-point perspective is in practice incompatible with truth to nature. By this, of course, we mean the truth of the representation of nature in painting, the natural visual truth that painters care about. Cézanne discovered some time in the 1880s that in order to represent nature "truly," in order to create what he called "a construction after nature,"[30] – nature as he had come to see it in its tensions and balances – he would have to introduce departures from the laws of single-point perspective. Some viewers, especially some critics, saw these departures as distortions. The "distortions" were at times attributed to primitive deficiencies in the artist's technique, a reaction that now itself seems naive. As J. A. Richardson puts it, "Nothing in his [Cézanne's] pictures is the result of accident, ineptitude, or whimsy. Every deformity has its formal justification."[31] We are tempted to agree, but then what can we mean any more by "deformity"? And where does the necessity for such deformity come from? Surely not from nature; and it was the artistic "realization" of nature that Cézanne said he was pursuing.

It is tempting to say that in modernist art deformities/distortions arise first in the mind of the painter, who then translates them to canvas where they become *symbolic* of deeper, imperceptible (non-visual) realities. And in fact for certain movements and schools contemporary with Cubism this was a primary aim and method. In 1909, Maurice Denis, who had painted the well-known *Hommage à Cézanne* at the turn of the century, published an essay called "Subjective and Objective Deformation." Here he justified increasingly pronounced departures in modernist painting, especially in symbolist painting, from the formal norms of Realism:

> Art is no longer only a visual sensation which we record, only a photograph, however refined it may be, of nature. No, it is a creation of our spirit of which nature is only the occasion. Instead of "working with the eye, we search in the mysterious center of thought," as Gauguin said. Thus imagination again became, as Baudelaire wished, the queen of the faculties. Thus we set free our sensibility, and art, instead of being a *copy*, became the *subjective deformation* of nature.

Or in our terms a distortion. But this distortion emerges intentionally from the artist's "thought," from non-visual meditation. This is no longer Cézannean "construction after nature." Denis continues:

---

30. Quoted by Read, *A Concise History of Modern Painting*, p. 18.
31. Richardson continues: "One must understand that, strictly speaking, distortion is not a characteristic of certain styles of painting; it is an attribute of pictorial order" (*Modern Art and Scientific Thought*, p. 36). In other words, of a superior order in the pictorial context–just as Relativity Theory gives superior measurements and only justifies them in context of the system of measurement (as opposed to absolutely and in themselves). Paul Laporte gives a particularly clear illustration of "distortion" in Cézanne in "The Space-Time Concept in the Work of Picasso," p. 27; and John Golding offers some careful speculation on how he may have arrived at his "deformations" in *Cubism*, p. 66.

"Do what you like, so long as it is intelligent," Gauguin said. Even when he imitates, the genuine artist is a poet. The technique, the content, the aim of his art warn him well enough not to confuse the *object* that he creates with the spectacle of nature which is the subject of it. The Symbolist viewpoint asks us to consider the work of art as an equivalent of a sensation received; thus nature can be, for the artist, only a state of his own subjectivity. And what we call subjective distortion is virtually style.[32]

In other words, Realism is itself a product of the imagination: for human beings there can be no single privileged reality because all perception of nature – what Denis simply terms "nature" as it exists for the artist – is inescapably subjective. There is thus no privileged norm or reality to depart from, and so what we had called "distortions" are the marks of individual artistic perception and representation, or "style."

Denis explains the symbolist/subjectivist departures from the norms of traditional Realism very clearly and economically. His explanation is useful because the perceived distortions of Cubism are often confused with symbolist or subjectivist or expressionist deformations. But the "distortions" of Cubism, like the "distortions" of Relativity Theory, are in most ways the reverse of subjectivist. Differing from the motives of the symbolists, subjectivists, and expressionists, the aesthetic impulse of the cubists was always an impulse toward the external world. As we shall see, they share this impulse with the great realists.[33] But like Cézanne the cubists were after a richer, more accurate representation of external nature. Like Cézanne (and like Einstein), Picasso and Braque during their brilliant joint development of Cubism from 1907 to 1914 never abandoned the premiss of an external reality nor the enterprise of its accurate representation. Like Einstein and like Cézanne they understood that the conventional rules for the description of nature had reached the limit of their application, that representation required new methods and new resources.

In *The Rise of Cubism*, Daniel-Henry Kahnweiler describes the early development of the movement in a way that leaves no doubt about its representational motives:

In the winter of 1908, the two friends [Picasso and Braque] began to work along common and parallel paths. The subjects of their still-life painting became more complex, the representation of nudes more detailed. The relation of objects to one another underwent further differentiation, and structure, heretofore relatively uncomplicated – as, for example, in a still life of the spring of 1907 whose structure forms a simple spiral – took on more intricacy and variety. Color, as the expression of light, or chiaroscuro, continued to be used as a means of shaping

---

32. In Chipp, *Theories of Modern Art*, pp. 106, 107.
33. Art historians have repeatedly pointed out that the cubists aimed at giving a more complete and accurate presentation of reality, or in John Golding's words, that "cubism . . . was an art of realism" (*Cubism*, p. 198). There is of course a distinction to be made between the techniques and aims of what we have called Realism and the intention to represent what cubists thought of as reality–though Golding's terminology does not help with that here.

form. Distortion of form, the usual consequence of the conflict between representation and structure, was strongly evident.[34]

In other words, the motive for the distortion as "the usual consequence of the conflict between representation and structure" was essentially the same as in Cézanne's works – the product of a "conflict between representation and structure" in Kahnweiler's 1915 formulation.

But the distortions even in the earliest cubist paintings are more extreme (as measured by formal departures from realist conventions or by the reactions of viewers) than any of Cézanne's. Why? We have seen that in *Les Demoiselles d'Avignon* (1907) Picasso broke away from the "spatial illusionism" of single-point perspective and from "the classical norm for the human figure."[35] We treated the departures from realist perspective as part of the initial difficulty of Cubism, its participation in the epistemic trauma of Modernism. The deformation (or as it was sometimes seen, the mutilation) of the human form arouses additional resistance; and in Cubism it has an additional justification. In 1911, the cubist painter and theorist Jean Metzinger put it like this: "To draw, in a portrait, the eyes full face, the nose in semi-profile, and to select the mouth so as to reveal its profile, might very well – provided the craftsman had some tact – prodigiously heighten the likeness and at the same time, at a crossroads in the history of the art, show us the right road."[36] So, the cubist portrait would be a more exact representation of reality *because* of what appear to be its distortions, just as Relativity Theory provides a more accurate model of the physical world *because* it dispenses with Euclidean and other ideal and static norms.

Cézanne attempted to represent nature as its constructions strike the eye. As has often been observed, he is in this sense the last of the great realists as well as the most important precursor of Modernism in painting. Picasso and Braque attempted to represent nature, or the object, as it exists in the mind's eye, in what we *know* about its visual reality. Since what we know about reality, about any object, is greater than what can be perceived from a single perspective, the limitations of single-point perspective are in fact distorting. Traditional perspective is literally *trompe-l'oeil*, visual deception.

We know what we know about objects in part because we have observed them over time. We know what the profile of the nose on the face that fronts us looks like because a moment ago we saw that nose from the side. (It goes almost without saying that our knowledge of the nose may not be photographic but affective: it may be a beloved or a detested nose. It may even be conceptual rather than literal, an imagined nose. It makes no difference to our point here.) Similarly we know what the bottom and the stem and

---

34. In Chipp, *Theories of Modern Art*, p. 253. Kahnweiler was a friend and associate of both Picasso and Braque, an art dealer who was a major early force in establishing Cubism as a movement and in marketing cubist paintings. The passage quoted was written in Switzerland in 1915.
35. Edward F. Fry, *Cubism*, p. 13. For our discussion of *Les Demoiselles d'Avignon* see pp. 32–3 above.
36. Jean Metzinger, "Cubism and Tradition," in Fry, *Cubism*, p. 67.

the bowl and the rim of our wine glass look like because we have held it in our hand on so many occasions of solace and respite. In other words, we know what we know about objects because we have observed them over time and in motion, during what Paul Laporte calls "kinesthetic experiences":

> Picasso's "distortion" is . . . the product of a new vision of "objective reality." In its intended completeness, this new vision is obviously made up of kinesthetic experiences whose integral and functional relationship with the visual perceptions is clearly recognized. Geometry, to Picasso, is not an end in itself, but a means to develop a new pictorial idiom capable of expressing kinesthetic experiences.[37]

The truth to nature that Cubism pursues is thus primarily a visual, not a metaphysical or symbolic one. Cubists are interested above all in the representation of visual experience – for them it maintains aesthetic primacy over psychological, spiritual, social, or political experience. In Cubism, truth to nature is *the truth that we know about its visual reality*. Cubism attempts to represent on a two-dimensional static surface what we have learned about three-dimensional objects by means of time and motion. In order to do this, Cubism must depart from conventional perspective because that shows only what we know from one point of view at a single instant. And in spreading "kinesthetic" knowledge over a plane, stretching the canvas of this knowledge over the two dimensions available to painting, cubist representation requires what appears to be a radical distortion of forms. But these are distortions *relative* only to the imperatives of conventional realism just as the deformations of objects in Relativity Theory are distortions only from the static idealized forms of Euclidean geometry as sustained by the limitations of Newtonian mechanics. To the cubists themselves, the new techniques offered the means to a more accurate representation of the world, a more *realistic* representation. In the words of Fernand Léger, "The *realistic* value of a work is completely independent of all imitative quality."[38]

There is more than an analogy here with the "finite but unbounded" volume of the general relativistic cosmos, or its "centerless expansion."[39] Since the 1920s it has been recognized that distant galaxies in the universe are rushing away from our own Milky Way galaxy and that we live in what is termed an "expanding universe." One is naturally led by classical Newtonian Euclidean reason to ask "expanding into what?" or "expanding from what, and exactly where was the center of this expansion?" Like the cubist painters, Einstein and others chose to abandon "imitation" of certain Newtonian–Euclidean concepts such as "center" and "expansion" and to seek a "realistic" rendering

37. Laporte, "Cubism and Science," p. 252.
38. Fernand Léger, "The Origins of Painting and its Representational Value" (1913), in Fry, *Cubism*, p. 121. Of course Léger's use of the word "realistic" is intended to be provocative here—an aggrandizement of the aims of his nineteenth-century predecessors while in the same instant a dismissal of their mimetic means.
39. Mook and Vargish, *Inside Relativity*, pp. 191–195.

by a radical contextualization of these classical notions: in General Relativity the expansion is of space itself and occurs at all points of the universe at once. Such expansion is centerless. To achieve a more "realistic" description or conceptual rendering of astrophysical phenomena, physicists had to change the meaning of their language and literally to "distort" the Euclidean space in which they had embedded their work. As we all know, this revolution continues to produce results, scientific and artistic.

In modernist painting the new vocabulary extended well beyond the end of Cubism as a homogeneous movement. A masterpiece of Georges Braque's, *Le Billard* (1944) (Plate 6), will serve with exceptional accessibility to focus and summarize our discussion.[40] The central subject is a billiard table, an arena which has served countless Newtonian physics problems and demonstrations for teachers and students of mechanics. And now its flat, Euclidean–Newtonian surface has been fractured, the balls still in place on the table, the cues evidently as straight as ever, but the playing surface, the spatial environment in which the game is to be played, has been rendered useless – useless, that is, as far as our classical game is concerned. The table has been tilted toward the vertical and folded to correspond to the shape of the room, its own spatial context. The condition of the room surrounding the table is uncertain. The wooden molding and the wall surfaces seem to be sound; the leaded window panes are in good shape. But at the right side of the picture, a crack can be seen extending across the horizontal sill of the window, a crack which trails from the sill down along the wall where it is cut off by the frame of the picture. Another, more prominent vertical crack extends nearly in alignment with the main rupture of the billiard table surface and the cracked molding at the top left of the wall. What we see is not the representation of discrete objects standing in free and neutral space, but a representation of what Relativity Theory terms a *field*.[41] Lurking on the surface of the stand behind the billiard table is what might be a book. One wonders what title it might bear. Would it be a bound Volume 17 of the *Annalen der Physik* or a collection of Kafka's stories? Not very likely, and in fact it doesn't matter: both Einstein and Kafka would have understood Braque's game.

Finally, we want to add that in describing the plastic innovations of Cubism we do not imply that cubist painting is devoid of political or historical or social content. In Picasso's work, for example, allusions to earlier painting, to religion, to myth, to personalities, to political and social events are widely evident. In our description of *The Aficionado* (Plate 5) we paid tribute to the witty treatment of the subject in its non-visual as well as its visual elements.

40. In the Musée d'Art Moderne, Pompidou Centre, Paris. This is one of seven such studies, painted between 1944 and 1949 (Jean Leymarie, *Georges Braque*, note to plate 69). For our purposes it does not matter whether the viewer considers this late modernist masterpiece cubist in the strict historical sense. It relies on the spatial innovations of Cubism and presents the necessary deformations. We select it for its rich and luminous illustration of our argument.
41. We discuss fields in Chapter 5.

As Edward Fry has it: "a Cubist representation from 1909 to 1911 involved the direct visual observation of the world; previous knowledge of the motif, if any; mastery of the classical conventions of representation; and the simultaneous Cubist transformations of those conventions as the motif was being represented."[42] All of these elements are present, and we will return to them. Our point here, however, is that the unique "*Cubist* transformations" derive almost exclusively from a new representation of the visual world. To call these transformations "distortions" or "deformations" is to speak from a context that was being parochialized by transformations in the general culture itself, by the changing values of the cultural context. It is to speak from what had become the provinciality of traditional Realism.

Narrative

We have seen that distortion is a matter of context and expectation. What appear to be distortions are the departures from the scientific or aesthetic (or philosophical or political or commonsense) model that serves as a frame of reference. The innovations of Relativity Theory and of Cubism appear as distortions when viewed from the reference frames of classical physics or traditional Realism. When viewed from within Modernism, however, the previously apparent distortions become the means of achieving a more complete and accurate representation of reality. The shift in value is from prescriptive norms to contextual relationships; or, to apply the General Theory of Relativity to the culture of Modernism generally, how our geometry works depends on the presence of matter and energy – the immediate physical context. Given this inversion of relationships, distortion becomes at best a *relative* concept.

At first we might think that this process is merely a question of simple relativ*ism*: what looks like distortion from one point of view appears to be accuracy from another and vice versa. But Modernism, as represented by Relativity and by Cubism, actually changes the epistemology of the comparisons; that is, it calls into question the standards by which representations can be judged. Fundamental to the modernist process of transformation is a validation of plurality itself. Realism, in contrast, asserts that there exists one visible reality to imitate. Realism assumes that a picture painted at a point in time and space will imitate *the* reality painted, and that therefore all pictures of a reality painted near to each other in space and time will (allowing for significant stylistic differences) resemble each other. Cubism asserts not only that there is another way for the reality to be portrayed but that there exists in fact a plurality of visible realities accessible to representation at any instant. It is true, no doubt, that a camera would not record most of these realities but then the camera is designed to take a single pre-coordinated (realist)

---

42. Edward F. Fry, "Picasso, Cubism, and Reflexivity," p. 298. *The Aficionado* dates from the summer of 1912 but Fry's generalizations still hold.

impression (optical systems can be and have been designed to do otherwise). We have seen that Relativity Theory impressively validates plurality by its assertion that measurements depend upon the spatio-temporal coordinates of the observer so that there can be as many different correct measurements of a single event as there are observers.[43]

It is this process of unhooking our perception from a single, recognizable, *normative* reality that produces the distortions of Modernism. In an important sense this liberation is what Modernism is all about, and the consequences implied can seem momentous. Modernist aesthetics propose not just one possible approach to representation, but offer as a primary premiss the viability of varying and even contradictory (though not exclusive) interpretations or descriptions of objects and events. As we will see in the following chapter, latent in Relativity Theory is not simply the implication that many measurements of a reality are possible, but the correlative that individual perception of any single reality cannot be comprehensive. In Relativity Theory, any observation says as much about the context of the observer as it does about the reality observed. We are no longer the context-free abstractors permitted by the Newtonian worldview. This contextual and inescapable limitation of our perceptive powers makes Relativity Theory the quintessential physics of Modernism. It deals with the problem of plurality in our measurement of the natural world.

And just as Cubism asserts the primacy of this plurality in visual or spatial reality, so modernist narrative treats its temporal manifestations. Because narrative, in contrast to painting, is primarily a temporal art it can treat multiple realities in the process of formation. It is not an accident that Franz Kafka's "The Metamorphosis" has so often been seen as the epitome of Modernism in fiction. Almost all of the major modernist novelists deal at length and directly with instabilities in our perception of time, with its distortions and deformations.

Kafka has a one-page story called "A Common Confusion" that is made up entirely of relativistic failures in common Newtonian time:

> A common experience, resulting in a common confusion. A has to transact important business with B in H. He goes to H for a preliminary interview, accomplishes the journey there in ten minutes, and the journey back in the same time, and on returning boasts to his family of his expedition. Next day he goes again to H, this time to settle his business finally. As that by all appearances will require several hours, A leaves very early in the morning. But although all the surrounding circumstances, at least in A's estimation, are exactly the same as the day before, this time it takes him ten hours to reach H. When he arrives there quite exhausted in the evening he is informed that B, annoyed at his absence,

43. It is worth noting that the relativistic measurements are not *created* by the observers. The measurements are constrained by certain rules and invariant qualities (e.g. separation in spacetime). A cubist artist (from this viewpoint) has more freedom to make multiple aesthetically coherent observations.

had left half an hour before to go to A's village, and that they must have passed each other on the road. A is advised to wait. But in his anxiety about his business he sets off at once and hurries home.

This time he covers the distance, without paying any particular attention to the fact, practically in an instant.[44] And so on. Kafka's labeling of his actors as "A" and "B" gives the account the tone of a school physics problem – one to which there is no longer a unique solution. The ironies of the little parable are achieved by the counterpoint between the relativistic physical "distortions" in the temporal flow and the aspirations and anxieties of the figures A and B. Needless to say, A and B never meet. As the rapidly compounding ironies develop their full momentum, it becomes impossible to separate the subjective distortions (caused by preconceptions in A's and B's minds) from the deformations of "external" physical time and space. Does the same journey *actually* require a second, ten minutes, ten hours? But what do we mean by "actually"? We can no more, any more, determine what *actually* is than A can get to B to settle his business.[45]

Much of Kafka's writing is devoted to such indeterminate temporal and spatial disjunctions–so much that the adjective "Kafkaesque" has been coined in part to describe this "common" modernist "confusion." In "A Country Doctor" (1917, published 1919), the journey to save the wounded Christ/patient is completed almost instantaneously; the return home has just begun as the story ends, but it will be literally interminable, an eternal wandering. In another story, "The Hunter Gracchus" (written c. 1917), the hunter dies naturalistically in the Black Forest but his death ship loses its way. He is prisoner both of time and of eternity, trapped in time, forced to awaken daily but without respite in an eternal return without renewal.

The title of Kafka's "The Metamorphosis" denotes change, transformation, an altered state. A monstrous alteration is the premiss, the *donnée* of the tale. The "metamorphosis" refers immediately to the transformation of the protagonist into an insect, a process which is completed before the story begins and which in part provides a symbolic or, more accurately, parabolic revelation of the protagonist's spiritual state. We learn that Gregor has gradually and inexorably supplanted his father as head of the family and that he has sexual fantasies about his sister. But a metamorphosis as serious as his physical transformation, one that takes place during the whole course of the story, lies in the transformation of Gregor's will from tenacious aggrandizing to

---

44. Franz Kafka, "A Common Confusion," in *The Great Wall of China*, p. 129.

45. It is certainly possible that a modernist physicist may object that this particular tale cannot be truly "modern" because according to Relativity Theory there will be several "invariant" quantities upon which "A" and "B" can agree. No matter how their clocks might differ, they both must measure the same speed for light and the so called "interval" (a mathematical combination of time and distance measurements) must be the same for each, for example. But the mathematics of Relativity was not known to either "A" or "B" or probably even to Kafka and this "scientific" objection is quite beside our point. In modernist narrative as in modernist physics the whole question of the nature of time (and space) is up for grabs, and distortions abound in both.

abject self-effacement. The process of this inner metamorphosis provides the pathos and the comedy of the story: "He thought of his family with tenderness and love. The decision that he must disappear was one that he held to even more strongly than his sister, if that were possible."[46] Gregor's achievement of resignation follows a deeply traditional pattern in Western literature. In Kafka's writing it is paralleled by Joseph K.'s spiritual development in *The Trial* (1914, *Der Prozess*). What traditional religious literature does not contain, but what *The Trial* and "The Metamorphosis" show, is a radical ambiguity concerning what to make of the whole account.[47]

This modernist ambiguity is reinforced by what we might call the story's secondary distortions, especially a narration in which time is seen as deformable, clotted. Gregor's gradual resignation is paced by an accelerating temporal medium that appears to be inconsistent, perhaps perverse. When Gregor awakens in his new form he is late for work and time has already begun to pass him by: "He looked at the alarm clock ticking on the chest. Heavenly Father! he thought. It was half-past six o'clock and the hands were quietly moving on, it was even past the half-hour, it was getting on toward a quarter to seven."[48] Despite Gregor's awareness of his insect state, he believes that he can set everything right by being on time. But time, heretofore Gregor's ally in his work (he has been the early bird), can no longer be depended upon. Is Gregor's obsession with time a form of madness? Perhaps, but then it is a madness shared by his employers: at ten minutes past seven the chief clerk turns up to find out why Gregor didn't catch the early train.

The social satire here concerns the obsession of mercantile capitalism, and its business practices, with schedules and timing and the substitution of these mechanical elements for the more organic rhythms of life often nostalgically associated with pre-industrial society.[49] Gregor's metamorphosis seems to reinstate some of these earlier rhythms. In particular, time ceases to be the regular duration prescribed by Newtonian mechanics and becomes deformable, distended or compacted by Gregor's needs and fears. The story shows Gregor losing touch with clock and calendar time. Eventually, he can't remember whether Christmas has come and gone. Distances become relative (usually inversely proportional) to his moods and his abilities: "He was amazed at the distance separating him from his room and could not understand how in his

---

46. Franz Kafka, "The Metamorphosis," in *The Penal Colony*, p. 127.

47. Specifically religious allegory and parable, along with other forms of didactic writing, may of course strike us as unclear even in the interpretation of their central meaning. The biblical Book of Job and the Middle English poem *Sir Gawain and the Green Knight* can provide examples of such difficulties. The ambiguities there, however, are largely the product of historical and cultural distance. Such works are didactic: ambiguity may be among their heuristic devices, but it is not their aim or ultimate effect.

48. Kafka, "The Metamorphosis," p. 69.

49. Writing of Theodor Adorno's *Aesthetic Theory*, Astradur Eysteinsson observes: "Modernist writing, through its autonomous formal constructions, places us at a 'distance' from society, making it strange, whereby we come to see its reverse, but true, mirror image, its negativity" (*The Concept of Modernism*, p. 45).

weak state he had managed to accomplish the same journey so recently, almost without remarking it."[50]

Are these departures from the objective time of realist fiction meant to reflect the distortions of Gregor's failing perception? Perhaps, but we have no way of knowing for certain. Here, in violation of the narrative conventions of nineteenth-century Realism, we are not told and we cannot identify the line between "reality" and subjective perception. The story ends with the family's apparent return to normality after Gregor's oppression ends in his death, but this return is actually the reverse of reassuring since it entails a shift away from Gregor as the center of narrative consciousness and thus calls into question the point of view of all the earlier action. As in *The Turn of the Screw* we will never know the "true" state of things. Kafka's stories, like Joyce's and like Henry James's, like the paintings of Picasso and Braque, like the metric tensor describing the geometry of spacetime in General Relativity, present not imitations of *the* reality but representations of realities. In particular, "The Metamorphosis" leaves us with the implication that reality in and of itself may be inaccessible to perception and that the search for such reality always leads to ambiguity. This ambiguity, a logical consequence of pluralistic reality, is a theme as well as a technique of modernist fiction.

This level of uncertainty and ambiguity constitutes a departure from the conventions of traditional Realism. But Kafka's admirers have not seen it as a departure from *reality*. On the contrary, like the early apologists for Cubism, a number of Kafka's modernist readers saw in his writing the closest and most faithful depiction of a real world that had become distant, alien, evasive. What exist as distortions in terms of conventional Realism become, like the apparent deformations of cubist representation, a better approximation of human experience in the actual world. Kafka's work offered a better model of what modernist writers took to be the reality of their contemporary experience – and not merely the experience of their creative enterprise but of the twentieth-century world to come. Commentators like Félix Bertaux, writing a survey of German literature for French readers in the early 1930s, spoke of Kafka's "passion for clarity." Albert Camus, whose fictional representations of absurdity owe a lot to Kafka's writing, paid his fidelity to reality a handsome tribute: "And those inspired automata, Kafka's characters, provide us with a precise image of what we should be if we were deprived of our distractions and utterly consigned to the humiliations of the divine."[51]

The theme of inescapable ambiguity in the pursuit of reality pervades Kafka's work but it is by no means exclusively his concern. Throughout modernist narrative a multiplicity of reference frames produces a multiplicity of realities. A great deal of modernist fiction both demonstrates this and asserts it. Joseph Conrad's great short story "The Secret Sharer" (1910) begins with a long descriptive paragraph that suggests with every phrase the difficulty of

---

50. Kafka, "The Metamorphosis," p. 126.
51. Ronald Gray, *Franz Kafka*, p. 5. Albert Camus, *The Myth of Sisyphus*, pp. 97–98.

interpreting, or rather of decoding, reality. For example the narrator can see (among other opacities) the tops of a number of fishing stakes whose arrangement is unfathomable, indecipherable from his perspective, "a mysterious system of half-submerged bamboo fences, incomprehensible in its division of the domain of tropical fishes."[52] Presumably from beneath the surface the arrangement of the fishing stakes makes sense, has a logic dependent upon the movement of fish in this section of the Gulf of Siam. The incomprehensibility, the nonsense, is a matter of point of view. In the course of the story the narrator comes to the realization that the established coordinates – the norms – of legal, ethical, professional life are inadequate to deal with the demands on his authority, inadequate to guide him in his command.

Conrad, like Kafka, is preoccupied with the shortcomings of our rational systems in dealing with contemporary moral and ethical problems. In Conrad's work the emphasis seems to be less on fundamental epistemological and metaphysical questions and more on psychological and social experience. But Conrad's work belongs to the modernist enterprise of showing that what we take to be exceptional or grotesque manifestations may really lie at the heart of human reality. Kurtz in "Heart of Darkness" (1902) is seen early on as a kind of human distortion, a European who has permitted himself to "go native" and, worse, to yield to the monstrous temptation to become a god. Conrad's narrator comes to understand, however, that this deformation of European ideals is actually a kind of logical extension of universal human nature when the social inhibitions (seen as the redeeming lies and the practical obsessions of civilization) are removed.

Again, distortions and deformations are a matter of point of view. In *The Secret Agent* (1907), where Conrad deals darkly and comically with the monstrosities of terrorist political action and the inadequacy of establishment methods to counter it, the ironies manage to transform the moral context. The conspirators and the agents of the political establishment become obtuse reflections of each other. The moral confusion infects even the world of geometric forms:

> Mr Verloc [the secret agent], getting off the sofa with ponderous reluctance, opened the door leading into the kitchen to get more air, and thus disclosed the innocent Stevie [his mentally retarded brother-in-law], seated very good and quiet at a deal table, drawing circles, circles; innumerable circles, concentric, eccentric; a coruscating whirl of circles that by their tangled multitude of repeated curves, uniformity of form, and confusion of intersecting lines suggested a rendering of cosmic chaos, the symbolism of a mad art attempting the inconceivable.[53]

The archetypal symbol of formal perfection, of perfect order, and of geometrical completeness seems in Stevie's hands to represent cosmic anarchy. The

52. Joseph Conrad, "The Secret Sharer," in *Great Short Works*, p. 367.
53. Joseph Conrad, *The Secret Agent*, p. 76.

bankruptcy of traditional methods for protecting the political order, and the obtuseness of its agents, are symbolized by the transformation of the circle into a sign of disorder. In the hands of Stevie, the hands of a sentimental, humane idiot, the geometric emblem of containment develops radically centrifugal tendencies. Only idiots believe in the stability represented by the perfect Euclidean circle.

The large problem of cultural norms and the departure from them lies at the center of E. M. Forster's A *Passage to India* (1924). At first the problem is brought forth as a matter of cultural *relativism*, understood in differing degrees by characters such as Fielding, Mrs Moore, and Adela Quested. There are the British and there are the Indians. They see things differently. This difference in viewpoint is proper and natural and must not be disturbed as long as order is maintained. Order, to most of "the British," means British rule in India and the safety of British subjects. But in general the British must behave and see things in a British way and the Indians are expected to behave and see things in an Indian way. This is so clearly understood that it has in itself become a principle of social order and people who cross the line from one camp to another, as Fielding tends to do, may be regarded as destabilizing elements.

But cultural relativism is not Relativity. Nor is it necessarily a characteristic of Modernism, though it gained in status and prestige by the popularization of anthropological researches in the late nineteenth and early twentieth centuries. Moral and cultural relativism holds that no valid ethical or moral *judgment* can be made with regard to the superiority or inferiority of a culture or its internal practices because they are always valid for the culture in question. Relativity, on the other hand, is epistemologically rather than ethically liberal: it holds that there is no privileged vantage point from which one can *observe* culture or its practices. Relativity holds that the observer's measurements are always made from within the observer's system and will almost certainly differ from those made from outside it, from some other system (or culture). Relativistic thought implies not that England and India have equally valid ways of doing things but that (as the end of Forster's novel suggests) there is no reference frame from which an unbiased view may be had. It may be that an understanding of Relativity's epistemological implications would reinforce an observer's relativism but that would not be an inherently logical consequence.[54]

A *Passage to India* distinguishes between relativism and relativity, and helps us distinguish between them. Not surprisingly, the more open-minded characters find it much easier to adopt a posture of cultural relativism (as Mrs Moore at first does with Dr Aziz) than to accept the consequences of epistemological relativity. What troubles Mrs Moore most is that the hierarchical absolutes of her traditional religious faith begin to lose force in India:

---

54. Furthermore, it bears repeating that there *are* constants in Einstein's 1905 theory. We have previously mentioned the measured speed for light and the so-called "interval."

Mrs. Moore felt that she had made a mistake in mentioning God, but she found him increasingly difficult to avoid as she grew older, and he had been constantly in her thoughts since she entered India, though oddly enough he satisfied her less. She must needs pronounce his name frequently, as the greatest she knew, yet she had never found it less efficacious. Outside the arch there seemed always an arch, beyond the remotest echo a silence.[55]

Along with the increasing awkwardness with "God" (the ultimate objectifier) comes a loss of meaning in language and in social order. Ideological, ethical, and semiotic hierarchies cease to make sense. In the Marabar Caves, Mrs Moore has a brush with nihilism:

The crush and the smells she could forget, but the echo began in some indescribable way to undermine her hold on life. Coming at a moment when she chanced to be fatigued, it had managed to murmur, 'Pathos, piety, courage – they exist, but are identical, and so is filth. Everything exists, nothing has value'.[56]

With the challenge to her Western hierarchy of values – in A Passage to India this challenge is closely allied to Hindu devotional practice – life for Mrs Moore loses its meaning and she leaves India in spiritual despair. She has been brought – in a phrase from another of the novel's contexts –"to acquire disillusionment." What has led her to this condition are not the distortions or deformations of India, but the realization that no firm ground exists anywhere. Without an objectifier there can be no privileged hierarchy; without a hierarchy there are no norms; no norms mean no distortions. "Everything exists, nothing has value." It is not relativism but Relativity that gets to Mrs Moore.[57]

Thus there appears to be a failure of traditional Western absolutes in India – but they are not replaced with non-Western absolutes. Nothing (literally the "nothing" of the Marabar Caves) seems to replace them. The Hindu Professor Godbole has his religious affirmations – and these indeed occupy a mysteriously privileged center in the novel – but they are not accessible to Europeans or even to the Muslim Dr Aziz. In this way, India itself becomes a metaphor, in the British or Western mind of the reader, for the relative universe, the universe of curved moral and aesthetic space – ambiguous, pluralistically perceived space. India therefore becomes an image of the modern world – or at least of the modernist intellectual world – composed of discrete systems of time and space. The novel is about the search for an absolute reference frame and the failure to find one. What we are left with in A Passage to India is a plurality of perspectives, multiple perspectives. That plurality makes up modernist reality. That is what "India" is.

Aziz remarks to Adela Quested:

55. E.M. Forster, A Passage to India, p. 52.
56. Ibid., pp. 149–150.
57. Mrs Moore would not be satisfied with invariants. She wants her traditional absolutes.

"You keep your religion, I mine. That is the best. Nothing embraces the whole of India, nothing, nothing, and that was Akbar's mistake."

"Oh, do you feel that, Dr. Aziz?" she said thoughtfully. "I hope you're not right. There will have to be something universal in this country – I don't say religion, for I'm not religious, but something, or how else are barriers to be broken down?"[58]

The answer is that they are not to be broken down. The barriers, like Mrs Moore's crumbling hierarchies, are what we have left for reality, our points of view. India exists, but we do not and cannot see it together.

In this chapter we have attempted to establish a second major value of Modernism. This value might be briefly and abstractly characterized as the *contextualization of identity*. By this we mean that in Modernism objects and events lost the normative or essentialist identity that they were traditionally thought to possess in themselves. This is not to say that realistic objects and events had no context, social or ideological: they did of course, as considerable historical scholarship demonstrates. Indeed pre-modernist practices of measurement and of representation form no small part of such contexts. Our argument holds that in Modernism normative expectations underwent radical revision on the leading edge of culture, though even here we have used social and ideological contexts sparingly and selectively to illustrate the immense general change in value. In Modernism events and objects take on shape and function in relation to their immediate context, and the context in a high degree determines their dynamic and formal qualities. From the perspective of traditional Realism such modernist phenomena can appear as distortions because they depart from and characteristically threaten expectations based on established markers that traditionally determined identity.

58. Forster, *A Passage to India*, p. 145.

Chapter 4 From Reality to Observation

> Almost immediately, reality gave ground on more than
> one point. The truth is that it hankered to give ground.
>
> Jorge Luis Borges, "Tlön, Uqbar, Orbis Tertius"

In the preceding chapters we were concerned to describe ways in which modernist physics, painting, and narrative departed from their respective traditions. We showed this by identifying and discussing two values or general characteristics of Modernism, epistemic trauma and radical contextualization. These values shape the distinctive productions of the period in the three cultural diagnostics, and also serve to describe widespread reactions to modernist innovations. In our view, such reactions are neither naive nor accidental. The fact that intellectual culture, scientific and aesthetic "literacy," became in a very short period much more difficult to acquire may be the single most important fact about Modernism for the majority of those who come into direct contact with it. And although some of the modernist innovations we examine no longer cause the degree of primary bafflement they did at first, it cannot be said that the work of Einstein or Picasso or Kafka has yet become part of our easy apprehension of the cultural past. Most people still find such nineteenth-century precursors as Darwin, or Monet, or George Eliot considerably more approachable – despite their undoubted originality and richness. The persisting strangeness in Modernism suggests both the endurance of traditional habits of mind and the remarkable historical compression of the modernist revolution. It also reflects the self-conscious aim of modernist painters and writers to produce work of marked strangeness, an aspect of the avant-garde's social and aesthetic agenda.

In general, we tried to keep our preceding chapters more descriptive than analytical. We tried to say *what* in our opinion happened, what the departures in Relativity, in Cubism, in modernist narrative, look like historically. Our description, in order to emphasize the common characteristics across fields, was kept as free as possible from local, field-specific political and methodological controversies. No doubt some scholarly readers may feel that their specific disciplines deserve fuller treatment, a problem we addressed in our introduction (Chapter 1). And of course to describe modernist epistemic trauma and distortion we found it necessary to give brief sketches of the scientific and aesthetic traditions, especially of the Newtonian world model in the natural sciences and of nineteenth-century Realism in painting and narrative. Now, having offered some description of what happened, we are free to ask *how*.

The present chapter deals with a fundamental change in the perception of reality, in the kind of contact people saw themselves as having with the external or natural world. We identify this change as a shift in values from "reality" to "observation." Such a shift in values is difficult to describe. Formulations that possess the precision and accuracy necessary to comprehend it can seem cumbersome. Modernism is a dynamic, highly pressured, freakish period – and our perception of it is clouded by the fact that in many ways it is the period that produced us. At some point people who like to think seriously about science and art stopped talking about reality and started talking about the observation of reality. We gave up some of the dogmatism of objectivity (the unquestioning assumption that we could agree on and describe what exists independent of perception) and began to examine what we meant by our own attempts to describe whatever may be out there. As a fundamental correlative of this process, our relation to the media of space and time underwent a marked alteration. We have seen that this did happen. We turn now to an analysis of the new ideas and techniques, the new argument with the world.

Relativity

We have hinted at the immense prestige of the cosmic model based on Newton's mechanics, with its apparently inalterable and complete set of laws.[1] It seems almost unnecessary to insist on the endurance of this prestige: Newton's cosmos remains the dominant, commonsense, intuitive model for most people in much the same way that the conventions of Realism continue to dominate popular fiction and most of the visual arts aimed at wide audiences. Both realist aesthetic conventions and Newton's physics have ways of colonizing the epistemological territory, of presenting themselves as the truth (unmediated descriptions of *reality*) rather than as functional models. From their beginning Newton's descriptions of nature were treated not merely as aspects of an operational model of the cosmos but as essential descriptions of natural reality:

> Nature, and Nature's laws lay hid in night:
> God said, *Let Newton be!* and all was light.[2]

1. See pp. 16–25, 40–41 and 55–60 above; also Delo Mook and Thomas Vargish, *Inside Relativity*, Chapter 2, "The Classical Background."
2. Alexander Pope, "Epitaph Intended for Sir Isaac Newton, in *The Complete Poetical Works of Pope*, p. 135. Newton's prestige, what Marjorie Hope Nicholson calls his "deification," is discussed in her *Newton Demands the Muse: Newton's Opticks and the Eighteenth Century Poets*, p. vii and Chapter 1 (pp. 1–19).

Newton's laws shortly became, at least in the general culture, not merely descriptive but prescriptive – so that natural phenomena, in order to qualify as reality, had to conform to the Newtonian description.

Einstein undermined this coherent and rational structure by redirecting attention from the nature of reality to the nature of measurement, from what was taken to be our direct contact with nature to our observation of it. Physicists involved in this redirection were keenly aware of the epistemic change they were making. Werner Heisenberg writing in 1958 reflected that the modern physics of elementary particles "no longer describes the behavior of the elementary particles but only our knowledge of their behavior. The atomic physicist has had to resign himself to the fact that his science is but a link in the infinite chain of man's argument with nature, *and that it cannot simply speak of nature 'in itself.'*" Later in the same essay Heisenberg remarks that "When we [physicists] speak of the picture of nature in the exact science of our age, we do not mean a picture of nature so much as a *picture of our relationships with nature.*"[3]

The importance of this shift, pervasive and central to Modernism in general, can scarcely be overemphasized.[4] In his 1905 paper on Special Relativity Einstein did not ask what time *is*: he asked how we *measure* it. He asked what we *mean* by the time of an event. Einstein saw that all statements about temporal measurements are statements about simultaneous events, and that all statements about spatial measurements are also, ultimately, statements about simultaneous events.[5] Unlike Newton, he did not imagine a universe of independent phenomena but a universe of human beings measuring phenomena. Relativity is thus a theory of physical measurement, not a theory of physical reality. As Sir Arthur Eddington put it in 1920, "When a rod is started from rest into uniform motion, nothing whatever happens to the rod. We say that it contracts; but length is not a property of the rod; it is a relation between the rod and the observer. *Until the observer is specified the length of the rod is quite indeterminate.*"[6]

The startling advances of Special Relativity were made possible by this

3. Werner Heisenberg, *The Physicist's Conception of Nature*, pp. 28–29. See also the discussion by Gérard Mermoz, "On the Synchronism between Artistic and Scientific Ideas and Practices," p. 139.
4. We saw in our preceding chapters that this intellectual ground had been cultivated for some time. By 1905, when Einstein published his paper on Special Relativity, the prestige of absolute time, Newton's "duration," had declined among literary artists and intellectuals as well as among physicists like Ernst Mach. Mach (1836–1916) believed that physics (and philosophy) must be purged of all ideas and concepts not directly observable: all concepts must be defined in terms of direct sensory experience. Mach's book *The Science of Mechanics* (1883) attacked Newton's absolute time (and space) as operationally undefinable and hence without place in physics. Einstein admired Mach's book which "exercised a profound influence upon me . . . while I was a student. I see Mach's greatness in his incorruptible skepticism and independence" (Paul Arthur Schilpp, *Albert Einstein: Philosopher-Scientist*, I, 21). For an excellent brief account of Mach's attack on Newtonian absolutes and his influence on Einstein, see Jeremy Bernstein, *Einstein*, pp. 130–133.
5. See Mook and Vargish, *Inside Relativity*, pp. 53–85.
6. A. S. Eddington, *Report on the Relativity Theory of Gravitation*, pp. 8–9 (as throughout this study italics are the original author's, not ours).

shift of emphasis away from the phenomenon as a discrete event and toward the observation of the phenomenon. A Newtonian thinks of a rod as inherently possessing length. A post-Newtonian thinks of length as *resulting from an act of observation applied to the rod*. Einstein did not conclude that "everything is relative." Nor did he abandon his assumption that the observer observes an external, independent reality.[7] He did assume that for human beings it is the location in time and space that determines our measurements of that reality, that determines in fact what that reality is to us.

For example, consider an object such as Volume 17 of the *Annalen der Physik*, the volume containing Einstein's original paper on Special Relativity. We measured the pages of this bound journal in a university library and we found that the book has a length of 24 cm. and a width of 19 cm. We were able to measure this same set of dimensions time after time, day after day. The pages remained the same size. But now suppose that the book moves lengthwise through the library stacks at various speeds. We measure the dimensions of the moving book. The table below shows what Special Relativity predicts our measurements of its length will be:

Speed(km/sec.)	Length(cm.)	Width(cm.)
0	24.0	19.0
100,000	22.6	19.0
240,000	14.4	19.0
290,000	6.1	19.0
299,000	2.0	19.0

One's response to the table could be that Special Relativity is predicting that the book has undergone a "distortion" because of its motion. But if we accept this suggestion we are led to a quandary: what is the "true" shape of the book? Why does its measured length change but not its width? We have discussed such questions in detail elsewhere;[8] here it will suffice to say that according to the Special Theory the length that we measure from our viewpoint (at rest at our reading desk) will indeed decrease in the direction of its motion as shown in the table. The width of the book, being perpendicular to the direction of motion, will experience no shrinkage. As the speed becomes greater the measured length becomes shorter and the book's overall measured shape becomes flattened into a small plane moving with its face in the direction of motion.

In the preceding paragraph we have used the word "speed" rather freely. What speed of the book are we talking about? This point is crucial to our discussion. Suppose that instead of sitting at our library desk we are in a wheeled chair that is moving in the same direction as the book and at the

7. See Bertrand Russell, *The ABC of Relativity*, pp. 138–139; and Ilse Rosenthal-Schneider, *Reality and Scientific Truth*, pp. 70–71.
8. Mook and Vargish, *Inside Relativity*, pp. 78–83.

same speed with respect to the reading desk. Then the book has no speed as far as we are concerned. From our new viewpoint, according to the Special Theory, we will measure it to have a length (24 cm.) and a width (19 cm.) just as it did at rest on the library shelf. As our chair slows and the bound periodical pulls away from us at an ever increasing speed, we measure its length to be shorter and shorter. In other words, the "speed" that we have been talking about all along is the speed of the book with respect to us, *relative* to us – a measurement dependent on our viewpoint with respect to the book (specifically, how fast our viewpoint moves with respect to it). When we were at rest at the reading desk the speed of the book was also its speed with respect to the desk, but we can change the book's speed (and so its measured length) simply by changing our viewpoint (specifically by moving the book relative to the reading desk at various speeds). And now the quandary dissipates because we see that its premiss is incorrect. In our quandary we asked what is "the true" length of the book; we now see that according to Special Relativity, the length of an object depends on the object's coordinates as well as the coordinates (the viewpoint) of any observer (or measurer) of that length. And so there is no "distortion" of the book because there is no absolute or "true" shape for the book in the first place.

This may still leave a possible objection: whenever we have consulted this book on the shelves or on a reading desk in the library it always presented the same shape and the same dimensions and so that shape and those dimensions acquired a certain prestige. They seem to be "true" facts about the book because we could always verify them. The "real book" we think of is derived from observations made when the book is at rest with respect to us or moving at a very slow speed with respect to that of light. But if we were moving through the library at a high speed and glanced at the book on its shelf or on the reading desk it would show the same shape as it did moving past us through the stacks at that speed. So what at first seemed to be a "distortion" was due to our prejudiced viewpoint, our prejudice developed by our habit of always viewing the volume at a low speed. According to Relativity Theory the nature of "shape," the nature of geometry, depends on an observer's frame of reference.

Again, it is important to remember that none of the various measurements or observations that Relativity Theory describes has any direct application to what are sometimes called "psychological" or "subjective" phenomena: objects and events that exist only within an individual human mind. Relativity Theory describes a *relationship*, what Werner Heisenberg called an "argument with nature."[9] In Relativity Theory, a *measurement* is neither a subjective impression (a unique event in a single mind that cannot be fully communicated) nor a constant necessary description of an independent external object or event. A *measurement* in Relativity Theory may be seen as a kind of middle ground – literally a *mediation* – between the observer and the observed

9. Heisenberg, *The Physicist's Conception of Nature*, p. 15.

phenomenon. In postmodern critical terminology, observation is the *text* of Modernism.[10]

And this middle ground, we believe, is the characteristic epistemological location of Modernism. As we will see, it is shared with Relativity Theory by Cubism and by modernist narrative.[11] This middle ground is neither sub-jective nor objective, but a human observation of a reality assumed to be external to the observer. With respect to subjectivity and subjective phenomena, Relativity Theory has nothing to say. With respect to objectivity and objective reality, Relativity Theory premises its existence and deals with measurements of it that necessarily vary. In Relativity, measurement is what we have of reality.

There is a modernist riddle which asks whether zebras are white with black stripes or black with white stripes. The relativistic answer is that we have no way of knowing what color zebras are but we can observe the stripes.

Cubism

In one respect, the value shift from reality to the observation of reality in Cubism continues a transition already begun in late realistic painting. This is a change in emphasis from the subject as independent of representation and toward the representation of the subject. We have noticed this process at work in Impressionism with its concentration on light and color, on the imitation of the appearance of objects in nature. Cubism radically accelerates this change and in a sense completes it with the initiation of formal techniques that abandon or counter the illusion of realist depth. There is an important sense in which the new techniques bring the focus of attention to the act of representation itself, to the epistemological implications of painting as a self-conscious activity, and we will consider this in Chapter 6, on Reflexivity. Here we concern ourselves with the tendency in Cubism to draw attention away from what had been considered the significance of the objects represented and toward their new relation to the space in which they are represented.

The choice of objects that Picasso and Braque and then Gris made for their paintings does have significance. We find a good deal of repetition –

10. That is to say its language, its system of relationships, its production of meaning, what it knows. See for example Roland Barthes, *The Pleasure of the Text*, or the more accessible Elizabeth Ermarth, *Sequel to History*, pp. 3–18 ("Prologue: Why Text?").

11. And shared, we could argue, by Freud's psychoanalysis and especially psychoanalytic theory nearly contemporaneous with the Special Theory. By 1898, Freud had arrived at the conclusion that what caused hysteria (and perhaps other neuroses) was repression. However, what was repressed was not *reality*, an objective historical event, but the memory of a reality – that is to say a human construct analogous to a measurement in physics. Freud had determined, for reasons that remain in dispute, that the memory need not be an accurate reproduction of a *real* event but a mental construct or affective correlative of the event. The memory is to be seen as part of the psychological history of the patient; the real, external event – though not discarded or lost sight of by Freud – is not the primary focus of the analysis. Thus a modernist aspect of early psychoanalysis is that it deals primarily with an "observation" or "measurement" – with the middle ground that is Modernism's epistemological site. See Sigmund Freud, *Early Psychoanalytic Writings*, and especially the essays on "The Aetiology of Hysteria" (1896) and "Screen Memories" (1899).

the wine bottles and glasses, tables, musical instruments, lettering, certain facial features (noses, eyes, lips, moustaches), hands – and this repetition reflects a style of life that ultimately makes a loosely anti-bourgeois statement. So it cannot be said that the objects represented are without referential meaning, but they seem often to be chosen partly for the sake of their *minimal* importance in the mainstream traditional hierarchies of Western art, whose values were characterized by early modernist painters under the ironic collective term, "the Louvre." The characteristic cubist objects were chosen because they were conventionally regarded as unimportant in themselves: they throw the attention back on the treatment. Even Picasso's early cubist "portraits" do not present the public outer likeness or the intimate inner recognition that offers the traditional gratifications of this form. In fact the brilliance of the portraits lies precisely in their calling our attention to the problematics of "likeness" and "portrait".

In a marked, fully conscious departure from its historical background, the "Louvre" tradition of Western painting (which the major cubists knew very well), Cubism clearly deflects our interest from the subject to its representation. In this process it derogates the specific importance of the historically or religiously or sentimentally significant subject. The focus of our attention has been shifted from the traditionally important subject (Christ on the Cross, the Mona Lisa, Manet's Olympia or Whistler's mother) to the techniques of representing the subject, the aesthetics of composition, the formal arrangement. What is significant about Picasso's *Portrait of Ambroise Vollard* (Plate 7) is not the subject (his distinctive features, his support of modernist art, his aesthetic intuition). What is important in Picasso's portrait is how Picasso presents Ambroise Vollard. Just as Relativity Theory refocused attention away from the nature of reality and toward the nature of measurement, of observation, so Cubism refocused attention away from what was being represented and toward how it was being represented. Cubist paintings from 1907 to 1914 are not independent of their subjects any more than Relativity Theory sees itself as independent of nature. But like Relativity Theory, Cubism occupies that middle ground between external reality and subjectivity. Like the measurements of Relativity Theory, the cubist paintings of this period are highly constructed mediations between external reality and the mind of the viewer.

Here again we need careful distinctions in order to give an accurate account of the nature of the change. Perhaps the most common errors in cultural history are claims of novelty for "innovations" that can be found active in earlier periods and movements. It is true that realistic paintings (and realistic novels, and Newton's laws of motion) become possible by means of conventions that mediate between observer and object; and that in this sense spatial conventions of realistic representation in the plastic arts are "mediations," and indeed have been called that.[12] The immense difference is that now the

---

12. See Edward F. Fry, "Picasso, Cubism, and Reflexivity," p. 596; and Elizabeth Ermarth on the "Rationalization of Sight," in *Realism and Consensus in the English Novel*, pp. 16–24.

mediation calls attention to itself *as a mediation.* In the transition from Classicism and Realism to Modernism, our entire relation to the reality represented has been changed. It is one thing for a Renaissance master of representation, Raphael for example, to declare (by means of a painting): "The Madonna existed; here is how she might have appeared." We know that this painting is *his* vision, a vision consciously idealized from present reality, modeled or not. We are not dealing with the external "real" world in all its imperfections. What interests us here are not the social or religious or even the strictly optical qualities of the work but the conventions of representation. These conventions assert that if we were standing where the artist was painting we would have seen what he has painted; that what he has painted might be a luminous approximation of Mary with her baby as they existed fourteen and a half centuries before; and that this representation has immense significance primarily *because the subject has immense significance.* And the same could be said for painting of secular subjects: Rembrandt's self-portraits, Hogarth's streets, David's historical scenes. Only the context of the subject's significance would vary. In pre-modernist conventions of representation significance may be religious or individual, sentimental or social, philosophical or historical, but the traditional conventions imply that the subject empowers and invests the representation with significance.

No cubist painting accepts this. Cubist paintings say, "This is what I *observe* and *have observed* about this visual reality. I offer it to you as an *observation.*" Cubist paintings are improvisations on the representation of visual reality, on what we take to be space and the relations of objects to space. The mediation, the observation and representation of the visual reality, has become the primary subject of the painting. Whereas the success of the classicist or realist painting at least in part depends upon its ability to hide, to keep latent, the act of mediation, the cubist representation places this act at the center of our consideration. We can point out, for example, that in the vast tradition of religious painting no act of representation however masterly, not even Raphael's, could have the status, the prestige, the claim to our interest, of the Madonna herself. And even when the represented subject is not sacred but assertively profane (a Courbet nude, for example) our attention is focused on it by the very premises of the convention. But Picasso's act of mediation might supersede his subject, might interest us more than a wine bottle, a scrap of newsprint, or Ambroise Vollard.

This is largely because Picasso's act of mediation is not a study of a wine bottle in the same sense that Raphael's painting is a study of the Madonna. Raphael's mastery of space, its representation and mediation, serves to present his visual conception of a subject. Picasso's is an explicit statement about the nature of visual experience – of forms, of spaces, of colors and of the relation of these quantities to each other. Where the classical representation centers the subject, the cubist statement centers the representation. And as a result of this shift of emphasis away from the content of observed reality and toward the observation of formal relationships, Cubism was liberated to alter the representational space of painting in ways strongly analogous to the alteration of space in Relativity Theory. The fact that direct influence between Einstein in central Europe and Picasso and Braque in France was unlikely or impossible does not detract from our description of Modernism.[13] What matters to us is that during the years from 1905 to 1915 in both the natural sciences and the plastic arts the medium of space – long considered neutral, homogeneous, "free" – suddenly developed formal and physical properties of compression and extension, of variation, assertion, influence.

Part of this change in painting appeared as an attempt to be true to the two-dimensional painting surface, an aspiration of Cézanne's.[14] Unlike Cézanne, however, Picasso and Braque were willing to reject explicitly the *trompe l'oeil*, the illusion of depth, of realist painting. Kahnweiler recalls Picasso's deliberate efforts to work this out: "In the spring of 1908 he resumed his quest, this time solving one by one the problems that arose. He had to begin with the most important thing, and that seemed to be the explanation of form, the representation of the three-dimensional and its position in space on a two-dimensional surface."[15] The conventions of single-point perspective had begun to seem not merely inadequate to the visual experience of nature (as Cézanne found them) but actually an *unreal* limitation on the representation of visual experience. In the words of Jacques Rivière, one of the most perceptive early commentators on Cubism, "Perspective is as accidental a thing as lighting. It is the sign, not of a particular moment in time, but of a particular position in space. It indicates not the situation of the objects, but the situation of a spectator. . . . Hence, in the final analysis, perspective is also the sign of an instant, of the instant when a certain man is at a certain point."[16]

But if realist perspective is discarded as too limiting, how is the three-dimensionality, the solidity, what is sometimes called the "sculptural" quality of objects to be represented? Clement Greenberg has managed what seems to us a technically accurate description that also accommodates the experience of non-specialized viewers, a feat that makes it worth quoting at length:

> Picasso and Braque began as Cubists by modeling the depicted object in little facet-planes that they took from Cézanne's last manner. [See Plate 8, *The Big*

13. See Chapter 1, pp. 3–6 above; and Linda Dalrymple Henderson, "The Question of Cubism and Relativity," Appendix A of *The Fourth Dimension and Non-Euclidean Geometry in Modern Art*, pp. 353–365.
14. See, for example, Clement Greenberg, "Cézanne, " in *Art and Culture*, pp. 54–57.
15. Daniel-Henry Kahnweiler, from *The Rise of Cubism* (1915), in Herschel B. Chipp, *Theories of Modern Art*, p. 252.
16. Jacques Rivière, "Present Tendencies in Painting" (1912), in Edward F. Fry, *Cubism*, p. 77. It is in this sense that, as Edward Fry puts it, "All the critics of cubism, both during its life span and afterwards, agree that its intentions were basically realistic. It is certainly easy to recognize how much more dispassionately realistic it was than such other styles of the period as futurism or German expressionism. An indication of this ultimate reliance on the visual world is the fact that a true cubist painting contains as subject-matter only those objects which might plausibly be seen together in one place. The real problem, therefore, is the precise nature of cubist reality, compared with the treatment of reality in earlier art, and whether or not the character of this cubist reality changes with the evolution of the style" (ibid., p. 36).

Trees (1902–4).] By this means they hoped to define volume more vividly, yet at the [same] time to relate it more firmly to the flatness of the picture plane. The threatened outcome of this procedure was, however, to detach the object from its background like a piece of illustrated sculpture. So, eliminating broad color contrasts and confining themselves to small touches of yellow, brown, gray and black, Picasso and Braque began to model the background too in facet-planes – the way Cézanne in his last years had modeled cloudless skies. Soon, to make a less abrupt transition from object to background, and from plane to plane inside the object, the facet-planes were opened up, and at the same time rendered more frontal – whence the *truncated* rectangles, triangles and circles that made up the characteristic vocabulary of Picasso's and Braque's Analytical Cubism. The contour and silhouetting lines of the depicted object became increasingly blurred, and the space inside the object faulted through into surrounding space, which, in turn, could be seen as infiltrating the object.[17]

The picture surface was thus no longer composed of objects standing in free space, but of constituents (the "little facet-planes" otherwise known as "cubes") that make up both the objects and their surrounding context (see Plates 5 and 7, Picasso's *The Aficionado* and *Portrait of Ambroise Vollard*). The absolute distinction between objects and the space in which they were supposed to "stand" is thus obliterated. With the identity (or at least increasing similarity) of the basic compositional elements of objects and their surrounding context it became possible to present the entire composition on a single general plane or (more accurately) a series of interconnecting shallow planes corresponding to or approximating the pictorial surface. All this became possible provided the artist could withstand the shock of withdrawal from the sustaining traditional conventions of Realism, a withdrawal that as we have seen was felt as epistemic trauma.

The use of the facet-planes as the basic compositional elements also supported the ambition of cubists to present what we *know* about a visual reality as well as what we see at any given instant. A glance at Picasso's *Aficionado* (Plate 5) shows that the facets themselves often help to indicate the objects represented, but as facets they can be used to represent any hypothetical point of view. And as we know, objects could be presented as seen from what in Realism would be different viewpoints on a single plane. The cubists could thus be true to the two-dimensional surface of painting and to what they might "know" about the visual reality of the object-spaces.

What seemed and may still seem "difficult" or "distorted" about this arises from its incompatibility with traditional Realism. Realism gave us the expectation that a single picture surface will represent reality at a single instant in time viewed from a single perspective in space. But this expectation is a

---

17. Greenberg, "Master Léger," in *Art and Culture*, pp. 98–99. Greenberg goes on to point out the similarities, and the debt, of this technique to Impressionism. A more sophisticated description of this process, aimed at showing its complex relationship to classical Realism, may be found in Edward Fry's "Picasso, Cubism, and Reflexivity," pp. 298–299.

realist convention, not a natural law or even a necessary experience of normal perception. After all, viewers of the world are often in motion themselves and are in the act of viewing moving objects.[18] The identification of the picture surface with an instant of time is an aesthetic convention based on certain arbitrary epistemological assumptions. When cubists represented more than one aspect of an object on a single surface they were violating a convention in much the same way that length contraction in Special Relativity violates the Newtonian–Euclidean convention of the undeformability of objects in motion.

It is in this context that we need to understand the popular talk about "simultaneity" in Cubism. Robert Delaunay used the word "Simultanéisme" to describe the combination of different aspects of figures and objects in the same painting.[19] Despite invocations of the "fourth dimension" in some of the writing contemporary with the development of Cubism, we have not found in the use of the *term* "simultaneity" important analogies to Einstein's essential definition of it in the Special Theory. The actual cubist *practice*, however, suggests important parallels. Paul Laporte has made accurate and reasonable use of these: "*The object of the painting is no longer an infinitesimal point in time manifest in an infinite space, but an event in time manifest in a finite space.*"[20] How is this perceived? According to Laporte a cubist painting represents experience of objects acquired over time by moving around them, freezes them simultaneously in space. "Through [Picasso's] kinesthetic experiences he participates in the dimension of time. But if time stops being measured as time, it resolves itself into the ever present dimension of space. . . . In Picasso, time is frozen into the 'distortions' of two-dimensional space."[21]

But what is of greatest significance to our present value, involving the shift from the consideration of reality to the consideration of the observation of reality, is that with such discussions as the inevitably awkward one of simultaneity in painting a fresh interest opens up. We are no longer locked into the limiting dichotomies of subject and treatment, world and observer. We can begin to move from one side to the other, to explore without interruption the unceasing interaction of the object and its space.[22] The old categories lose their integrity in our experience and we begin to inhabit the middle ground of observation itself. This was a profound discovery of early Modernism. In an essay of 1912, Maurice Raynal shows his awareness of it in a comment on the futurist school:

18. An observation often made by the futurists, who receive limited attention in Chapter 5.
19. Herbert Read, *A Concise History of Modern Painting*, p. 94. See also Fry, *Cubism*, pp. 32, 133.
20. Paul Laporte, "Cubism and Science," p. 255.
21. Paul Laporte, "The Space-Time Concept in the Work of Picasso," pp. 30–31.
22. As phenomenology did in philosophy from Husserl on. "Husserl rejected the Cartesian notion of a preexisting reality out there waiting to be discovered and argued instead that all consciousness must be 'consciousness-of' something. By 1913 he elaborated his revolutionary theory that an act of consciousness and its object are but subjective and objective aspects of the same thing" (Stephen Kern, *The Culture of Time and Space*, pp. 204–205).

The futurist painters provide a convenient example. Many of them have tried, in their pictures, to render the real movement of various objects; however, the perception of a real movement presupposes that we know some fixed point in space which will serve as a point of reference for all other movements. But this point does not exist. The movement which the futurists have perceived is therefore only relative to our senses and is in no way absolute.[23]

The physics here, as with all contemporary critical discussions of early Cubism, is Newtonian. But Raynal's critical awareness, carefully occupying the middle ground between absolute and subjective, aligns itself with Relativity as a comment on observation.

Picasso, Braque, and other cubists found the new ambiguity concerning the representation, or presentation, of reality liberating and invigorating. It gave them an unlimited arena for visual exploration and for epistemological play as well. Early in 1910, Braque painted a realist *trompe-l'oeil* nail, complete with its own shadow, at the top of his *Violin and Pitcher*, as if the painting were hung from a fastener represented within it.[24] The newspaper lettering often found in cubist compositions, the "JOU" at the beginning of JOURNAL, alludes at once to the news, to the present day, and to play ("jouer" – also to feign, fool, frolic, mock and toy with; and even to wager and gamble). The games played and the wagers placed (the "jeux") are usually witty, sometimes witty and coarse, sometimes perhaps a little repetitious. But they are very strong games and their game status is in itself a value, a statement of liberation, and a device for undermining what these artists often presented as the blind self-importance of traditional ("Louvre") representation.

In what is usually taken as the first cubist collage, Picasso's *Still Life with Chair Caning* (1912) (Plate 9), we see the "JOU" clearly lettered in the upper left quadrant of the oval, and in fact the work is a multilevel game in which the new art asserts its breezy freedom and its immense possibility. In the first place the chair caning referred to in the title is not "real" caning at all but oilcloth with a print of chair caning on it. Picasso has glued oilcloth printed with a pattern of chair caning to the surface of his composition. In other words he has attached a prefabricated realist illusion to his cubist presentation. Those who take it to be actual caning for an actual chair are already deluded. But that, of course, is the point. Realism is not really about reality at all, any more than Cubism is about reality. It is part of the *jeu* (game) of Cubism to point this out and part of its *joue* (cheek) to do so at the expense of the literal-minded observer looking for realist likeness. As William Rubin puts it in his telling analysis, "For Picasso, collage, construction, and *papier collé* were [not primarily] about 'reality' . . . . They were about alternate ways of *imaging* reality."[25] To crown his achievement and to stress the unresolvable nature of the duality (as Realism has it) between reality and representation, Picasso

---

23. Maurice Raynal, "Conception and Vision" (1912), in Fry, *Cubism*, p. 95.
24. There are several examples of this. See John Golding, *Cubism*, p. 106.
25. William Rubin, *Picasso and Braque: Pioneering Cubism*, p. 37.

chose to frame the *Still Life with Chair Caning* with a custom-made endless mariner's rope surrounding an oval composition which images aesthetically and epistemologically the modernist collapse of origins into results, or of reality into the representation of reality.

In our next two chapters, on Fields, Abstraction, and Reflexivity, we will be discussing certain later tendencies of Cubism, including implications for Modernism of the development of what art historians have called "synthetic" Cubism from the earlier "analytic" Cubism, a change in style and emphasis that began early in 1912, approximately at the time of the *Still Life with Chair Caning*. Here we wish only to emphasize that the development of Cubism during World War I and indeed during the mid-1920s did nothing to reverse the modernist shift in emphasis and attention from reality to observation. For most modernists, the literary as well as the visual artists, the war did little to increase the prestige of reality. On the contrary, in Cubism as in literature the movement toward observation and toward representation was confirmed by the universal catastrophe. The arrival of what has been termed "crystal" Cubism attests to this. As Christopher Green puts it:

> Order remained the keynote as post-war reconstruction commenced. It is not surprising, therefore, to find a continuity in the development of Cubist art as the transition was made from war into peace, an unbroken commitment to the Latin virtues along with an unbroken commitment to the aesthetically pure. The new Cubism that emerged, the Cubism of Picasso, Laurens, Gris, Metzinger and Lipchitz most obviously of all, has come to be known as "crystal Cubism". It was indeed the end-product of a progressive closing down of possibilities in the name of a "call to order".[26]

After the war, aesthetic positions became more self-conscious, more decidedly taken *as positions*, more defensive. The war gave a kind of dogmatic prestige to certain existing epistemological vectors of early Modernism. It also added an awareness of fragility, an obsession with the clarity of one's position, as if human consciousness were etched in glass, easily fractured. The war confirmed the avant-garde attitude that aesthetics was the place to live – and not only because it provided an escape from ugliness and vulgarity (a clear pre-war agenda) but also because it seemed the only arena in which sudden, brutal, gratuitous violence could be countered. Art seemed – to use Hemingway's great colloquial metaphor – the clean well-lighted place.[27] So that again, and now for new social reasons, we see that what became central and valuable in Modernism was not the nature of reality in itself, but the nature of our observation of and relation to it, the ways in which we can control and represent it. Picasso said of the "reality" of analytic Cubism that "It's not a reality you can take in your hand. It's more like perfume – in front of you,

---

26. Christopher Green, *Cubism and Its Enemies*, p. 37.
27. See Ernest Hemingway, "A Clean, Well-lighted Place."

behind you, to the sides. The scent is everywhere but you don't quite know where it comes from."[28]

Narrative

When during the beginning of the modernist period it became possible to conceive of the external world, "reality," not as an existence in itself but (so far as human beings are concerned) as a plurality of perceptions and measurements,[29] it followed that the traditional distinctions between time and space began to blur or realign themselves. Such realignment was permitted by a shift of value from the supposed contemplation of independent being in itself to the contemplation of the perception of being, a shift from "reality" to "observation."

A clear example of this revision of temporal and spatial categories may be found in the popular use of the term "simultaneity." When early analysts of Cubism spoke of "simultaneity" they meant the representation in cubist art of more than one perspective, or of what would represent more than one perspective in the tradition of optical verisimilitude. A cubist painter could represent, for example, the profile and frontal view of a nose or the side and base of a wine glass in a single composition. Since these differing views can be collected only over time, for example by walking around the nose or wine glass, a two-dimensional plastic representation of them could be characterized as developing "simultaneity." In his discussion of this discovery, Paul Laporte observes that "it seems that the only possible procedure of integrating the kinesthetic with the visual experience in painting is by breaking through the absoluteness of Euclidean geometry, and by re-assembling the shattered fragments of visual perception on the basis of their temporal cohesion."[30] In Cubism each painting is a *reassemblage* that forces various "fragments," perspectives or aspects gathered over time, into a single visual "instant," a "simultaneous" mental construct represented in a single visual frame.

The temporal achievement of "simultaneity" in Cubism corresponds to a pervasive spatial metaphor in early modernist fiction, that of "point of view." The phrase is often associated with the work of Henry James, in part because he commented on the problem in prefaces to his novels and in part because in his work the philosophical, psychological, and above all aesthetic possibilities are explored with unprecedented depth and resonance. We have seen that in *The Turn of the Screw* the entire meaning of the narrative depends on the

28. See William Rubin, *Picasso in the Collection of the Museum of Modern Art*, pp. 72, 206. Picasso is quoted by Rubin in *Picasso and Braque: Pioneering Cubism*, p. 59, n. 74.
29. See our discussion of Ortega's doctrine of "perspectivity" in Chapter 1.
30. Laporte, "Cubism and Science," p. 253. Laporte prefaces this comment with an observation from Einstein: "That there is no objective rational division of the four-dimensional continuum, indicates that the laws of nature will assume a form which is logically most satisfactory when expressed as laws of the four-dimensional space-time continuum."

degree of credibility the narrator/governess generates, on how completely we are able to trust her.[31] What becomes interesting in modernist narrative is not so much the nature of events themselves on the one hand and the feelings of the characters on the other (the realist "objective"/"subjective" dichotomy) but the negotiated middle ground, the *relation*, the *measurement*, the *observation*. This is what we have called the characteristic epistemological location of Modernism. What the fiction is about seems to be neither the objective world nor the subjective perceiver but their interaction.

Relativity Theory may be considered the expression of a geometry of spacetime. As we have seen, Cubism valorizes the geometry of the entire pictorial space rather than focusing on what are represented as discrete objects located in what is supposed to be neutral (realist) space. Correspondingly, much important modernist narrative gives primacy to a geometry of time rather than to the individual actions of discrete characters moving in supposedly neutral time. This narrative temporal geometry is presented by a variety of means, but the most important of these is a new depth and variety of the handling of point of view. The time of modernist narrative is *observed* time, time embodied in individual perception. This is not the consistent duration of social experience in *Middlemarch* or the sweep of history in *War and Peace* but time as actually resident in human awareness and measurement.

Marcel Proust's *À la recherche du temps perdu* comprises one of the greatest extended explorations of a geometry of time in modernist fiction. As presented in the first novel of the series of seven, *Swann's Way* (1913), this is a geometry of affective time, time of the feelings, an emotional, inner time deeply involved with memory. The narration plays with the relation of this affective time to historical or chronological time. The Swann who appears in Part I, "Combray," is the Swann who has already been through his love affair with Odette, but this affair is not recounted until the second part, "Swann in Love." In historical or realistic time Swann falls in love with Odette at approximately the moment of the narrator's birth, and we are given parallels, both emotional and figurative, between the narrator's story and Swann's. These parallels are both temporal and affective: the narrator's waiting for his mother's goodnight kiss in Part I, Swann's abasement in love, the narrator's boy love for Gilberte (daughter of Swann and Odette) in Part III. The unending iteration of longing and humiliation that emerges from the novel as a human condition is affirmed and reaffirmed by the aesthetic structure, the structure of the novel as it presents time, and in the numerous parallels in the chronological planes of action that resist chronological sequence as the visual planes of cubist painting deny realist perspective.

Objects in Proust's temporal geometry exist primarily in affective time; their "objective" or "historical" existence pales beside the emotional intensity of the narrator's regard for them. This can be illustrated by means of a well-known passage concerning a church at Combray:

31. See pp. 43–47 above.

all these things made of the church for me something entirely different from the rest of the town; a building which occupied, so to speak, four dimensions of space – the name of the fourth being Time – which had sailed the centuries with that old nave, where bay after bay, chapel after chapel, seemed to stretch across and hold down and conquer not merely a few yards of soil, but each successive epoch from which the whole building had emerged triumphant.[32]

The church is a time ship, propelled by the intensity of the narrator's feeling, with its movement through the centuries – and its conquest has been over time, over "each successive epoch."[33] But what empowers the geometry of time in Proust is precisely that interaction of imagined time, affective time, and the older, Newtonian, realist time. The church at Combray exists in both geometries.

An equally powerful contrast between realist and affective time is presented in a discussion of certain Italian cities that the youthful narrator plans to visit:

> They became even more real to me when my father, by saying: "Well, you can stay in Venice from the 20th to the 29th, and reach Florence on Easter morning," made them both emerge, no longer only from the abstraction of Space, but from that imaginary Time in which we place not one, merely, but several of our travels at once, which do not greatly tax us since they are but possibilities, – that Time which reconstructs itself so effectively that one can spend it again in one town after one has already spent it in another – and consecrated to them some of those actual, calendar days which are certificates of the genuineness of what one does on them, for those unique days are consumed by being used, they do not return, one cannot live them again here when one has lived them elsewhere.[34]

By giving the narrator temporal coordinates, realistic "objective" coordinates, the narrator's father has changed the nature of the cities. He has removed them from the realm of the imagination, a realm in which we can make several voyages in the same time, and placed them in that exclusive, lesser, and realistic space that can accommodate only one object in one place at one time.

The prospect of his Italian journey thrills and delights the narrator, but it threatens a loss as well. It would be a loss to the narrator to have his imaginary cities transformed from their romantically decorated existences to unique points on an itinerary in realistic space. And the reader feels the threat of this loss as well. The reader knows that these celebrated places will not meet the boy's highly crafted expectations. It is perhaps just as well that

---

32. Marcel Proust, *Swann's Way*, p. 75.
33. Perhaps bringing to mind descriptions of Special Relativity as substantiating a "four-dimensional space-time continuum" (Albert Einstein, *The Meaning of Relativity*, p. 33; cited by Laporte, "Cubism and Science," p. 253). Time was often referred to as a "fourth dimension" in the years leading up to the publication of *Swann's Way* in 1913.
34. Proust, *Swann's Way*, pp. 506–507.

an illness prevents him from making the trip, for by now the narrator's emotions and their correlatives have become our object of interest – the subject has become the object – and a loss to the imaginative field entails a substantive loss to the reader's store of value, the reader's investment, in the work. This impoverishment that occurs when beloved objects are taken from the realm of the imagination and relegated to mere objectivity, to mere "reality," becomes the lost time, the "temps perdu," of Proust's masterpiece.

Proust's world is manifestly a world observed, perceived, felt. The existence of an objective, real world moving through historical, neutral time – those "unique days" that are "consumed by being used" – is acknowledged but devalued. The reader finally feels it to be *impertinent* in the strictest sense. The world that counts is the world that exists as the narrator feels and observes it. The Odette of value is the Odette crystallized by Swann's passion, the Odette of Swann's imagination.

The Dublin of Joyce's *Dubliners* (1914) is another world validated by affective time. It consists of multiple viewpoints and perspectives and ultimately exists only in them. Joyce's narrators and (in the case of third person narration) his centers of consciousness move in a world that the reader assumes exists in its own right independent of human perception, just as nature exists beyond measurements in Einstein's Relativity Theory. But like nature this world enters human consciousness only through the unique viewpoints of individual observers. Collectively they offer fragments of a city, Dublin; but these fragments, like Proust's objects, have interest for the reader as *observations*, emotionally charged negotiations, occupying that middle ground between subject and object. The fragments do not fully become fragments of external "reality"; nor do they remain exclusively internal or psychological phenomena. The fragments of perception in *Dubliners* are of course unthinkable without the centers of consciousness that express them, and they are equally unthinkable without the grim, dense, unaccommodating world that brings them forth.

One way of describing the fundamental epistemological instability of modernist art and literature is to point out that when the world loses its status as neutral, external existence on which agreement can be reached by empirical or realist methods then the status of any representation of that world becomes problematic. We saw in our discussion of Cubism that the authority of a cubist painting lies in its power to engage a viewer, to present itself as a valid and interesting observation. Picasso's *The Aficionado* (Plate 5), for example, is not *the* reality of the bullfight fan, but an observation of the fan that engages the viewer. What makes it all possible is Picasso's assumption that the viewer already has some knowledge of bullfighting, of fans, of more traditional forms of representation, of a great many other matters on which his observation can thus provide a kind of comment. In order for the cubist painting to work at all, an implied and usually somewhat ironic comparison needs to be made. This comparison can be highly complex but it remains essential to our ability to receive the representation. In *Dubliners* such invited and implied comparisons are also in play. The protagonists of the stories nearly always have some vision of themselves or of their world that conflicts with what the world offers. Their lacerating disillusionment, or the continuing slide downward into disillusionment, provides the dominant emotional develop-ment of the stories and renders them repeatedly affecting.

But in the temporal medium of narrative Joyce has at his disposal another technique as well, and this is the use of parallels or echoes, "counterparts" (the title in fact of one story) that provide margins of reference for the narrators or centers of consciousness. Because "reality" no longer has its neutral, objective status, the "world" can no longer absolutely inform the characters as it can inform Pip in *Great Expectations* or Levin in *Anna Karenina*. Instead, as in Special Relativity, one must gain an appreciation of one's own system by means of a comparison with another. In "Two Gallants," Lenehan envies Corley, wonders about his success with women, lives vicariously and parasitically alongside him. He can measure his own humiliation and failure by comparing it with Corley's "success" in conning money from a prostitute. Similarly, in "A Little Cloud" Little Chandler, the center of consciousness character, envies his travelling friend Gallaher. Little Chandler tries painfully to account for his apparent relative poverty of experience. The reader's perception that he may have a deeper awareness than the vulgarian Gallaher only means that the reader has yet another frame of reference, suggested by narrative appeals to an experience wider than that of either of the characters. The somewhat enigmatic title of the story "Counterparts" in fact suggests all that finally can be known, and all that can be known are relative identities. The alcoholic Farrington seems literally swamped with doubles: his lecherous, vain, choleric boss; his fraudulent, mooching fellow drinkers; even his wretched little son. As the center of consciousness he finds himself surrounded by echoes of his own condition, echoes of his own cowardice, vanity, rage. The relative identities parallel and define his own. They are his counterparts, right down to the terrified servile child in him.

Readers may have a wider frame of reference than the protagonists, but both readers and characters are inescapably dependent on parallels, on com-parisons, on other unique, individually perceived frames of reference for their ultimate disillusionment. *Dubliners* refuses to resolve this disillusionment, though it offers examples of noble acceptance. The characters do not arrive at an absolute, *tragic* awareness that offers them the solace of contact with the absolute or the "real."[35] They hover between illusion and disillusionment.

There is no escape from the mirror world of Dublin. The parallel systems, counterparts, are the bars of the prison (which becomes the labyrinth of the

---

35. An arguable exception is Gabriel in "The Dead," as he seems to arrive at a generous and deep understanding of his lack of understanding. What he understands is that to him his wife and romantic love and the world itself are incomprehensible and that he is therefore among the many dead. That is, what he understands is precisely his lack of connection. The other "epiphanies" in *Dubliners* – however they may reveal the essence of the protagonists – remain relative in the sense that they provide insights not into the order of things, the "truth," "reality," but into the subjects themselves, into the natures of the observers.

mythological Daedalus in *Portrait of the Artist as a Young Man*, 1916). The stories parallel and counter each other, generalizing the themes without objectifying the city. The power of *Dubliners* is highly synergistic and the power of the collection is much greater than simple collective power. It is the power of authentic relativity, power derived from measurement by another system.

When we think of the modernist treatment of systems – cultural, religious, bureaucratic, epistemological – we go almost inevitably to Franz Kafka. The conflict between systems pervades his fiction. He consistently imagines a double universe inhabited by two systems, but in his fiction one of these is privileged. Joyce creates a world in which absolutes have proved bankrupt, leaving behind the sad prisons of disillusionment which in their isolation his characters perceive as their world, their "Dublin." In Kafka's narratives there is the familiar context of everyday business and mundane relationships (the bank, the village) and there is the opaque world of divine and absolute but incomprehensible law (the Court, the Castle). Kafka's narrators and protagonists rush about trying to "measure" or to "understand" the "other" system but their measurements, observations, and all attempts to generalize from their experience are in process of continuous collapse.

This representation of collapse in the attempt to measure the absolute (that which is immeasurable, *unobservable*) is what Albert Camus admired when he spoke of Kafka's precision in treating our relation to the divine. For Camus, a late modernist with a profound understanding of early Modernism, this attempt to relate to the divine approximates a desire for direct contact with and representation of reality. But the unknowable or "dense" nature of reality precludes such contact and representation.[36] What we have instead, according to Camus, is the opportunity given by choosing to accept the unending tension of our authentic relation to reality.

This relation is the famous "absurd" of existentialist art and thought. It is Kafka's chief subject. In an exquisite "Meditation" published in 1913 and titled "The Trees" he gives a dizzying image of our tenuous relation to the world:

> For we are like tree trunks in the snow. In appearance they lie sleekly and a light push should be enough to set them rolling. No, it can't be done, for they are firmly wedded to the ground. But see, even that is only appearance.[37]

The little parable deals with the propensity of reality to give way, to show itself unstable, illusory, at every approach. The tree trunks look ready to roll, but upon closer examination they are welded to the earth, but upon still closer examination even this is only an "appearance," and so on into infinite ambiguity.

One of the passages Kafka deleted from *The Trial* treats this instability in another way:

36. Albert Camus, *The Myth of Sisyphus*, pp. 97–98, 16.
37. From Franz Kafka, *The Penal Colony*, pp. 39–40.

As someone said to me – I can't remember now who it was – it is really remark-able that when you wake up in the morning you nearly always find everything in exactly the same place as the evening before. For when asleep and dreaming you are, apparently at least, in an essentially different state from that of wakefulness; and therefore, as that man truly said, it requires enormous presence of mind or rather quickness of wit, when opening your eyes to seize hold as it were of everything in the room at exactly the same place where you had let it go on the previous evening. That was why, he said, the moment of waking up was the riskiest moment of the day. Once that was well over without deflecting you from your orbit, you could take heart of grace for the rest of the day.[38]

In their different ways, each of these two passages undermines the realist assumption of reality as neutral, consistent, stable, uninterruptedly "out there." What both passages substitute for the old faith in reality are perspectives: we feel ourselves to be sleekly mobile, like tree trunks in the snow; alternatively, we feel ourselves firmly wedded to the ground; but both impressions are merely impressions, merely "illusions": reality itself remains inaccessible. So too our impression of the stability and continuity of our arrangements, the placement of the furniture in our room, is illusory. It requires great mental athleticism (presence of mind and quickness of wit) to maintain the inner impression of continuity, to find everything in the room where we left it the evening before.

Does this mean that without this presence of mind the furniture, "reality," *actually* moves about during the night? Does it mean, even more radically, that there may be no "tree trunks," no selfhood? Kafka does not go quite so far. What it means is that we do not know what happens during the night, and that our sense of external and internal stability – the temporal stability or the continuity of the world on the one hand and the self on the other – is a matter of negotiation, what we have called the epistemological middle ground occupied by Modernism. In Kafka this process of keeping the self and the world in view is one that requires constant effort, unremitting attention to the details of our impressions. Kafka's protagonists, the characters which Camus called "inspired automata," possess the qualities most suited to the eternal questioning of their experience and to the analysis of others' experience. Their lack of heroism corresponds aesthetically and philosophically to the lack of available certitude; their selfishness, their meanness, correspond exactly to the oppressive absurdity of their experience.

Although many of the metaphors governing perception in Kafka's narratives are spatial (the furniture in the room), his treatment of the medium of time, the medium of narrative itself, is more significant. Just as Cubism deals in a new way with the measurement of space so the obsessive concern of modernist narrative is with the possibilities of continuity and discontinuity in time. In Cubism, as in Relativity Theory, space is deformable. In modernist fiction,

38. Franz Kafka, *The Trial*, pp. 257–258.

again as in Relativity Theory, time is deformable. In *The Trial*, Joseph K. opens a storeroom door in his familiar workplace, the bank, to find the warders who had initially guarded him during his arrest at the beginning of the novel about to be whipped. They protest that K.'s complaint against their behavior led to this punishment. The whipping begins: "Then the shriek rose from Franz's throat, single and irrevocable, it did not seem to come from a human being but from some martyred instrument, the whole corridor rang with it, the whole building must hear it." K., beside himself, tries to get the Whipper to release the warders. He fails. The next day, still preoccupied with the whipping, K. again opens the door: "Everything was still the same, exactly as he had found it on opening the door the previous evening. The files of old papers and the ink bottles were still tumbled behind the threshold, the Whipper with his rod and the warders with all their clothes on were still standing there, the candle was burning on the shelf, and the warders immediately began to wail and cry out: 'Sir!'"[39]

Here time has passed in K.'s world: it is the evening of the day after he first opened the door on the whipping scene, on the event. But in the world of the Court the same time has not passed. The furniture has moved in K.'s world but not in the world of the Court. The deeper horror of the event lies not in the torture meted out to the conventionally corrupt warders but in the evidence of temporal discontinuity between the two systems. Kafka's use of time is essentially relativistic. The two systems do measure time differently. And here the disjunction is too lucid and precise for readers to attribute it entirely to K.'s subjective distortions as it may be possible to attribute the acceleration of time in "The Metamorphosis" to Gregor's slowing perceptions. In *The Trial* time measurements (perceptions of continuity) differ as they do in Relativity Theory, and this difference receives extended and intense articulation throughout.[40]

This amounts to a metaphysical departure from realist conventions. In realist literature that contains fundamental religious assumptions (the novels of Dickens or of Dostoevsky, for example), the divine world contacts the human world in the course of events, often by means of "coincidences" that point to the engagement of the divine with the human.[41] We have seen that in fiction underpinned by a providential worldview the ultimate objectifier is the divine. According to the premises of this fiction, absolute time and space, absolute reality, are effectively maintained by providential arrangement

39. Ibid., p. 89.
40. At this juncture an important difference between Kafka's philosophical/theological treatment of time and time in Relativity Theory needs to be acknowledged. Although in Kafka's world the divine system intrudes into, interrupts, the mundane (K. can be arrested and executed), there is no intelligible, reliable communication between the time of the everyday world (the bank) and that of the divine (the Court). In Kafka, the times of human aspiration and of divine intention remain incommensurable. We can draw a contrast with Special Relativity and say that in Kafka there are no Lorentz transformations or Minkowski diagrams whereby events in another system can be calculated in one's own.
41. See Thomas Vargish, *The Providential Aesthetic in Victorian Fiction*, pp. 7–10.

and temporal reality may be measured by its degree of correspondence to divinely ordained absolutes. The world is real and intelligible to us because of its connection with them. But in Kafka this connection has become radically incommensurable, unintelligible. This is where Kafka's Modernism comes in. He speaks to us not of the nature of reality but of the nature of our attempts to perceive and to understand it. These remain always incomplete, always in process (the German for *The Trial* is *Der Prozess*). "There is a goal," one of Kafka's reflections has it, "but no way."[42] But because Kafka's protagonists cannot accept the inaccessibility of ultimate reality, the human condition in his works is a condition of searching, a metaphysical search that always ends in failure. That this failure sometimes contains a hint of redemptive transcendence suggests the depth of Kafka's religious metaphysic. The barest possibility of the infinite is, as Pascal observed, enough. But it is a metaphysic embedded in modernist representation.

The shift in value from that assumption of direct contact with an objective temporal world, contact that was a premiss of Realism, to the more tentative measurements and observations of Modernism carries political as well as religious consequences. Some of the more worrying of these are suggested in Joseph Conrad's *The Secret Agent*, which appeared as a serial in 1906 (one year after the Special Theory) and in book form in 1907 (the year of *Les Demoiselles d'Avignon*).

The Secret Agent has as its central event an aborted terrorist attempt to blow up the Greenwich Observatory. At first glance the attempt to explode the installation where Greenwich Mean Time (that standard of Newtonian order) is measured looks anarchistic and is meant to look that way. The "agent" of the outrage is a putative anarchist named Verloc who is in fact a double agent, working at the same time for a repressive, reactionary empire (czarist Russia, perhaps) and also for the British police. Verloc attempts the crime at the bidding of a Mr Vladimir, a diplomatic representative and secret agent of (probably) the czar. His regime, in agreement with other repressive regimes, holds that the British authorities are dangerously permissive in matters of political law and order; Vladimir therefore prods the secret agent Verloc to implement an atrocity, an outrage that will by public outcry force the authorities to stamp out the anarchists and revolutionaries. In this way a liberal Britain will be forced to suppress revolutionary elements and to comply with the interests of a reactionary Europe – or more exactly with the interests of those regimes most vulnerable to the forces of anarchy or revolution. In this enterprise the slothful Verloc employs his compassionate retarded brother-in-law Stevie to place the explosive. In the attempt Stevie trips over a tree root and blows himself to pieces, leaving the observatory and British legal processes intact.[43]

42. Franz Kafka, *The Great Wall of China*, p. 166.
43. For interesting suggestions on the symbolic role played by Stevie and his relation to GMT, see Randall Stevenson, *Modernist Fiction*, pp. 119–122.

The lethal anarchist called "The Professor," the only fearless and therefore the most dangerous "agent" in the novel, supplies the bomb; he is at work on "the perfect detonator," a device that would function with temporal perfection to set off the dynamite. He has not succeeded in constructing it, so the present device proves not to be, in the Professor's phrase, "fool-proof."[44] It is, in fact, highly vulnerable to fools – most notably the pathetic Stevie. With almost farcical rapidity, the novel compiles multiple ironies dealing with political, bureaucratic, and domestic mistiming.

Obviously the attempt to explode the measurement of Greenwich Mean Time has resonance for our subject. The anarchists are supposed to be threatening the very means by which we order our lives. But Conrad identifies the plotting force behind the anarchists as coming from foreign reactionaries, who wish to break down the liberal protection of civil liberties in Britain. In the view of Privy Councillor Wurmt, "The general leniency of the judicial procedure here, and the utter absence of all repressive measures, are a scandal to Europe." Wurmt's chief, Mr Vladimir, has thought through the various possible outrages with a view to obtaining the maximum middle-class public reaction. Political targets are too familiar; religious ones are open to misinterpretation. An outrage against culture or art, such as a bomb in the National Gallery, would not be taken seriously: "It's like breaking a few back windows in a man's house." No, he has decided,

> "The demonstration must be against learning – science. But not every science will do. The attack must have all the shocking senselessness of gratuitous blasphemy. Since bombs are your means of expression, it would be really telling if one could throw a bomb into pure mathematics. But that is impossible. . . . What do you think of having a go at astronomy? . . . The whole civilized world has heard of Greenwich. The very bootblacks in the basement of Charing Cross Station know something of it. See? . . . Yes," he continued, with a contemptuous smile, "the blowing up of the first meridian is bound to raise a howl of execration."[45]

Mr Vladimir, though politically repellent, is a student of modernist political culture. He knows where the epistemic trauma can be found: in an attack on Newtonian time.

In the narrative structure of *The Secret Agent* the disjunctive placement of events and the violations of regular chronological development reinforce the assault on standards of Newtonian time. The first three chapters set up the Verloc domestic situation and the pressure on Verloc from the embassy (Mr Vladimir). We also see something of the rag-tag collection of self-styled anarchists and revolutionaries. Then at the beginning of Chapter 4 we get the first news of the explosion from Ossipon, who believes it to be Verloc who has been blown up because the Professor tells him he gave Verloc the

44. Joseph Conrad, *The Secret Agent*, pp. 93, 99.
45. Ibid., pp. 55, 67, 67–68.

explosive. Then we see Inspector Heat and the Assistant Commissioner at work. *Then* in Chapter 8 we return to the domestic affairs of the Verlocs (Winnie's mother is leaving) *before* the explosion, and we work toward the evening of the day of the outrage. These shifts present difficulties, but thanks to the unchronological placement of events in Chapters 4 to 7 we read all of the rest of the book with foreknowledge of the explosion. About half-way through Chapter 9 we are brought again to the moment that concludes Chapter 8, when the Assistant Commissioner was looking at the Verlocs' shop: now in Chapter 9 he calls at the shop and speaks to Verloc. In the remaining four chapters the narrative proceeds in realist "chronological order," but by this point a non-sequential, abrupt, modernist temporal geometry has succeeded the comforts of Greenwich Mean Time.

These apparently arbitrary shifts in the presentation of events mean that the true revolutionary in this somber novel is the ironic narrator. We see that it is only the narrator who knows why Mr Verloc's code symbol is delta (Δ), a conventional symbol in mathematics or physics to express a change. The fear of uncontrolled change provides the dominating motive for most of the actions in the novel. The failure of those in authority to find a principle and method by which social and political change can be governed leads to the pervasive nihilism of *The Secret Agent*. This nihilism is permitted by the loss of absolute frames of reference. There is no natural or divine order to which to appeal. There are no providential coincidences – only foolish accidents. The heavens seem to be fulfilling their function on a fatigued, hungover, pro forma basis: "And a peculiarly London sun – against which nothing could be said except that it looked bloodshot – glorified all this by its stare. It hung at a moderate elevation above Hyde Park Corner with an air of punctual and benign vigilance."[46] Established authority is still alive, but not well – and some rather grim changes (of the sort encouraged by the explosive Professor) may lie in wait.

This problematic of temporal change in a world without absolutes became a persistent theme throughout modernist literature. Conrad, Proust, Gide, Joyce, Woolf, Forster, Kafka, and Mann all treat it with seriousness. But no modernist writer dealt with the problem in such intensity and depth as William Faulkner. Jean-Paul Sartre was right in saying that his "metaphysic is one of time," though he was wrong in his assessment of Faulkner's statements on human freedom.[47] And of direct relevance to the modernist treatment of time and freedom is the fact that Faulkner knew of Relativity Theory and made use of it in his first great novel.

The Sound and the Fury (1929) comprises four narratives that tell the story of the doomed Compson family, and especially of the daughter Caddy who is the voiceless center and heart of the drama. Each of the first three narratives

---

46. Ibid., p. 51.
47. Sartre went on to miss Faulkner's commitment to human dignity and freedom. See Paul André Harris, "Time Spaced Out in Words: From Physics to Faulkner," Chapter 2.

is told in the first person by one of the brothers: the idiot Benjy, the suicidal Quentin, and the sociopathic Jason. Of immediate interest to us, Quentin's narrative of the day of his death, July 2, 1910, contains what must be veiled references to Relativity. According to Julie M. Johnson, "Quentin would have taken this physics course during the 1909–1910 academic year, his only year at Harvard. The Special Theory of Relativity had been published four years previously. It is therefore logical that his physics class would have been exposed to the highly proclaimed new theory of the budding genius, Albert Einstein."[48] Johnson goes on to offer some persuasive evidence that certain aspects of the Special Theory receive ironic or parodic illustration in Quentin's attempts to affect the passing of time.

These possibilities are interesting, but in themselves they do not deal with the nihilism consequent on the effects of change in a world bereft of certitude. The greatness of *The Sound and the Fury* begins with the intensity with which the threat of meaninglessness is realized; with the boldness of its title, plucked from Macbeth's great statement on the failure of human time to yield significance:

> Tomorrow, and tomorrow, and tomorrow
> Creeps in this petty pace from day to day,
> To the last syllable of recorded time,
> And all our yesterdays have lighted fools
> The way to dusty death. Out, out, brief candle!
> Life's but a walking shadow, a poor player
> That struts and frets his hour upon the stage
> And then is heard no more. It is a tale
> Told by an idiot, full of sound and fury,
> Signifying nothing.[49]

Macbeth's despair is the despair of time to provide a reason for living. His image is an image of fools preposterously asserting meaning in time, the medium

---

48. Julie M. Johnson, "The Theory of Relativity in Modern Literature: An Overview and *The Sound and the Fury*," p. 226. If 1910 sounds a little early for the freshman Quentin to be taught Special Relativity it helps to remember that *The Sound and the Fury* appeared in 1929 – in plenty of time for the popularized theory to be absorbed by Faulkner, who probably was not constrained by the precise chronology of the development of the Harvard science curriculum. Johnson goes on to make some other telling observations: "Quentin is the only [narrator] who is in a different space-time system. Benjy and Jason are both in Jefferson, and both narrate their sections during Easter weekend, 1928. Quentin, on the other hand, is at Harvard, and his narrative is set in 1910. . . . Quentin's spatial dislocation affects his perspective by aggravating his sense of alienation and loss. From his position in the North, he sees the South, Yoknapatawpha County, and his family from within another inertial system; and as we learn in *Absalom, Absalom!* he is torn between love and hate. . . . I believe that in his series of aimless streetcar rides Quentin is hoping the paradox of the clocks is true, and he is trying to move fast enough to slow time, if not to stop it" (p. 227). "His eye blackened, Quentin leaves his friends and takes another trolley back into town. It is twilight, 'that quality of light as if time really had stopped for a while' " (p. 229).
49. William Shakespeare, *Macbeth*, V.v. 19–28.

Plate 1 Edgar Degas, *Le Tub*, 1886. Musée d'Orsay, Paris.

Plate 2 Paul Cézanne, *Fruits, serviette et boite à lait*, *c.* 1880. National Gallery of Scotland, Edinburgh.

Plate 3 Paul Cézanne, *Nature morte au panier*, 1888–90. Musée d'Orsay, Paris.

Plate 4 Pablo Picasso, *Les Demoiselles d'Avignon*, 1907. The Museum of Modern Art, New York.

Plate 13 Pablo Picasso, *Girl with a Mandolin*, 1910. The Museum of Modern Art, New York.

Plate 12c (*left*) Henri Matisse, *The Back, III*, bronze, 1916. The Museum of Modern Art, New York.

Plate 12d (*right*) Henri Matisse, *The Back, IV*, bronze, 1931. The Museum of Modern Art, New York.

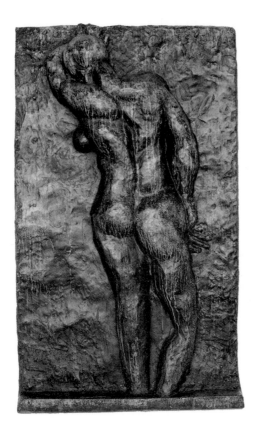

Plate 12a (*left*) Henri Matisse, *The Back, I*, bronze, 1909. The Museum of Modern Art, New York.

Plate 12b (*right*) Henri Matisse, *The Back, II*, bronze, 1913. The Museum of Modern Art, New York.

Plate 11 Umberto Boccioni, *Development of a Bottle in Space*, silvered bronze, 1912. The Museum of Modern Art, New York.

Plate 10 Umberto Boccioni, *Dynamism of a Soccer Player*, 1913. The Museum of Modern Art, New York.

Plate 9 Pablo Picasso, *Still Life with Chair Caning*, 1912. Musée Picasso, Paris.

Plate 8 Paul Cézanne, *The Big Trees*, 1902–4. National Gallery of Scotland, Edinburgh.

Plate 7 Pablo Picasso, *Portrait of Ambroise Vollard*, 1909–10.
The Puskin State Museum of Fine Arts, Moscow.

Plate 6 Georges Braque, *Le Billard*, 1944. Musée National d'Art Moderne, Paris.

Plate 5 Pablo Picasso, *The Aficionado*, 1912. Kunstmuseum, Basel.

Plate 14 (*above*) Pablo Picasso, *Painter and Model*, 1928. The Museum of Modern Art, New York.

Plate 15 Juan Gris, *The Painter's Window*, 1925. Baltimore Museum of Art.

Plate 16 Pablo Picasso, *Portrait d'Olga dans un fauteuil*, 1917. Musée Picasso, Paris.

that reduces everything to vanity, to what vanishes, to "nothing." Macbeth's image of the world as a stage and of language (expressive time) as mere noise, is echoed without compromise in Faulkner's novel: "Then Ben wailed again, hopeless and prolonged. It was nothing. Just sound. It might have been all time and injustice and sorrow become vocal for an instant by a conjunction of planets." The mentally arrested Benjy is the literally realized idiot of Macbeth's metaphor for life as a tale told by an idiot, and it is Benjy who tells the first tale of *The Sound and the Fury.* We as readers are not idiots, but confronted with the enduring and universal pathos of vanity we may be no better off. In any case, we all of us live in time and so we can sympathize with Benjy's indignation: "For an instant Ben sat in an utter hiatus. Then he bellowed. Bellow on bellow, his voice mounted, with scarce interval for breath. There was more than astonishment in it, it was horror; shock; agony eyeless, tongueless; just sound . . . ."[50]

The substantive challenge of the novel is to find significance. Does the fact that it is humanly impossible to move beyond the *perspective* of individual narrators (points of view) imprisoned in their temporal cages offer the nihilistic conclusion that "it"–meaning *time* or *life*–signifies nothing? In this way *The Sound and the Fury* confronts what is an obsessive concern of literary Modernism, the order/disorder duality, and confronts it in temporal terms. Benjy is affirmative but hopeless; Quentin methodical but suicidal; Jason rational but nihilistic or (like the others only more evidently) solipsistic. Together they tell a story. For each of the two elder brothers time is an enemy. Quentin attempts to arrest it (ultimately in suicide), and Jason is at odds with it (always a little too late or too early to make the "killing" as measured by the clock that is the cotton market). Benjy is *sub*temporal and therefore can find momentary fulfillment in an inalterable memory of Caddy or in the reduction of time to arbitrary sequence as he rides around the square at the end, finding each landmark "in its ordered place."[51] But Benjy's level of solace is inaccessible to most of us.

What readers of this novel need is a margin of reference whereby the various points of view can be fitted into a system of measurement – not to bring them into agreement (which would be trivial) but in order to give them the missing significance, so that the tale signifies something, so that the narrative affirms value. What is needed is a kind of philosophical Lorentz transformation, an aesthetic Minkowski diagram.[52] The recovery of significance in *The Sound and the Fury* requires an appeal to another system. And Faulkner provides it in the fourth section, a third person past-tense narration with Dilsey as the moderating consciousness and the exceptionally validated point of view. This resort to a third person perspective, with its reassuring associations with the objectifying narrator of traditional Realism, is one aspect of the appeal to

50. William Faulkner, *The Sound and the Fury*, pp. 359, 400.
51. Ibid., p. 401.
52. See Mook and Vargish, *Inside Relativity*, pp. 96–100, 203–246.

another system. It invokes the varied assurances of Realism and also partakes of their limitations. At one level of interpretation it can be seen as a *retreat* into Realism and the epistemological premises of neutral homogeneous time and space. But this in itself does not bring meaning to the long saga of Compson decline and suffering, partly because the time covered by the final narration overlaps with only a small part of the events narrated by the Compson brothers and partly because it introduces largely new material on Easter Sunday 1928.

What the fourth and final narration does is to validate another epistemological system, another way of knowing the world, from the deteriorating Compson system. This other epistemology is the black system. In his narrative Quentin thinks, "They come into white people's lives like that in sudden sharp black trickles that isolate white facts for an instant in unarguable truth like under a microscope; the rest of the time just voices that laugh when you see nothing to laugh at, tears when no reason for tears."[53] Specifically, the final narration validates Dilsey's perspective. It distances us from Dilsey's consciousness as we cannot be distanced from Benjy or Quentin or Jason from within their first person narratives. The third person narrative stays on the outside of Dilsey's consciousness, and this helps to give her a dignity and a generosity that the others, including even the central, almost mythic Caddy, do not possess. It permits our parallel with the Lorentz transformations and Minkowski diagrams of Special Relativity, by which you do not *enter* the other system but *measure* it from your own.

Dilsey's viewpoint is not equated with reality or truth, as it might have been in nineteenth-century realist fiction. The narrator effectually objectifies her and her world, presents her as one reality among many. Dilsey, however, is allied to the narrator in her lack of self-absorption. She functions not as an objectifier but as a kind of *validator*. She is the margin of reference, the aesthetic and ethical touchstone for what happens. Most important, she shows us how significance may be achieved without absolutes and without generalizations; that it is achieved solely by point of view itself, the point of view of narrative, *achieved over time*. The narration enlists the apparent agent of nihilism, time, in the transcendence of nihilism – not in philosophical generalization but in personal perspective:

> "I've seed de first en de last," Dilsey said. "Never you mind me."
>
> "First en las whut?" Frony said.
>
> "Never you mind," Dilsey said. "I seed de beginnin, en now I sees de endin."[54]

She asserts that she has been a witness. She knows the stories of the others and has measured them. She has reached the completion of her own story in which they have their account. Her experience of the Compson "tale" validates that tale *because she has seen it*. The tale achieves significance not

53. Faulkner, *The Sound and the Fury*, pp. 211–212.
54. Ibid., p. 371.

because it is "reality," not because it is "true," not because it can be generalized in philosophical or ethical terms, but because it has been seen over time, because it has been *observed.*

In *The Sound and the Fury* we can see how completely Modernism has achieved the shift from reality to observation. One can say that in the final section of this novel events actually achieve reality by being observed. Dilsey realizes the Compson story. And for this reason, the tears that at the end "took their sunken and devious courses" down her face signify the value of the tale.[55]

---

55. Ibid.

Chapter 5 Field Models and Modernist Abstraction

Le contour me fuit.

Cézanne

Field Models

In the preceding chapter, we argued that observation as a middle ground between external "objective reality" and the internal "subjective observer" constitutes the characteristic epistemological location of Modernism. This represents a major change of value that took place at the intellectual forefront of European and American culture. Modernism devalues the realist premiss of an external universe conceived as independent of human perception and supplants it with the primacy of observation or measurement.

As we offered our description of this change in value, we found ourselves constantly in danger of raising a question that threatens the logical consistency of our analysis: if one replaces the realist observer and the realist object with a middle ground of observation, then what becomes of that realist distinction? Doesn't the very concept of observation require an observer and an object? In the realm of logic it does of course require them. But cultural history does not move by logic, and we believe that this question is in fact *not* resolved in much of the best work of the period. We could say that Modernism *wanted* the logical confusion consequent on what often seems the collapse of distinction between object and observer to remain unresolved. And that modernist physicists, artists, and writers derived considerable opportunity and effect from *not* resolving it.

This does not mean that modernist physics, art, and narrative did not address the loss of the neutral objective observer and of the stable, intelligible, rationalizable reality that is the realist observer's correspondent. We have seen that this loss coincided with the modernist preoccupation with observation. What was it that enabled Modernism to leave open the question of how one can focus on the act of observation without sustaining the dichotomy between observer and object? The answer, an answer that applies to Cubism and modernist narrative as well as to physics, lies in the development of the concept, metaphor, and method of the *field*.

104

The relation of field models in science to their application in literature has received some admirable scholarly attention.[1] The scope of our description of Modernism, however, requires a very general definition of "field," sufficiently general to qualify it as one of the *values* of the period, recognizably operative in physics, painting, and narrative:

A field is a spatial and/or temporal model or representation in which all constituents are interdependent and in which all constituents participate and interrelate without privilege.

We would agree that this definition is abstract, but it gathers flesh and function from what follows.

Relativity Theory

Mathematicians and physicists use the term "field" in several different senses. Mathematically a field is defined as any set of entities that obeys certain rules for manipulating and combining the members comprising the set. For example, all positive numbers constitute a field in the mathematician's sense because they follow appropriate rules of arithmetic. Physicists sometimes use the mathematician's field, but in physics the term commonly assumes a more empirical meaning, as illustrated by this discussion taken from a standard mathematical physics text:

Many physical quantities have different values at different points in space. For example, the temperature in a room is different at different points: high near a register, low near an open window, and so on. . . . Similarly, the gravitational force acting on a satellite depends on its distance from the earth. . . . In all these examples there is a particular region of space which is of interest for the problem at hand; at every point of this region some physical quantity has a value. The term "field" is used to mean both the region and the value of the physical quantity in the region (for example, electric field, gravitational field).[2]

The field of temperature values cited in the physics text exemplifies our general definition of field. The values of the temperature at points throughout the volume of a room constitute the "model" or "representation," to use the terms of our definition. The temperature values are interdependent (for example, a hotter radiator at one point will increase the temperature values throughout the room to some extent). The temperature values at *all* points interrelate to determine the field of temperature values. Yet the points in the room are "without privilege" in the sense that introducing a heat source at *any point* will increase the temperature at all other points.

Michael Faraday probably made the earliest use of the term "field" in the sense understood by physicists today. In 1845 he was studying the behavior

1. Especially by N. Katherine Hayles in *The Cosmic Web: Scientific Field Models and Literary Strategies in the Twentieth Century*, a work to which we are indebted methodologically as well as substantively; and also by Alan J. Friedman and Carol C. Donley in *Einstein as Myth and Muse*.
2. Mary D. Boas, *Mathematical Methods in the Physical Sciences*, pp. 248–249.

of various materials placed near the poles of a large magnet. In his laboratory diary entry for November 10 he writes, "Wrought with bodies between the great poles, i.e. in the magnetic field, as to their motions under the influence of magnetic force."[3] Prior to this diary entry he had used terms such as "magnetic force," "magnetic lines," "lines of force," or even "magnetic curves" in describing the influence of a magnet, but now he begins to refer to the magnet having a "field" around it. The field concept served Faraday in picturing both electrical and magnetic forces. In other minds Faraday's field would begin to take on a reality of its own: James Clerk Maxwell subsequently developed a full mathematical formulation of field theory for electricity and magnetism. In the equations of his electromagnetic theory Maxwell offered a mathematical embodiment of Faraday's fields.[4] Faraday's first use of the field concept as an aid in describing magnetic forces echoes down to contemporary physics where fields still often relate to the action of forces; the field represents both the magnitude and direction of a force acting on some entity at a given point in spacetime.

In order to see how the development of the field concept in physics reflects a broader value of Modernism in its literary and artistic manifestations, we can distinguish the physicist's way of thinking about forces before and after the development of field theories. The concept of a force is derived from the experience that distinct objects can affect one another's motions. Newton in his first and second laws of motion first gave the quantitative definition of force as it is used in physical science.[5] Any change in the state of motion of an object is attributed by Newton to the action of a force. But "force" so defined cannot be observed directly. Its presence is inferred by the behavior of an object upon which the force is supposed to act. Force, in other words, is an invisible, intangible agent defined in Newton's laws as responsible for the change in an object's state of motion.

The means by which an invisible and intangible force is communicated from one object to another was somewhat problematic in classical physics. When two objects were observed to be in physical contact with one another it seemed "intuitively obvious" (to use a favorite phrase of physicists) that either object could exert a force on the other. This intuition probably developed because of the physiological response to muscle contraction in the human

3. Michael Faraday, *Faraday's Diary*, p. 331.
4. The physicist's notion of a field and Maxwell's use of this concept in his electromagnetic theory are discussed in detail for the non-scientist in Delo Mook and Thomas Vargish, *Inside Relativity*, Appendix D, pp. 260–285. Einstein has emphasized the importance of field theories in the development of physics: "Before Clerk Maxwell people conceived of physical reality – in so far as it is supposed to represent events in nature – as material points, whose changes consist exclusively of motions, which are subject to partial differential equations. After Maxwell they conceived physical reality as represented by continuous fields, not mechanically explicable, which are subject to partial differential equations. This change in the conception of reality is the most profound and fruitful one that has come to physics since Newton" (Albert Einstein, "Clerk Maxwell's Influence on the Evolution of the Idea of Physical Reality," p. 44).
5. Mook and Vargish, *Inside Relativity*, pp. 31–45.

body as it "exerted forces on" (that is, changed the state of motion of) other objects. The difficulty with force transmission arose when physicists studied influences between objects not in direct contact. The forces observed between remote magnets, charged objects, and, ultimately, the gravitational influence between distant masses were often called "actions-at-a-distance" to distinguish them from forces exerted by objects in contact. Fields were devised to describe actions-at-a-distance. Contact forces needed no such artifice.[6]

The transition from descriptions of forces based on "action-at-a-distance" to field models mirrors the distinction we draw between the observer–object duality of Realism and the epistemic middle ground of Modernism. Consider a common example. A classical physicist has been holding a book in her hand; she then releases the book so that it falls to the floor. She understands the fall of the book to represent the phenomenon of "gravitation," and her knowledge of Newtonian physics has led her to believe that the mass of the earth exerts an attractive force on the mass of the book. Despite the fact that the earth and the book are not in direct contact, it seems in no way unusual to the classical physicist that the earth should exert a gravitational force on the book across empty space. She focuses her attention on two tangible *objects*, the book and the earth, and she is well aware that her Newtonian explanation pictures the earth reaching out across space and somehow tugging on the book from afar, but this action-at-a-distance seldom if ever bothers her.

Newton himself, however, showed dissatisfaction with actions-at-a-distance. In a letter to his friend Richard Bentley in the 1690s Newton wrote:

> It is inconceivable, that inanimate brute matter, should, without the mediation of something else, which is not material, operate upon and affect other matter without mutual contact, as it must be, if gravitation, in the sense of Epicurus, be essential and inherent in it. And this is one reason I desired you would not ascribe innate gravity to me. That gravity should be innate, inherent and essential to matter, so that one body may act upon another at a distance through a vacuum, without the mediation of any thing else, by and through which their action and force may be conveyed from one to another, is to me so great an absurdity, that I believe no man, who has in philosophical matters a competent faculty of thinking, can ever fall into it.[7]

But in the minds of his successors, any misgivings about innate gravity were overwhelmed by the efficacy and mathematical simplicity of Newtonian

---

6. As modern physics (particularly quantum theory) developed, physicists began to think of contact forces in terms of fields as well; however, because of the quantum mechanical uncertainty inherent in the position of a particle of matter, "contact" between particles is not a useful idea in the quantum realm. Particles regarded by classical physicists to be "in contact" are now thought to influence one another through the action of fields. When I hold a book in my hand, for example, I usually adopt the classical view and think of the book as being "in contact" with my hand. In the modern view, the molecules comprising the book and the molecules comprising my hand are not really in contact. Both sets of molecules are surrounded by "clouds" of electrons, and the electric fields of these electron clouds exert mutually repulsive forces which act on the hand and the book to keep them somewhat separated.

7. Sir Isaac Newton, *Principia*, II, 634. See also Mook and Vargish, *Inside Relativity*, pp. 148–149.

gravitation. It was not until Faraday's development of the field concept that physics adopted the sort of mediator Newton required between two interacting bodies, that "any thing else, by and through which their action and force may be conveyed from one to another."

Suppose a physicist versed in General Relativity also drops a book and watches as it accelerates to the floor of her room. She understands that the earth's mass establishes a gravitational field, meaning that the earth has some- how modified the properties of surrounding spacetime.[8] The dropped book is *immersed* or "participates" in the modified spacetime, meaning that the book is acted upon directly by the field at the book's location. A classical physicist might even say that the book is acted upon by the portion of the field with which the book is "in contact" at its location in spacetime. According to General Relativity Theory, the book responds to the action of the proximate field by following a mandated path (mathematically speaking, a "geodesic") in spacetime, and this geodesic takes the book to the floor of the room.

Before the post-classical physicist released her book it was following a different geodesic in spacetime. As long as the book was being held it was under the strong influence of fields (largely electrical) established by molecules in the physicist's hand, and these molecular fields completely overwhelmed the field established by the much more distant earth. The fields due to the physicist's hand caused the book to follow a geodesic in spacetime contiguous with the geodesic followed by the hand itself. But the molecular fields originating in a hand are effective only over an extremely small distance from the molecules comprising the hand. When the hand released the book, the fields surrounding the book changed dramatically; the gravitational field established by the earth dominated all other fields and the book's geodesic changed: it fell to the floor following the geodesic dictated largely by the earth's gravitational field.

In the history of science, the introduction of the field concept into physics can be viewed as a response to the sorts of criticisms raised against actions- at-a-distance by Newton in his letter to Bentley. From the perspective of our analysis of cultural values in the modernist period, the development of field theory and, especially, its incorporation in General Relativity was a central scientific manifestation of Modernism. It bears repeating that the "practical" (or operational) definition of a field is based on supposed measurements of some physical property (temperature in the physics text example cited above, or forces in the example of the dropped book) at any point in spacetime. The field is defined to predict correctly the results of those measurements. Thus, as we observed earlier, modernist physics shifts the focus of theory from the objects establishing the field (the only focus of classical theory) to

---

8. In the original formulations of field theory the modification was only to the properties of space. After Einstein's publication of Special (1905) and General (1916) Relativity the modification represented by a field was extended to include the temporal as well as the spatial environment so that after 1916 physicists would speak of the modified properties of "spacetime." The precise meaning of the temporal modification of fields is discussed for non-scientists in Mook and Vargish, *Inside Relativity*, especially pp. 151–152 and 163–168.

the intermediate field that is supposed to exist in the spacetime around the objects, a field that correctly predicts measurements. In the action-at-a-distance analysis of the dropped book our concern was only with two tangible entities, the earth and the book. Classical physicists assert as a "law of nature" that any two such masses will experience a gravitational attraction. The field analysis, in contrast, focuses attention on the measurable properties of the spacetime surrounding the objects – properties represented by the intangible fields established around the two objects.

So far we have emphasized the conceptual shift from forces as actions-at-a-distance to forces as manifestations of fields, modifications of the properties of spacetime that serve to predict the results of measurements. But there are two other aspects of field theory that are important to our analysis: matter can alter the properties of surrounding spacetime (that is, matter can alter surrounding fields), and fields in spacetime possess attributes formerly ascribed to matter. The distinction between matter and the properties of the space the matter occupies became blurred.

In 1905 Einstein concluded that matter and energy are two manifestations of the same entity now sometimes called "mass," sometimes called "energy," and even "mass-energy."[9] Maxwell's studies of electromagnetism had made it clear that electric and magnetic fields bear energy and therefore these fields possess certain attributes of matter. This connection was strengthened by the theoretical prediction and subsequent experimental verification that electromagnetic waves can carry momentum and exert forces like any particle of matter. Fields, then, assumed properties formerly ascribed to matter and the properties that had distinguished the "abstract" fields and "tangible" matter began to dissolve. The dissolution was enhanced by the role of matter in determining fields in spacetime. Properties of fields are known by measurements that observers choose to make. For example, devices called magnetometers and electrometers can determine the strength and direction of magnetic and electric fields in spacetime; another measuring apparatus can be used to measure the pressure exerted by the passing electric and magnetic fields as they propagate in an electromagnetic wave. The energy contained in the electromagnetic field can also be determined, and the mass equivalent of this energy can be calculated. At the same time that these properties of the fields in spacetime are being measured, the fields themselves, through the equations of General Relativity, function to influence the structure of spacetime. Moreover, the influence of fields, of mass-energy, on spacetime extends throughout the whole universe. Newtonian gravity originating in mass also extended throughout the universe, but it did so as an action-at-a-distance. In the modernist view, it is fields that extend throughout space and that determine measurable properties throughout spacetime.

9. Particle physicists speak of "particle fields" and picture the production of mass from the energy of certain fields in spacetime. This area of contemporary physics is called "quantum field theory" and it involves a still developing combination of quantum mechanics and relativity.

Just as Newton's gravitational theory is mute on the question of why gravity should exist as a force or why Newton's law of gravitation should work as well as it does, so too are General Relativity and modern field theories mute about the ultimate "reasons" for their utility. Relativity and other field theories, as we have often observed, focus not on ontological or metaphysical questions but on measurements – the epistemological middle ground of Modernism. The field equations of General Relativity are used to predict what physical measurements will be obtained at various points in spacetime. Again, the field equations do not address the issue of the "true" structure of spacetime (the "true" geometric scheme of the cosmos or the "true" history that is applicable). Given the distribution of mass (either matter or its equivalent energy) in the cosmos, the theory predicts what measured values one will obtain at any location in spacetime (that is, what readings a physicist will obtain at any measured position and at any measured time).

Terms like "the fabric of spacetime" or Hayles's "cosmic web" have been introduced to suggest the properties of universality and interconnectedness engendered by the field concept in physics. But neither of these formulations adequately suggests either the three-dimensionality of the geometric situation or, more importantly, the temporal dimension of fields. We have tried to explain elsewhere how in Relativity Theory the presence of mass (as manifested in matter or its equivalent energy) influences time.[10] We have emphasized in the present work that in modernist physics "time" means time's measurement – the value read from a clock. Perhaps the ultimate clock is the observable structure of the cosmos itself. By making appropriate sorts of astrophysical observations,[11] certain properties of the cosmos (for example, the average density of matter, or the average temperature characterizing regions of space) through time can be estimated. Another way of putting this would be to say that the fields *determine* or *define* the temporal structure of the cosmos – determine its history, as manifested by certain measurable cosmic properties. One possible field structure will indicate that the universe is eternal, with no discernible beginning or end in time; another possible field configuration characterizes a universe that had a definite beginning and that will continue to expand in volume for ever. Still another field leads to the prediction of a universe that will expand in volume for a while and then begin contracting. The point is that the fields are not just geometric specifications of possible measurements, they are fields in space*time* and as such serve to predict "historical" or temporal measurements as well.

For minds trained to view the world through Newtonian eyes, general relativistic field predictions of cosmic history can provoke their own special epistemic trauma. The geometric structure of the cosmos (a structure, of course, defined by the results of measurements that one makes) predicted by Einstein's field equations is unlike any that a Newtonian could predict. For

10. Mook and Vargish, *Inside Relativity*, pp. 151–152.
11. Ibid., pp. 195–199.

example, that the universe may exist without boundaries does *not* necessarily mean that the universe is infinite in volume.[12] Cosmic geometric systems that are finite in volume and finite in time but without boundaries are one of several possible predictions of General Relativity. Another example is provided by the classical temptation to seek a "center" to geometric entities. In classical or traditional physics and metaphysics, one way to ascribe privilege to a geometric point is to demonstrate that the point is at or near a cosmic "center." In the geometry of General Relativity, this badge of privilege is denied. There is no "center" to the relativistic cosmos. Even though the universe is expanding in volume as time goes on, the expansion does not take place as movement away from a "center." The general relativistic expansion occurs at *all* points in space. There is no spatial privilege in modern cosmology. Indeed, one sort of cosmic history (now out of favor among cosmologists but nonetheless consistent in principle with General Relativity) called the "steady-state" cosmology, denies temporal privilege as well as spatial privilege. Not only are all points in space on an equal basis, but so are all times in the cosmos. The universe has no beginning and no end, it simply *is* with no one time in history bearing any more significance than any other time.[13]

While the "big bang" model of cosmic history (now generally in favor among cosmologists) does acknowledge a special time at which the universe originated (the "big bang" or "creation event") and views cosmic history as a temporal progression from that point, there is a variation on such models that seeks to diminish the privilege of the moment of origin by robbing it of uniqueness. In a "cyclic" cosmological model, the universal origin (the big bang) is followed by an expansion that slows and comes to a stop; the universe then begins to contract and ultimately contracts back into a "big bang" state from which a new cosmos is born. In recycling the cosmos spatially and temporally, such universes posit a multiplicity of creation events.

The importance and depth of the change represented by Einstein's theory was recognized in the very title of his 1916 paper "Die Feldgleichungen der Gravitation": "The Field Equations of Gravitation." It was not the field approach *per se* that was important in Einstein's contribution but the fully developed description of the gravitational field in spacetime. He was articulating a mathematical framework for an epistemological middle ground in physics and in so doing was (in our terms) reflecting his participation in Modernism. The concern of Relativity Theory was not the determination of what was real or true, but what measurements would show.

Another way to put this would be to say that while General Relativity was a *field* theory, the field itself lacks ultimate physical importance. The only connection between the field theory and our perceptions and activities in the cosmos is made by the act of measurement. The act of observation, the actions of the observer thus become paramount. It is the observer executing

---

12. Ibid., p. 187.
13. Cosmological models are discussed in ibid., pp. 184–195.

measurement protocols that gives the field meaning and utility. Furthermore, the mere presence of an observer and her measuring apparatus will cause a change in the properties of spacetime, according to the General Theory. That is, the observer becomes an unavoidable influence on the field structure she is trying to measure. The whole notion of "objectivity" becomes highly problematic as field theory helps to erode the distinction between subject and object in science.[14]

Cubism

In the preceding chapter we described what we are now identifying as the *field* of a cubist painting. We observed the incorporation into Cubism of the technique of depicting objects in "little facet-planes" that Picasso and Braque probably took from Cézanne and their extension of this technique to the background as well, again after Cézanne's last manner. (see Plate 8, Cézanne's *The Big Trees* (c. 1904)). Braque and Picasso found that the facet-planes could be opened up to allow for transitions within the object and within the background and between the object and the background, giving rise to the "truncated" rectangles, triangles, and circles that make up the characteristic vocabulary of analytical Cubism.[15] These developments eroded the demarcations between objects and the space surrounding them because the objects and the space were presented by means of the same visual constituents. Object-space and background-space leaked into each other, participated in the reciprocal representation, and became a *field* according to our definition. The spatial flow between background and object creates the "interdependence" of the painting's constituents while the facet-language permits their common participation without privilege.

Because the development of the facet-planes is so central to the dissolution of the distinction between object and space, this contribution of Cézanne – regardless of how it can be related to his own aesthetic aims – may be seen

---

14. This problem becomes even more acute and mathematically explicit in the quantum theory where the measurement protocol becomes a conceptual and mathematically intimate part of any system under study. Quantum mechanics further expanded the notion that observers become inseparably part of the observed, and the mathematical formulation of quantum mechanics incorporates an explicit mathematical expression of this into the very structure of the theory. The quantum theory began in 1900 with Max Planck's introduction of a quantum of energy to explain the way that heated objects emit electromagnetic radiation (for example, light). Over the next three decades the theory was developed into a complete mechanical view of the world. The inherent indeterminacy in measurements and the probabilistic interpretation of the mathematics of quantum mechanics was established between 1925 and 1930. Hayles describes the erosion in these terms: "there is no such thing as observing this interactive whole from a frame of reference removed from it. Relativity implies that we cannot observe the universe from an Olympian perspective. Necessarily and irrevocably, we are within it, part of the cosmic web" (*The Cosmic Web*, p. 49). Hayles here refers to the multiplicity of valid but different measurements of events in spacetime predicted by Relativity Theory. We further emphasize that our participation in the cosmic "web" or, to use our terminology, the spatial and temporal fields, extends to our direct influence on the fields themselves.
15. Clement Greenberg, "Master Léger" (1954), in *Art and Culture*, pp. 98–99. See Chapter 4 above, pp. 4–85.

as the single most important source of Cubism's revolutionary achievements. Unlike the smaller constituents of Impressionism – the tiny dots, strokes, touches of color – which were of course capable of eroding the outlines of objects to a degree, the facet-planes could actually *assert* the interpenetration of object-space and background-space and so ultimately establish the integrity or identity as a single field of that formerly dualistic space. To draw an analogy from physics, the breakthrough came with the discovery of the applicable *quanta*, which in painting were the visual *units* comprised of strokes or hatches of paint that could be interpreted as volume, that could make a statement about the formal space they represented.

We can see this by looking at details from representative cubist paintings from 1911 to 1913, such as Picasso's *The Aficionado* (1912) (Plate 5) or *Portrait of Ambroise Vollard* (1909–10) (Plate 7) or contemporaneous works such as Braque's *Le Portugais* (1911–12) or Léger's *La Femme en bleu* (1912).[16] Here we see what in realist terms ought to be the solid integral objects like the head or facial features or body of Braque's Portugais leaking out into the surrounding space, or the interfusion of Picasso's bullfight fan with the paraphernalia of his obsession or even the tendency of such interfusion pushing modernist art toward the abstract as with Léger's *Femme en bleu*. We can see that the object, surface, and background or surrounding space are all made up of the little facet-planes and that these visual quanta mold the space and the objects alike.[17] Space and object become indistinguishable; the aesthetic focus or *privilege* of objects in realist paintings is undercut in the interest of fresh formal unities. As in General Relativity Theory, the objects are also a kind of energy, perhaps more concentrated or denser or more richly defined than the rest of the field.

The relationship between "space" and "objects" (or "matter") is a complicated one in modern physics, as in Cubism, and we believe it important to make such comparison as clear as possible. Only by doing so can we go beyond simple analogies and establish the common value represented by "the field." We have seen that in Einstein's General Theory, certain properties of "space" (the geometric and temporal rules followed by objects in any region of space) are determined by the distribution of mass (objects) in space. Thus the presence of matter helps to define the properties of the very space in

16. All at the Kunstmuseum, Basel.
17. William Rubin makes a valuable distinction between what the "fusion" of object and background meant for Braque and what it meant for Picasso: "The importance Braque attributes to the picture field, as against Picasso's stress on the physiognomic of particular forms, is also expressed in the priority he gives the spatial continuum. Picasso starts with the objects that inhabit this continuum. Braque, as he himself said, was 'unable to introduce the object until I had created the space for it.' Braque's insistence on dissolving distinctions between figure and ground, a characteristic of his Cubism throughout, follows from this position. . . . While Picasso also exploited the new fusion of figure and ground to great advantage in his work of 1910–11, his real interest in the fragmentation of objects lay in the opportunity it gave for pushing their physiognomic into a world of new signs" (*Picasso and Braque, Pioneering Cubism*, p. 26). This is a valuable distinction, but for our present purposes it serves chiefly to confirm that both cubists exploited the development of the spatial field in their painting.

which the matter is located. Furthermore, we remember that Einstein was able to show in his earlier Special Theory that mass (matter) and energy are two manifestations of the same fundamental entity. Energy, then, like mass, influences the properties of space in which it moves. So "space" and its trans-actions with matter and energy define the characteristic behavior (geometric and temporal) of any measuring apparatus. Even to speak of "space" having "properties" as though it were some tangible entity shows the erosion in the distinction between "empty space" and space containing matter. So in Cubism as in physics the space itself can be regarded as another kind of object, perhaps less dense and less associated with familiar, vaguely Euclidean, forms. The cubist hatching or facet-planes, the visual quanta or primary constituents of the representation, make it all possible.

For the clearest available summary of where this takes us, we turn again to Greenberg:

> All pictorial space became as one, neither "positive" nor "negative," insofar as occupied space was no longer clearly differentiated from unoccupied space. The depicted object was not so much formed as precipitated in clusters of facet-planes – which in their turn could be conceived of as formed by the vibrating and expanding echoes of the depicted objects. By means of design and drawing, the Cubists brought to a culmination what the Impressionists, when they let forms emerge as clots of color touches from an ambiance of color touches, had begun: the old distinction between object-in-front-of-background and background-behind-and-around-object was obliterated – obliterated at least as something felt rather than merely read.[18]

Here Greenberg describes a field according to our definition of it: a spatial and/or temporal model or representation in which all constituents are inter-dependent and in which all constituents participate and interrelate without privilege. "What has insinuated itself into modernist art is the . . . notion of space as a continuum which objects inflect but do not interrupt, and of objects as being constituted in turn by the inflection of space."[19] It is significant that much of Greenberg's description of the cubist field could apply to the cosmic field of General Relativity. As an acute late modernist critic of art and literature, Greenberg himself participates in the value structure of the period, including the priority accorded to the development of fields, though he perhaps does not identify them as such. In fact, the development of the field model solved for modernist thinkers similarly perceived problems in both painting and physics: how to represent more completely what we can measure; how to incorporate into our representation the fullest possible observation of the world we perceive.

In Cubism the influence of the field extends well beyond its initial develop-ment during the analytic period. In the following chapter we will have more

18. Greenberg, "Master Léger," *Art and Culture*, p. 99.
19. Greenberg, "On the Role of Nature in Modernist Painting" (1949), *Art and Culture*, pp. 172–173.

to say about what is widely termed synthetic Cubism in which the picture field itself becomes a kind of final and only certainty and the visual continuum of the painting surface the effective reality.[20] For the present we can suggest the scope of the development by turning again to Braque's 1944 study, *Le Billard*, painted thirty-five years after the developments we have been discussing (Plate 6).[21] The space represented in the room, like space in General Relativity Theory, collects and incorporates the "objects": the billiard table, the cues, the chair, the balls suspended on the nearly vertical green felt. The space literally "curves" or bends. The usual signs of Euclidean geometry – right angles, perpendiculars, circles, triangles, parallelograms – are all travestied in the interest of what we might call the "geodesics" of the composition. What we see is no less than a visual event in relativistic spacetime, an event that asserts the interdependence of represented object and represented space, of the integrity of the field.

In the plastic arts beyond Cubism the value of the field (according to our definition of it) was widely and independently demonstrated. Matisse, for example, was at the same period (1907–12), or even earlier, profoundly engaged in studying the interrelation of the object with its surrounding space: "I have never abandoned the object. The object is not of such interest by itself; it is the environment which creates it. . . . The object is an actor. . . . It is not perceived alone by itself, but evokes a group of elements."[22] In the work of Matisse and his followers the object may be said to organize the space around it, but the terminology is revealing. As in the work of Picasso, Braque, and other cubists, the duality between object and space has not been completely discounted but remains at a vestigial or verbal level.

In modernist painting and sculpture, it was left for the Italian futurists to break most radically with the space–object duality, and it was they who most fully developed what might be called a "field theory" of modernist painting, one that in terms of our cultural history complements and transcends (as the futurists themselves argued) the more static, spatially oriented achievement of the cubists. Although Italian Futurism does not carry the immense influence of Cubism and did not in the end produce a corresponding legacy of great painting, its theoretical basis brings us closest to our definition of field. During its brief period of development and articulation (1909 to about 1915), Futurism arrived at important and striking parallels with General Relativity, though of course without adopting Relativity's new concept of the field (which would have been chronologically impossible).[23]

---

20. Ibid., p. 173.
21. For our earlier treatment see Chapter 3, p. 66. This is one of a series of studies of billiard tables that Braque did late in his career – this one to be found in the Centre Georges Pompidou, Paris.
22. Henri Matisse, "Testimonial," 1952, quoted in Herschel B. Chipp, *Theories of Modern Art*, p. 142.
23. Linda Dalrymple Henderson has pointed out that any sense of "field" in Boccioni's art probably derives from his assumption of an ether that Relativity discarded ("Modern Art and the Invisible Waves and Dimensions of Occultism and Science"). This would necessarily have been the case with most modernist painters who had an interest in science. The field value is a general value of Modernism and not limited to Relativity Theory and its now dominant enlargement

The primary aim of the Italian futurists was to find a new solution to the problem of representing motion, first in language but then more interestingly in painting and sculpture. Obsessively conscious of heralding a new era, the futurist painters and their first theorist and mouthpiece, F. T. Marinetti, saw the primary and contemporary value of their age as *speed* or *velocity*. They asserted their views in the form of numerous manifestos from 1909 to 1914, usually read aloud at raucous and sometimes pugilistic demonstrations (so that the manifesto and the demonstration actually became new art forms of the futurist movement, distinguishing it radically from Cubism).[24] Among their most important programmatic productions was *Futurist Painting: Technical Manifesto*. In the words of Herbert Read, "The manifesto of 1910 is a logical document. It begins by declaring that a growing need for *truth* can no longer be satisfied by form and color as they have been understood in the past: all things move and run, change rapidly, and this universal dynamism is what the artist should strive to represent. Space no longer exists, or only as an atmosphere within which bodies move and interpenetrate. Color too is irides-cent, scintillating; shadows are luminous, flickering."[25]

The futurist emphasis on dynamism (one of their favorite words) and on a universe in which space is a context or "atmosphere" for matter in constant and often violent motion makes their theoretical statements highly evocative of General Relativity and also of the emphasis in modernist fiction on the deformation of time. For example, the *Technical Manifesto* declares:

> To paint a human figure you must not paint it; you must render the whole of its surrounding atmosphere.
>
> Space no longer exists: the street pavement, soaked by rain beneath the glare of electric lamps, becomes immensely deep and gapes to the very center of the earth. Thousands of miles divide us from the sun; yet the house in front of us fits into the solar disk.
>
> Who can still believe in the opacity of bodies, since our sharpened and multiplied sensitiveness has already penetrated the obscure manifestations of the medium? Why should we forget in our creations the doubled power of our sight capable of giving results analogous to those of the X-rays?

of the concept. We perhaps need to reiterate our methodological assumption that all cultural diagnostics – scientific and aesthetic – will contain much of importance that here goes untreated for reasons of clarity and space.

24. See especially Marjorie Perloff, "Violence and Precision: The Manifesto as Art Form" in *The Futurist Moment*, pp. 80–115; also Ester Coen, *Umberto Boccioni* and Marianne W. Martin, *Futurist Art and Theory*. The most important painters of the movement included Umberto Boccioni, Carlo Carrà, Luigi Russolo, Giocomo Balla, and Gino Severini. In a chapter on "What Divides Us from Cubism" in his book on futurist painting and sculpture, Boccioni wrote: "Emotion in modern painting and sculpture sings of the gravitation, the displacement, the reciprocal attraction of forms, masses, and colors: which means *movement*, and that is the interpretation of forces. To fix beforehand as its sole end the integral analysis of volumes and physical bodies is a dead stop" (quoted in Coen, *Umberto Boccioni*, p. 244). This was how he and other futurists distinguished Futurism from what they saw as its static (or "dead") contemporary, Cubism.

25. Herbert Read, *A Concise History of Modern Painting*, pp. 109–110.

Our bodies penetrate the sofas upon which we sit, and the sofas penetrate our bodies. The motor bus rushes into the houses which it passes, and in their turn the houses throw themselves upon the motor bus and are blended with it.

The construction of pictures has hitherto been foolishly traditional. Painters have shown us the objects and the people placed before us. We shall hence-forward put the spectator in the center of the picture.[26]

A number of vigorous assertions are offered here and we can see a convergence on the general idea of the field, though that word is not used. The violent rejection (typical of manifestos) of certain basic distinctions central to Realism shows us the way to this fundamental value of Modernism: the object may no longer be fully distinguished from surrounding "space"; in fact the neutral space of Realism "no longer exists"; objects themselves are no longer opaque or discrete – they penetrate and are penetrated by their surroundings; and the observer is no longer outside the system of representation but a part of it, "in the center of the picture." All these moves are characteristic of a modernist assertion of the field, as is the declaration (remarkable in that it anticipates the publication of General Relativity by five years) "THAT MOVE-MENT AND LIGHT DESTROY THE MATERIALITY OF BODIES."[27]

By thus building movement (in Relativity Theory the "dimension" of time) into their aesthetic program the Italian futurists arrived at what we can call a field theory of painting, beautifully realized in their best work – for example in Boccioni's *The Dynamism of a Soccer Player* (1913) (Plate 10). Realist conventions that had dominated Italian art since the second half of the fifteenth century had been based on static perspectives, just as Newtonian mechanics, the famous laws of motion, were derived from a fundamentally absolute model of spatial and temporal measurement in an unaccelerated reference frame.[28] When the futurists made the striking assertion that "movement and light destroy the materiality of bodies" they meant that the realist distinctions between space and matter, context and object, needed to be replaced with a comprehensive theory of representation that would be free of what they had come to see as an arbitrary duality.

As might be expected, this program works at least as well in sculpture as in painting. Umberto Boccioni provided the clearest and most complete theoretical document in his *Technical Manifesto of Futurist Sculpture* of 1912. Boccioni saw this statement as an application to sculpture of the doctrine set out in the 1910 technical manifesto on futurist painting:

Why should sculpture remain behind, tied to laws that no one has the right to impose on it? We therefore cast all aside and proclaim the ABSOLUTE AND COMPLETE ABOLITION OF DEFINITE LINES AND CLOSED

26. *Futurist Painting: Technical Manifesto* (first published as a pamphlet in Milan in 1910, then translated with Marinetti's guidance and published in the catalogue of the London exhibition of futurist painting in March 1912), in Chipp, *Theories of Modern Art*, pp. 289–290.
27. Chipp, *Theories of Modern Art*, p. 293. Capitals in the original pamphlet.
28. As discussed in the preceding section.

SCULPTURE. WE BREAK OPEN THE FIGURE AND ENCLOSE IT IN ENVIRONMENT. We proclaim that the environment must be part of the plastic block which is a world in itself with its own laws; that the sidewalk can jump up on your table and your head be transported across the street, while your lamp spins a web of plaster rays between one house and another.

Not only is a sculpture of the same substance and subject to the same laws as the environment, but the environment itself may be seen as a part of the "plastic block"; or, in other words, the world itself is governed by the laws that govern sculpture. They exist in the same field:

The thing that one creates is nothing other than a bridge between the EXTERIOR PLASTIC INFINITE and the INTERIOR PLASTIC INFINITE; thus objects never end, and intersect with infinite combinations of sympathetic harmonies and clashing aversions.[29]

Instead of discrete objects located in neutral space we have an interaction, a middle ground, a field of play.

If we look at one of his most successful realizations of this argument, *Development of a Bottle in Space* (1912) (Plate 11) we can see how completely Boccioni himself was able to convey the integration of what in Realism would have been the object in what would have been its neutral, homogeneous, unformed space. But in this sculpture the bottle is represented as influencing its surrounding space and the space is sculptured. The concentric circles that spiral around the central form echo that form by repetition and amplification. From the perspective of modernist aesthetic criticism, the sculpture seems to be "an analytical experiment on the relation between an internal space and an external one . . . the planes . . . are . . . no longer boundaries to the object but [act] as communication and connection between these two spaces, as a means to restore the unity of the space beyond the empirical limits of things."[30] And that is the unity we have been calling "field."

In Boccioni's words, "To render a body in motion, I definitely do not present the trajectory, that is, the passage from one state of repose to another state of repose, but force myself to ascertain the form that expresses continuity in space."[31] The radical innovation of *Development of a Bottle in Space* lies not in the simple suggestion of movement by means of a static spatial medium – many realist paintings and sculptures represent moving objects – but in the achievement of a form that embodies motion, in this case the "development" of the bottle. We have seen that the multiple perspectives of cubist paintings imply a dynamic *knowledge* of an object in that they represent more than one perspective "simultaneously," a visual awareness of different aspects that must be acquired over time. What Futurism (at its most successful)

---

29. Chipp, *Theories of Modern Art*, pp. 302, 304. Boccioni's capitals.
30. G. C. Argan and M. Calvesi (*Umberto Boccioni*, Rome, 1953) are quoted by Coen, *Umberto Boccioni*, p. 215.
31. In an exhibition catalogue of 1913, quoted in Coen, *Umberto Boccioni*, p. xxix.

added was a formal incorporation of the experience of motion, of "velocity" or "speed," into the work itself. As Boccioni put it:

> A horse in movement is not a stationary horse that moves but a horse in movement, which is something else, which must be conceived and expressed as something completely different. It means that objects in movement must be conceived otherwise than in the movement they have within themselves. This means finding a form that will be the expression of this new absolute: Speed, which is a truth no genuinely modern temperament can ignore. It means the study of the aspects life has assumed in velocity and in the consequent simultaneity.[32]

A futurist art work is thus not an object moving from one point to another such as we see in realistic motion pictures, but a representation that incorporates the motion itself; and consequently a bottle that used to be thought of as an essentially self-contained object in neutral space now becomes something inseparable from its surroundings. The bottle cannot be said to exist independently, statically in a space, but must be represented as engaging and enlarging its context. As in General Relativity, matter participates in defining the nature of space and time just as matter may also be viewed as a quality of the energy existing in and determining the geometric properties of space and time. Futurism complemented Cubism by integrating the "dimension" of time into visual representation and so arriving at another modernist application of the value of the field.

Narrative

Modernist narrative deals extensively and explicitly with the collapse of realist distinctions into formal and ethical fields, into representational models or fictions in which all constituents are interdependent and in which constituents participate and interrelate without privilege. The positivist premiss of a privileged observer is treated thematically and with masterful and destructive irony in Kafka's "In the Penal Colony" (1919), a short story we discussed in relation to epistemic trauma at the end of Chapter 2. Here the center of consciousness character is a foreign "explorer," distinguished for his experience of varying cultures, who thinks of himself as a neutral observer and who is asked by the New Commandant of the penal colony to review its archaic system of justice. Versed as he is in the principles of cultural relativism, the explorer nevertheless allows himself to take a position:

> The explorer thought to himself: It's always a ticklish matter to intervene decisively in other people's affairs. He was neither a member of the penal colony nor a citizen of the state to which it belonged. Were he to denounce this execution or actually try to stop it, they could say to him: You are a foreigner, mind your own business. He could make no answer to that, unless he were to

32. From *Pittura, scultura, futuriste* (1914), quoted in Coen, *Umberto Boccioni*, p. xxxiii.

add that he was amazed at himself in this connection, for he traveled only as an observer, with no intention at all of altering other people's methods of administering justice. Yet here he found himself strongly tempted. The injustice of the procedure and the inhumanity of the execution were undeniable.

The explorer sees himself as trapped, especially when he learns that his refusal to condemn the apparently monstrous torture of the old system can be represented as support for it. He chooses to follow his own ideas of due process and to condemn the old system of justice – whereupon its advocate, the officer who administered it under the Old Commandant and who has argued all along that the archaic system is "most humane and most in consonance with human dignity," sacrifices himself to it.[33]

Very few readers of Kafka's parabolic story would support the officer and the old system. After all, readers in 1919 were used to thinking of themselves as neutral observers of realist texts like the explorer in his travels. But in Kafka's ironic treatment of the paradoxes of justice, the officer has a point. His system, after all, rationalized guilt. The condemned persons eventually (at about the sixth hour) deciphered the script being inscribed on their bodies and experienced a sublime revelation. Their sufferings were significant, not absurd, and thus the system of justice justified itself and gave the guilty person a final "dignity" – in implied contrast with the vaguely promised due process of the new regime. This archaic dignity the explorer fails to consider and in fact he lacks the knowledge necessary to recognize it. He cannot read the "scripts" on which the precepts of the old system are written, the sacred texts that validate and rationalize it. He tries, but he cannot make out the words. And this failure defines his fraudulence as a neutral observer; his ignorance, human and inescapable, forces him to become a participant in the ethical field – in it rather than above it. "In the Penal Colony" tells us that there are no more observers.[34]

Formally as well as thematically the relation of the field model to modernist literature has been observed by a few critics and scholars. In their study of *Einstein as Myth and Muse*, Carol Donley and Alan Friedman offer this explanation:

> A major artistic problem in the 20th century is that of inventing forms capable of carrying the indeterminisms, ambiguities, pluralities, uncertainties, and antitheses characterizing modern ways of seeing. Many writers use field forms as functional contemporary structures, since the fields can continuously adjust to accommodate discontinuities within their "range."
>
> Essentially these open forms express field relationships in which each

33. Franz Kafka, *The Penal Colony*, pp. 206, 212.
34. Ibid., pp. 218–219. In Joseph Conrad's *Victory* (1915), the protagonist Heyst explains that after falling under the influence of his nihilist father he could no longer participate in the human world: "I started off to wander about, an independent spectator – if that is possible" (p. 161). This dissociation destroys him at the end when it leads to the loss of Lena, and again there are no living "independent spectators."

individual or event interacts with all other elements within the field. A shift in
any one element alters the field so that the whole complex fluctuates.

Friedman and Donley illustrate the use of the field in modernist fiction in
several texts, among them Virginia Woolf's remarkable novel *The Waves* (1931),
composed like a chamber music sextet from the interior voices of six characters
who conceive their individual identities by means of their lifelong relation
to each other:

> The six figures change as they separate and come together. Bernard, on his way
> to meet his friends at Hampton Court, remarks, "In a moment, when I have
> joined them, another arrangement will form, another pattern. . . . Already at fifty
> yards' distance, I feel the order of my being changed." All relationships in the
> field shift each time one of the figures comes through the swing doors at Percival's
> farewell party. Rhoda and Jinny, at their coming-out party, both feel the changes
> in the field every time another person comes into the room. In Rhoda's frame of
> reference, each newcomer frightens her as the field changes and she cannot find
> her place in it. "The door opens; the tiger leaps. The door opens; terror rushes
> in; terror upon terror, pursuing me." Jinny, on the other hand, primed and ready,
> welcomes the door's opening as her potential lovers keep entering the field. As
> Woolf commented in her diary, "Never in my life did I attack such a vague and
> elaborate design. Whenever I make a mark, I have to think of it in relation to a
> dozen others."[35]

We can go beyond this valuable analysis and establish more extended
parallels in *The Waves* to the development of the field model in modernist
physics. For example, the six characters all admire a schoolboy hero named
Percival, in himself entirely conventional and solid: "He is conventional; he
is a hero." In other words, Percival's virtues, precisely because of their con-
ventionality, permit the six characters, however different from each other,
to agree in their admiration of him. They organize a farewell dinner party as
Percival leaves for public service in India. Bernard says, "We have come
together (from the North, from the South, from Susan's farm, from Louis's
house of business) to make one thing, not enduring – for what endures? –
but seen by many eyes simultaneously."[36] Here Percival the heroic still centers
the design and the others form around him. In fact Percival's importance
lies precisely in centering the design. He is that lovely anachronism, a hero.
But his contemporary context, the relativistic, modernist universe – the
universe as field – has no center and no place for centers.

Woolf illustrates this centerless universe by means of a later dinner party
for the six characters after Percival dies from the conventional but sub-heroic
accident of falling from his horse. Because this second dinner party takes
place without Percival it lacks a center. Instead, as Friedman and Donley

35. Friedman and Donley, *Einstein as Myth and Muse*, pp. 136–137.
36. Virginia Woolf, *The Waves*, pp. 123, 127.

point out, we see that the six characters form a field: Bernard says, "There at the door by the Inn, our meeting-place, they are already standing – Susan, Louis, Rhoda, Jinny and Neville. They have come together already. In a moment, when I have joined them, another arrangement will form, another pattern. What now runs to waste, forming scenes profusely, will be checked, stated. I am reluctant to suffer that compulsion. Already at fifty yards' distance I feel the order of my being changed. The tug of the magnet of their society tells upon me." We can see that Woolf has used the physical metaphor of the magnetic field, and although the six characters now have no center of affection and value to locate them, and although they are left centerless and in this sense bereft, they are neither lost nor devoid of a dynamic geometry of relationships. But realist identity, the firm contours of individualized personality, the discrete signatures of defined character in social space familiar to us from nineteenth-century novels, is dissolved. As Bernard puts it in his old age, "what I call 'my life,' . . . is not one life that I look back upon; I am not one person; I am many people; I do not altogether know who I am – Jinny, Susan, Neville, Rhoda, or Louis: or how to distinguish my life from theirs."[37]

Woolf goes farther still, to the point of an almost complete rejection of realist conventions for character. Bernard at the end feels his "self" slipping away: "For this is not one life; nor do I always know if I am man or woman, Bernard or Neville, Louis, Susan, Jinny or Rhoda – so strange is the contact of one with another." He feels he lacks vocabulary, language, adequate to his fluid or field state: "'But how describe the world seen without a self? There are no words.'" Self disappears into the collective social matrix as observer moves into field in modernist physics or subject into space in cubist and futurist art. There is no view of the world from a single privileged perspective. The world becomes knowable only through participation within the field. Bernard, who at the end of the novel speaks for all six characters (his voice has become their voices in the last chapter) says, "And now I ask, 'Who am I?' I have been talking of Bernard, Neville, Jinny, Susan, Rhoda and Louis. Am I all of them? Am I one and distinct? I do not know. We sat here together. But now Percival is dead, and Rhoda is dead; we are divided; we are not here. Yet I cannot find any obstacle separating us. There is no division between me and them. As I talked I felt, 'I am you.' This difference we make so much of, this identity we so feverishly cherish, was overcome."[38]

In *Absalom, Absalom* (1936), William Faulkner took the multi-narrator novel well beyond Woolf's achievement in *The Waves*. Faulkner's narrators attempt to tell the story of Thomas Sutpen and his explosive success and decline in fictional Yoknapatawpha County. There are four "inside narrators" – Mr Compson, Rosa Coldfield, Quentin Compson, and Shreve McCannon –

37. Ibid., pp. 210, 276.
38. Ibid., pp. 281, 287, 288–289.

who not only tell the story but have a personal relation to it; and there is one third person narrator who comments on the inside narrators and their relation to the action. The inside narrators not only tell their versions of the tale but also engage in speculation about each other and about the accuracy and imagination of each other's narration and the distortions caused by each other's preconceptions. To Quentin, the most perceptive and reserved of the inside narrators, their identities seem to blend into each other in their narrative function. In a passage famous for its treatment of the nature of modernist narration, he notices how closely he and his Harvard roommate Shreve resemble his father in their speculation on the Sutpen story:

> Maybe we are both Father. Maybe nothing ever happens once and is finished. Maybe happen is never once but like ripples maybe on water after the pebble sinks, the ripples moving on, spreading, the pool attached by a narrow umbilical water-cord to the next pool which the first pool feeds, has fed, did feed, let this second pool contain a different temperature of water, a different molecularity of having seen, felt, remembered, reflect in a different tone the infinite unchanging sky, it doesn't matter: that pebble's watery echo whose fall it did not even see moves across its surface too at the original ripple-space, to the old ineradicable rhythm thinking Yes, we are both Father. Or maybe Father and I are both Shreve, maybe it took Father and me both to make Shreve or Shreve and me both to make Father or maybe Thomas Sutpen to make all of us.[39]

Again, from being a story told by a single observer the nature of narrative has become plural and collective, has become a field. In this field the narrator participates in and influences the events being narrated, so that individual narrative identity can be overtaken and subsumed by the narrative itself in much the same way that observers of the relativistic universe must take into consideration their own participation in that universal field.

In *Absalom, Absalom!* the narrators by means of their imaginative effort actually become the actors whose story they are imagining, so eventually Shreve and Quentin take turns narrating: "So that now it was not two but four of them riding the two horses through the dark over the frozen December ruts of that Christmas Eve: four of them and then just two – Charles-Shreve and Quentin-Henry."[40] One acquires knowledge, achieves understanding, only by entering the field, by participating in and thus helping to create the story. Here the field is an imaginative field, a field created by Quentin and Shreve as they *become* Henry and Charles. As in Woolf's *The Waves*, though even more richly and completely, individual identity with all its distinctions so valued in the realist tradition, dissolves into the field. Here one arrives at significance within events only by encouraging such dissolution.

In his short story "Delta Autumn" (1941), Faulkner again plays with the dissolution of identity in time, but here it is not primarily a question of the identity of individual characters but of the land, the river delta, and its diminish-

---

39. William Faulkner, *Absalom, Absalom!*, p. 210; his italics.
40. Ibid., p. 267. We examine the implications of Shreve and Quentin's *creation* of the story, their "truth of the imagination," in our next chapter, on Reflexivity.

ment. The mathematical or physical symbol for change (Δ),[41] the *delta* in the story, works on several planes of significance. It is a diminishing or dissolving area of wilderness in which the center of consciousness character, Ike McCaslin, used to shoot game during his childhood and youth. The shrinking of the delta as a wilderness parallels the loss of masculine honor in the current coarse exploitation of women (the black mother and child abandoned by McCaslin's younger relative) and the unraveling of the hunter's code of conduct (the doe dishonorably shot at the end of the story). The "delta" is also at once a symbol for *space* (the wilderness) and *time* (McCaslin's life, which is diminishing): "He seemed to see the two of them – himself and the wilderness – as coevals, his own span as a hunter, a woodsman, not contemporary with his first breath but transmitted to him, assumed by him gladly, humbly, with joy and pride, from that old Major de Spain and that old Sam Fathers who had taught him to hunt, the two spans running out together."[42] This vision of dignified valediction itself dissolves in the concluding helplessness and betrayal.

The narrative field here includes the river delta, the hunting ethos, the ethical responsibility of men toward women, and the motives of the chief actors in the story. These different aspects move in one direction, together, interacting, inseparable. McCaslin, technically the story's center of consciousness, also participates in the movement of the narrative field toward the dissolution of standards, toward moral degeneration, in that he sees no possibility for his younger relative Roth Edmonds to act honorably toward the young woman. McCaslin thinks, "*Maybe in a thousand or two thousand years in America . . . But not now! Not now!* He cried, not loud, in a voice of amazement, pity, and outrage: 'You're a nigger!' "[43] His treatment of her, though not as coarsely selfish or culpable as Edmonds's, contrasts tellingly with her courage and capacity for love. McCaslin, with all his ethical nostalgia and hatred of moral entropy, effectively helps shoot the doe, and what tells us this is his unprivileged participation in the total formal and thematic field.

Our final illustration of the adaptation of field models by modernist fiction comes from a story by Jorge Luis Borges, "The Garden of Forking Paths" (1941). Here the use of the field model is completely conscious, replete with allusions to Einstein and the universe of General Relativity. The sinologist murdered by the narrator bears the name "Stephen Albert." He has solved the riddle posed by the narrator's ancestor, who wrote a novel and devised a labyrinth – an apparently incoherent manuscript and a labyrinth that was never found. Stephen Albert has discovered that the novel and the labyrinth are one and the same, "an enormous guessing game, or parable, in which the subject is time":

---

41. In Faulkner's story the delta is inverted, "this inverted-apex, this ∇-shaped section of earth" ("Delta Autumn," p. 343). The inverted delta, called a "del" or "nabla" in physical science and mathematics, is also a symbol representing minute changes in a quantity. We remind the reader that Verloc's code symbol in Conrad's *The Secret Agent* is a delta, as discussed in Chapter 4 above.
42. Faulkner, "Delta Autumn," p. 354.
43. Ibid., pp. 340–341, 361.

"The explanation is obvious. *The Garden of Forking Paths* is a picture, incomplete yet not false, of the universe such as Ts'ui Pên conceived it to be. Differing from Newton and Schopenhauer, your ancestor did not think of time as absolute and uniform. He believed in an infinite series of times, in a dizzily growing, ever spreading network of diverging, converging and parallel times. This web of time – the strands of which approach one another, bifurcate, intersect or ignore each other through the centuries – embraces *every* possibility."[44]

This exquisite metaphorical description of Einstein's universe is anticipated and alluded to throughout Borges's story. It reminds one of Max Born's comment that Einstein's "suggestion of a finite, but unbounded space is one of the greatest ideas about the nature of the world which has ever been conceived."[45]

Modernist Abstraction

Related to the value of the field in the intellectual history of Modernism but much more troubled by conflicting definitions is the problem of abstraction. In the contemporary response to all three of our cultural diagnostics – Relativity Theory, Cubism, modernist narrative – we find criticism of what was felt to be a rapidly increasing abstraction, approaching the incomprehensible or un-bearable. This association of Modernism with the abstract remains active: popular opinion often equates all Modernism in painting and sculpture with abstract art; modernist poetry and narrative bears the charge of being dissociated from reality or from that particularized reality common in Realism; and Relativity Theory seems remote in part because of its association with the loss of the mechanics of Newton. Much of what we have to say about this can be found in our Chapters 2 and 3, under the headings of "Epistemic Trauma" and the shift in value, "From Normative to Contextual," and we will not attempt a comprehensive discussion of abstraction in Modernism. But we can address this problem directly in order to see precisely what values drive it, or in other words what kind of abstraction Modernism supports and requires. We can do this by discussing our three cultural diagnostics in relation to each other.

Our first observation must be that Modernism is not characterized simply by an increase in the degree of abstraction, as if abstraction were a simple quantity and Modernism a simple vehicle. We can illustrate the complexity of the topic by observing that Realism, like all epistemological systems (epis-temes), had its abstraction too. The premises that permitted Realism – underlying assumptions about the nature of space, time, and representation – may be viewed as highly abstract.[46] In Modernism we find a specific kind of abstraction, an abstraction best defined by distinguishing it from the

---

44. Jorge Luis Borges, "The Garden of Forking Paths," in *Ficciones*, pp. 99, 100. We should add that this story also contains allusions to quantum mechanics (in particular the so-called "many-world" interpretation of quantum theory), probability, and number theory.
45. Born is quoted in Ronald W. Clark, *Einstein: The Life and Times*, pp. 270–271.
46. See Elizabeth Deeds Ermarth, *Realism and Consensus in the English Novel*, pp. 3–92.

particularities of Newtonian mechanics because it was in the abandonment of these that modernist abstraction came to be most fully felt. We have seen that in its break with Realism, Modernism and its manifestations appeared to be difficult, compressed, radically simplified. Relativity Theory, cubist painting, early twentieth-century poetry and fiction all seemed to cause difficulty by leaving something out, by taking away (literally *abstracting*) coordinates of time and space or indices of moral and aesthetic importance that had given meaning to preceding achievements in these areas. It is precisely this "taking away" or abstracting from Realism the authority of its own sustaining abstractions – nothing less than a *de-coordination* of the mainstream tradition of representation in the West – that constitutes the unique quality of modernist abstraction and not the obvious departure from natural and social particularity (the realistic details of "object" or "event").

Relativity Theory

The modernist commitment to streamlining and simplification by means of abstraction (taking away) may be seen in Einstein's work from his paper on Special Relativity through the General Theory to his final commitment to a unified field theory. The paper on Special Relativity laconically (simply!) removed the necessity for ether theory.[47] The opening pages of this 1905 paper, where the central notions of Special Relativity Theory are developed, may be seen as an entirely characteristic work of Modernism in its omission (abstraction) of all but the simplest mathematics and in its enviable freedom from scholarly machinery. And even when in the General Theory the mathematics became much more difficult, Einstein was concerned to assert that the underlying principles must be *simple*: "Equations of such complexity as the equations of the gravitational field can be found only through the discovery of a logically simple mathematical condition which determines the conditions completely or (at least) almost completely."[48] It was part of his development as a modernist that Einstein came to believe that "our experience justifies us in believing that nature is the realization of the simplest conceivable mathematical ideas."[49] Of course it does not follow that such simple ideas will be easy to grasp.

47. We believe it to be no accident that what may be the first use of "streamline" can be traced to James Clerk Maxwell (1873) whose work helped inspire Einstein's formulation of Special Relativity; and that the word comes into use in hydrodynamics around 1885–1906, at the beginning of the modernist period. Maxwell did not invent the term "streamline" to suggest simplification or abstraction, meanings the term acquired later, but a simplification or abstraction is exactly what the streamline, as a geometric artifice, was. To describe the complex motion of the myriad particles comprising fluid flow, the streamline abstracts from the true motion a representation of the average motion of the fluid in a region of space and greatly simplifies the description of fluid flow. For the dismissal of the ether from post-classical physics see Mook and Vargish, *Inside Relativity*, pp. 69–79, 280.
48. Quoted by Carl Friedrich von Weizsacker, "Einstein's Importance to Physics, Philosophy, and Politics" in Peter C. Aichelburg and Roman U. Sexl (eds) *Albert Einstein: His Influence on Physics, Philosophy and Politics*, p. 163.
49. Quoted by Henry Margenau in Paul Arthur Schilpp (ed.) *Albert Einstein: Philosopher-Scientist*, I, 254–255.

The popular association of simplicity with ease of comprehension does not work in Modernism. As we saw in our fourth chapter, realist representation (including scientific models, painting, and fiction) justified itself in terms of direct perception of reality, no matter how fully endowed that reality might be with abstractions like the neutrality of space and time or how dependent it might be on methodologies themselves sustained by abstract values like verification or universality. Such "direct perception" – as exercised in, for example, George Eliot's *Middlemarch* or Newtonian models of the solar system or Michelangelo's *Last Judgment* – could in practice be highly complex. Modernism, with its own different difficulties, focuses on the observation of reality, the nature of measurement or of representation itself. It tends (as we have seen) to deal with what we termed the epistemological middle ground, the field, and thus to avoid classical and realist complexity. But the principles and values, the abstractions sustaining pre-modernist traditions of scientific investigation and aesthetic representation, have come over five centuries to seem characteristics of reality itself. The abstractions of realistic representation went underground.

We can see how all this works by using the example of the field in the departure of modern from classical physics. In what sense is a field more abstract than the traditional empirical paradigm of neutral observer and objective reality? Scientific models, like works of art, are abstractions in that they use signs to represent something else. Like some paintings, some scientific models are more abstract than others. From the time of Newton until the middle of the nineteenth century, the formulas of physics were expressed in terms of directly measurable quantities such as position, speed, mass, and acceleration. Then, as we have remarked above, Maxwell used Faraday's idea of a field to describe electromagnetic phenomena in his equations. A field in physics is not something tangible, but a mathematical structure that describes measurable properties of spacetime. In principle, one could experimentally define an electromagnetic field in a region of space (the verb often used is "to map out" the field) by placing an electric charge of known magnitude at various points in space and measuring the magnitude and the direction of the electrical force experienced by this charge at each of the test points.[50] The results of these measurements are sometimes illustrated by drawing an arrow at each of the test points with the length of the arrow being proportional to the magnitude of the electrical force and the direction of the arrow indicating the direction of the force at that point. The imagined and infinite aggregate of all of the arrows characterizing all points in a region of space comprises a map of the electric field in this region of space.

Maxwell's equations are expressed in terms of electric and magnetic fields.

50. Here, of course, the experimenter must beware of the effect that the test charge introduced to determine the field is having on other charges that are establishing the field. In practice this is accomplished by making the magnitude of the test charge smaller and smaller until further reduction has no noticeable effect on the measured field.

In a typical application of Maxwell's model one calculates the field and then, if necessary, goes through another step to predict the action of that field on an actual object. In such an application the field represents a level of abstraction once removed from the Newtonian descriptors of the physical world. A mass or an electrical charge or a magnet is tangible. These tangibles are the currency of Newton's laws. In contrast, Maxwell's equations use fields as currency and one cannot directly "pick up" a field the way one can a charge or a magnet or a mass. This is the sense in which we mean that Maxwell's electromagnetic field equations and Einstein's General Relativity field equations are more abstract than Newton's laws of motion and of gravitation.

We can see this clearly by glancing at the development of Einstein's epistemological premises between the Special Theory (1905) and the General (field) Theory (1915). Einstein began his career as a Machian positivist.[51] Indeed, the 1905 Special Relativity paper contains vivid thought experiments involving directly observed and quantifiable properties of ordinary objects (positions, times of observations). But in creating the General Theory, Einstein adopted the mathematics of tensor calculus, which describes electromagnetic or gravitational fields in a particularly compact form – compact and, because the field tensors are still further removed from direct observations of the world, more abstract by positivist standards. Einstein was led to the belief some time in the course of his development of General Relativity that scientific "truths" about nature could be determined by mathematical manipulation of abstract mathematical entities alone: "nature is the realization of the simplest conceivable mathematical ideas. I am convinced that we can discover by means of purely mathematical constructions the concepts and the laws connecting them with each other, which furnish the key to the understanding of natural phenomena. . . . In a certain sense, therefore, I hold it is true that pure thought can grasp reality as the ancients dreamed."[52]

The epistemological shift here is profound. From the science of Faraday, created literally by hands-on work with apparatus in the laboratory, we have jumped to the modernist approach of Einstein, created by calculational effort and expressed in terms of intangible fields, fields that must undergo further mathematical processing to articulate the predictions of theory in terms of directly observable quantities.

Cubism

In 1911, the poet and critic André Salmon published an anecdote in which a young painter asks Picasso whether one should paint feet "round or square." Picasso annihilates the novice by asserting that "there are no feet in nature!"[53] Picasso implies that "feet" is an aesthetic construction, essentially relevant not to nature but to culture, or in this case to art, to the formal priorities

---

51. See Jeremy Bernstein, *Einstein*, p. 130; and Albert Einstein, "Autobiographical Notes," in Schilpp, *Albert Einstein: Philosopher-Scientist*, I, pp. 21–30.
52. Albert Einstein, "On the Method of Theoretical Physics," pp. 17–18.
53. Quoted in Edward F. Fry, *Cubism*, p. 68.

of painting. Feet in paintings are not natural feet (that is, direct observations of feet in nature as they pretend to be in realistic art). Does this make the representation of "feet" (and there are plenty of them) in Picasso's modernist painting more abstract or less abstract than it would be in Realism? The answer, like the answer to similar questions about Relativity, must be complex. Picasso's observation makes feet more abstract in the sense that they lack realist particularity, the unique characteristics of a particular pair of feet imagined to exist in the world outside the painting; but less abstract in that they are not representations of anything else but themselves: their full and complete and unique existence lies right there on the canvas and requires no abstract assumptions concerning the nature of external space and its representation in plastic art.

The space of single-point perspective from the Renaissance through to nineteenth-century Realism is premised as neutral and homogeneous space in which independent objects are located. This space, supposed to be everywhere uniform and constant and based upon the values of uniformity and neutrality, serves to separate objects from each other. Such Renaissance-realist space, intangible and invisible, certainly satisfies most of the conditions for an abstraction. The spaces that preceded it in medieval art and that followed it in post-impressionist painting actually may be viewed as less abstract. In the words of Clement Greenberg, "space as that which joins instead of separating also means space as a total object."[54] Thus we again confront a paradox of abstraction: that as painting moves away from realist representation of independent, particular objects in single-point perspective and toward the representation of space-as-object or as the *field* of spatial interaction it becomes less dependent on the abstract premises of Realism. As painting moves toward what has come to be called "abstract" art – "non-representational" art like that of Mondrian or Malevich – it actually becomes less dependent on abstract principles and premises. So we can say (wickedly but all the same accurately) that what abstract art abstracts from Realism is in fact the privilege of realist abstractions.[55] It is complications and paradoxes such as this one that give discussion of abstraction a bad name in cultural and intellectual history.

In any case, experts on Cubism generally agree that when Braque and Picasso found their work approaching the non-representational or non-figurative or non-objective (all these terms are used), both artists "recoiled."[56] They

---

54. Greenberg, *Art and Culture*, p. 173.
55. Here is Kasimir Malevich in 1927: "In the year 1913 in my desperate struggle to free art from the ballast of the objective world I fled to the form of the Square and exhibited a picture which was nothing more or less than a black square upon a white background. The critics moaned and with them the public: 'Everything we loved is lost: We are in a desert. . . . Before us stands a black square on a white ground'" (quoted in Alfred H. Barr, *Cubism and Abstract Art*, p. 122).
56. "Recoiled" is Douglas Cooper's term in *The Cubist Epoch*, p. 51. He sees Picasso and Braque as approaching "total abstraction" from time to time between the summer of 1910 and the spring of 1912. John Golding in his *Cubism*, puts the relation of Cubism to abstract painting like this: "The fact that Cubism gave birth to so much abstract art may be one of the reasons why it was so often misunderstood by the public, and even occasionally by serious critics and historians....

chose, like Cézanne and Matisse and the great majority of post-impressionist and modernist painters, not to lose sight of the object. For this reason among others it is often said that the aim of Cubism was essentially to represent reality more accurately and completely. This might be helpful if modernist painters generally regarded as "abstract" – such as Mondrian, Malevich, or Kandinsky during important periods – did not also profess to be representing a more urgent or higher or more complete reality.[57] But if Cubism sticks with the object, then we are brought back to the question so many of its original viewers asked: why not stick with the methods of Realism and *its* abstractions? In 1912 Roger Allard, a poet and critic, addressed the problem with respect to abstraction in this way:

> What is cubism? First and foremost the conscious determination to reestablish in painting the knowledge of mass, volume and weight.
>
> In place of the impressionist illusion of space, which is founded on aerial perspective and naturalistic colour, cubism gives us plain, abstract forms in precise relation and proportion to each other. Thus the first postulate of cubism is the ordering of things – and this means not naturalistic things but abstract forms. Cubism feels space as a complex of lines, units of space, quadratic and cubic equations and ratios.
>
> The artist's problem is to bring some order into this mathematical chaos by bringing out its latent rhythm.
>
> In this way of looking at things, every image of the world is the point of convergence of many conflicting forces. The subject of the picture, the external object, is merely a pretext: the *subject* of the equation. This has always been true; but for many centuries this basic truth lay in a deep obscurity from which today modern art is seeking to rescue it.[58]

Allard suggests that Cubism is interested in particulars (objects, "naturalistic things") primarily as they manifest formal relationships. We can see that much of this description of the aims of Cubism could be applied to Einstein's 1915 General Theory of Relativity. Both Cubism and General Relativity are underpinned by the same values, essentially those of the field model, where every point (each image), to use our own definition of "field," participates and interrelates with all other points without privilege. Relativity presents this mathematically; Cubism visually.

In Cubism and Relativity Theory, the function of abstraction is similar. As Paul Klee (who was influenced by Cubism and who painted in 1914 an

All the true Cubists had at one time or another come near to complete abstraction, but each of them had almost immediately retracted and reasserted the representational element of their art" (p. 198). See also Christopher Green, *Cubism and Its Enemies*, pp. 47, 221–242.

57. In modernist painting the use of abstraction could be and generally was justified by an appeal to an overarching scheme or force, usually metaphysical; or by an appeal to some underlying imperative, usually seen as cosmic or natural: e.g. Mondrian and the universal; van Doesburg and "harmony"; Kandinsky and theosophy; Kupka with Goethe and Schopenhauer and theosophy (see Green, *Cubism and Its Enemies*, p. 228 for a summary of this point).

58. Roger Allard, "The Signs of Renewal in Painting" (1912) in Fry, *Cubism*, p. 70–71.

exquisite non-figurative *Homage to Picasso*) put it: "'Abstract?' To be an abstract painter does not mean to abstract from naturally occurring opportunities for comparison, but, quite apart from such opportunities, to distil pure pictorial relation. . . light to dark, color to light and dark, color to color, long to short, broad to narrow, sharp to dull, left–right, above–below, behind–in front, circle to square to triangle."[59] Like Allard, Klee defines abstraction in painting as a focusing on the dynamics of representation and not on the degree of removal from objects in nature. In Klee's use of the term, non-figurative modernist painting might be no more "abstract" than the Cubism of Braque and Picasso or indeed the Realism of Rembrandt and Ingres.

The relation between Cubism and abstract painting has been treated with precision and clarity by a number of art historians,[60] and we will not attempt to summarize their work here. Our point however – that modernist abstraction is best understood not in terms of a loss of realistic detail but in terms of shifting the frame of reference away from the object and toward the spatial dynamics of representation (the plastic field) – can be clearly illustrated by an account of Piet Mondrian's movement away from cubist principles toward non-figurative or non-objective painting. Douglas Cooper shows him arriving in Paris in 1911 with a background in Symbolism and in Post-Impressionism, coming under the influence of Braque, Picasso, and other cubists, and using this new knowledge of space to arrive at his distinctive "abstractions":

> Mondrian had, as it were, seized on the basic structural principle of Cubism and rejected the rest, for he believed that art was above reality and that the painter therefore should not be concerned with it. These paintings then are a sort of intellectual shorthand with no representational purpose, for Mondrian's aim was to achieve a static balance of lines and colours which would satisfy the eye without troubling the mind, would evoke by intuition an experience of reality and at the same time induce a state of spiritual calm. . . . A brief experience of handling the pictorial language of Cubism enabled Mondrian to pursue another type of reality through a personal non-figurative idiom, which he elaborated with a thoroughness which commands our fullest respect.[61]

Mondrian's choice to apply cubist techniques to a non-figurative art led to the influential minority report his work became. He shows us that the development of non-objective art from cubist techniques was not a necessary progress but a matter of individual choice. The great cubists – Picasso, Braque, Léger, and Gris – while they approached and even experimented with non-objective representation, stuck in the end to the object and the object-space as opened up by Cubism. Their painting continued to occupy the middle ground of the field.

59. Paul Klee, *Notebooks*, I ("The Thinking Eye"), 72.
60. The most helpful studies include Barr's *Cubism and Abstract Art* (1936), Cooper's *The Cubist Epoch* (1970), Green's *Cubism and Its Enemies* (1987), and Rubin's *Picasso and Braque: Pioneering Cubism* (1989).
61. Cooper, *The Cubist Epoch*, pp. 140–143.

One last example will conclude this discussion – and though it doesn't come from Cubism directly it shows very well that the loss of realist particularities does not, in art, necessarily lead in the direction of the loss of the object or of the representational function of the object. Matisse sculpted a series of four nude female backs between 1909 and 1931 (Plates 12a–d), each one abstracting more naturalistic detail than the preceding. They lose realist detail without losing representational force.

Narrative

Much of our discussion of abstraction in Relativity Theory and Cubism can be transposed into temporal terms and applied to modernist narrative. A few brief examples will show how this works. In our discussion of *The Sound and the Fury* we saw that the Compson story – essentially a narrative of loss and despair – was brought back from the threatening abyss of nihilism, of "signifying nothing," by the act of witnessing, of observing. It was the observation of the events by the enduring Dilsey that raised them above the sordid and chaotic. Her observation and participation in the narrative field provide a much-needed guide for the reader who wants to understand the tale. Dilsey leads such a reader into a kind of active participation in the development of significance, a kind of participation that was effectively unknown in realistic fiction (which of course had its own discipline and demands). Thus *The Sound and the Fury*, by dropping the lucid temporal coordinates of realist narrative and with them the premiss of neutral time and space, escapes some of the abstraction of Realism and imposes its own by refocusing attention on to *how* the story gets told and how it develops meaning. *Absalom, Absalom!* takes this departure and this refocusing farther still: Quentin and Shreve are not merely auditors or observers of the Sutpen saga but participate in its creation as agents from within the imaginative field.

Thomas Mann's novel *Doctor Faustus* (1949), told in putatively traditional realist style by an old-fashioned academic humanist Serenus Zeitblom, actually undertakes the radical project of offering an historical account of Modernism and its implications from within the Germany of the Third Reich. Subtitled *The Life of the German Composer Adrian Leverkühn as Told by a Friend*, the old-fashioned "realist" narration attempts to deal with the loss of orientation and meaning, the loss of religious and humane values, by means of language dependent on those values. The effect of this attempt is to show the appalling inadequacy of the traditional language to *say* what is going on. For example, Zeitblom, who has resigned his academic post, separated himself from his children, and put his life at risk, is able to describe his reaction to the Holocaust only in pathetically rationalized terms: "I have never, precisely in the Jewish problem and the way it has been dealt with, been able to agree fully with our Führer and his paladins." Even when he permits himself to express his outrage, his words seem incommensurate with the evil he wants to condemn: "the outrageous contempt of reason, the vicious violation of the truth, the cheap, filthy backstairs mythology, the criminal degradation and confusion of standards; the abuse, corruption, and blackmail of all that was good, genuine, trusting, and trustworthy in our old Germany."[62] Such language is eloquent, clear, general, and accurate; but as a depiction and condemnation of Hitler's Germany it falls short, seems weak; it is the language of humanistic Realism – rational, coherent, pathetically abstract.

What in *Doctor Faustus* comes to represent the other side, the emerging demonic value structure that develops in the course of the modernist period and culminates in the Third Reich, does not share this weakness. The new ethos is not humane and it does not require the same kind of naturalized abstract premises for its coordination. Instead the new ethos is concrete, tactile, primitive, folkish. In the novel it receives its fullest expression in the new music of the protagonist, Adrian Leverkühn. This music and its theory is based on the work of Arnold Schönberg, and although Leverkühn is not a thinly disguised Schönberg (who was still living when the novel was published), the theoretical discussions of his new, serial or twelve-tone music clearly and consistently borrow from Schönberg's theory and composition.

Leverkühn detests tonal music and all music based on harmony; he associates such music with what he calls the "subjective" – a music that succeeds by means of a kind of psychological trick (much as realist painting succeeded by means of the illusionism of single-point perspective). In contrast, Leverkühn values the concrete dissonances of polyphony. He even sees harmonic music (whose great figurative representative in the novel is Beethoven) as a kind of perversion of the true:

> "A chord [in harmonic music] is meant to be followed up by another, and so soon as you do it, carry it over into another, each one of its component notes becomes a voice-part. I find that in a chordal combination of notes one should never see anything but the result of the movement of voices and do honor to the part as implied in the single chord-note – but not honor the chord as such, rather despise it as subjective and arbitrary, so long as it cannot prove itself to be the result of part-writing. The chord is no harmonic narcotic but polyphony in itself, and the notes that form it are parts. But I assert they are that the more, and the polyphonic character of the chords is the more pronounced, the more dissonant it is. The degree of dissonance is the measure of its polyphonic value. The more discordant a chord is, the more notes it contains contrasting and conflicting with each other, the more polyphonic it is, and the more markedly every single note bears the stamp of the part already in the simultaneous sound-combination."[63]

62. Thomas Mann, *Doctor Faustus*, pp. 8, 175.
63. Ibid., p. 74. There is an interesting connection with Cubism here, noted by Edward Fry: "As Apollinaire remarked, a chair will be understood as a chair from no matter what point of view it is seen if it has the essential components of a chair . . . or as Picasso remarked to Leo Stein, the brother of Gertrude, before 1914: 'A head . . . was a matter of eyes, nose, mouth, which could be distributed in any way you like – the head remained a head', a mode of thought analogous to the method of composition by tone-row in the music of Schoenberg and of other twelve-tone composers" (*Cubism*, p. 39).

In other words, Leverkühn has denied or deleted or abstracted the relationships privileged by the abstractions that govern harmony.

Whether or not such claims would satisfy serious musicologists, here in *Dr Faustus* Mann has established a resonant dichotomy; or rather he has had his humanist narrator establish one. Zeitblom, infinitely attracted to Adrian and his music, finds inescapable associations between the development of a *keyless* music and the destruction of the humane values of the old Germany. When Leverkühn sells his soul to the devil for the now relative time of modernist music, the realist abstractions that sustained harmony are lost and with them the social values, like compassion and individual freedom, that such abstractions sustain. We have, therefore, more than a hint in this novel that for poor Zeitblom at least the Modernism of Leverkühn, and by quite permissible extension Modernism in the general culture, has a regrettable association with totalitarianism. Whether or not a reading of the full text asserts such an association will remain (in the accustomed ambiguity of late modernist fiction) a question for each reader. The fact, however, that such an association can be posited indicates a profound ambivalence toward the new music and what it might stand for. And yet the Faustian bargain – given the bankruptcy of the old humanism – seems inevitable. Again we arrive at that paradox of modernist abstraction: it consists (as in Schönberg's music) of the taking away of the privileges of the harmonious abstractions of realism.

Finally, as a coda to our discussion of modernist abstraction, we glance at Borges's troubling little *jeu d'esprit* called "Funes, the Memorious" (1942). Borges's narrator meets a boy, Ireneo Funes, who in falling from a horse has acquired a capacity for total recall. He remembers everything, and not just everything in the external world but everything he has thought about or imagined:

> A circumference on a blackboard, a rectangular triangle, a rhomb, are forms which we can fully intuit; the same held true with Ireneo for the tempestuous mane of a stallion, a herd of cattle in a pass, the ever-changing flame of the innumerable ash, the many faces of a dead man during the course of a protracted wake. He could perceive I do not know how many stars in the sky.

The distinction is between the abstracting quality of ordinary human memory and the endless detail of specific reality that Ireneo is compelled to recall. "The truth is that we all live by leaving behind," says the narrator.[64] In other words, some kind of abstraction is necessary to thought and even to life.

The story provides an ultimate indictment of the abstract premises of Realism, which imagine the perception and representation of real objects in neutral space and which do not acknowledge the streamlining required for all significant acts of mind. Ireneo's capacity is immense, and so is his bondage to realist detail:

---

64. Borges, *Ficciones*, pp. 112–113.

He was, let us not forget, almost incapable of general, platonic ideas. It was not only difficult for him to understand that the generic term *dog* embraced so many unlike specimens of differing sizes and different forms; he was disturbed by the fact that a dog at three-fourteen (seen in profile) should have the same name as the dog at three-fifteen (seen from the front). . . . It was very difficult for him to sleep. To sleep is to be abstracted from the world. . . . In the overly replete world of Funes there were nothing but details, almost contiguous details.

Ireneo dies at the age of twenty-one, "of a pulmonary congestion."[65] He has achieved (though only in his own mind) a kind of fulfillment of naive Realism, the recollection of the world in its complete and detailed "reality." In this troubling fictional speculation, the act of leaving behind, of abstracting, saves us from the infinite detail of the world. Or, to apply this thought to the natural sciences, in the words of the modernist philosopher Bertrand Russell, "Physics is mathematical not because we know so much about the physical world, but because we know so little. It is only its mathematical properties that we can hope to discover."[66] Only, that is, its abstractions.

65. Ibid., pp. 114–115.
66. E.M. Hafner, "The New Reality in Art and Science," p. 388.

Chapter 6 Reflexivity

The observ'd of all observers

(Ophelia on Hamlet)

Our final comprehensive value for this study of Modernism is that of *reflexivity*. This in many ways is the most difficult to discuss because it relates in considerable depth and complexity to the other sustaining characteristics treated in our preceding chapters: epistemic trauma, departure from normative realist conventions, the focus on observation rather than reality, the development of the field, and a particular kind of abstraction. Constituted by these values, a distinct historical definition of Modernism emerges – as a coherent, unified period of advanced intellectual activity. Its various constituents overlap and reinforce each other in a shifting but continuously recognizable dynamic.

Reflexivity bears directly on this unity and these relationships. By reflexivity we mean the tendency of a system or period to refer to itself, to develop a dynamic internal coherence that shows self-referentiality as a primary characteristic.[1] In modernist art and literature this appears most frequently in an awareness of being avant-garde, of leaving the less new, the more traditional, behind. But this is a fairly superficial application of the value of reflexivity. In the major manifestations of Modernism, in all three of our cultural diagnostics, reflexivity is the method by which we arrive at significance; reflexivity is the means by which meaning develops.

A system or model or episteme is reflexive when it acknowledges itself as one system among other possible systems, one model of the world among other possible models, one mode of thought aimed at reaching certain ends and limited culturally and historically by its underlying values. Systems, models,

---

1. Our emphasis here is on "primary." As Hilary Lawson points out, "Reflexivity, as a turning back on oneself, a form of self-awareness, has been part of philosophy from its inception, but reflexive questions have been given their special force in consequence of the recognition of the central role played by language, theory, sign, and text" (*Reflexivity: The Post-Modern Predicament*, p. 9). As the title suggests, Lawson is largely concerned with a particular aspect of reflexivity, essentially how one can discuss the problem of reflexivity given the epistemological limits that reflexivity asserts (because the discussion itself is subject to those limits). Interesting and entertaining, Lawson's technical discussion is in somewhat peripheral relation to our cultural history.

and methods of thought that do not allow for these basic limitations are not reflexive. Vaclav Havel, in an essay on "Politics and the World Itself," has described with powerful eloquence what the recent historical costs of a lack of reflexivity in governmental and corporate leadership have been:

The modern [i.e. the entire post-Renaissance, not specifically modern*ist*] era has been dominated by the culminating belief, expressed in different forms, that the world – and Being as such – is a wholly knowable system governed by a finite number of universal laws that man can grasp and rationally direct for his own benefit. This era, beginning in the Renaissance and developing from the Enlightenment to socialism, from positivism to scientism, from the industrial revolution to the information revolution, was characterized by rapid advances in rational, cognitive thinking. This, in turn, gave rise to the proud belief that man, as the pinnacle of everything that exists, was capable of objectively describing, explaining, and controlling everything that exists, and of possessing the one and only truth about the world. It was an era in which there was a cult of depersonal-ized objectivity, an era in which objective knowledge was amassed and tech-nologically exploited, an era of belief in automatic progress brokered by the scientific method. It was an era of systems, institutions, mechanisms, and statistical averages. It was an era of freely transferable, existentially ungrounded information. It was an era of ideologies, doctrines, interpretations of reality, an era where the goal was to find a universal theory of the world, and thus a universal key to unlock its prosperity.[2]

In this passage Havel treats certain historical and political consequences of positivist, empiricist Realism, the value structure which we have discussed at length as preceding Modernism, that system of conventions and premises which claims a direct approach to external reality and the ability to view it from without, from a posture of "depersonalized objectivity." In our terms Havel rejects the realist assumption that since we can observe reality directly in neutral homogeneous time and space we can manipulate it directly by manipulating – again from the outside – the coordinates that govern it. As we argued in our fourth and fifth chapters, the process of refocusing on the human acts of observation and measurement and on the participation of observer and observed in a common field has been going on for some time, for almost the whole duration of Modernism. Havel's appeal is thus to apply at last to politics the modernist values that drove advanced scientific and artistic activity at the beginning of the twentieth century. In this sense he attempts to bring the values of Modernism (and especially those that survive into Postmodernism) to public recognition. He thus provides us with a valuable confirmation of them. Havel argues that our decision-makers must now see their activity as taking place within limited systems that show an awareness of their identity as constructions, as human enterprises. He asks that politicians become reflexive by becoming aware of the necessary limitations of their systems.

2. Vaclav Havel, "Politics and the World Itself," pp. 9–10.

Relativity Theory

At the very beginning of his career, at the age of sixteen, Einstein asked himself the apparently childlike question that was to be answered ten years later in the Special Theory of Relativity. He asked himself what he would see if he were able to follow a beam of light at its own speed through space.[3] The way he formulated the question shows a new direction already taken. Einstein asked not about the nature of light in itself, but about the nature of light as contained in an observation. He did not seek information about its objective configuration independent of observers but about what *he* would see if he were an observer moving at light speed. His experiment was a thought-experiment, and he himself was a part of it – or, as we have put it, a participant, a constituent of the field.

In Einstein's autobiographical notes appears a section pertaining to a later period of his life, a formulation concerning scientific models, which he characterizes as his "epistemological credo":

> A proposition is correct if, within a logical system, it is deduced according to the accepted logical rules. A system has truth-content according to the certainty and completeness of its co-ordination-possibility to the totality of experience. A correct proposition borrows its "truth" from the truth-content of the system to which it belongs.[4]

If we remember that the "experience" in Einstein's phrase "the totality of experience" must refer to experience of the observation of reality rather than to reality itself, it seems clear that according to such a credo there can be no "truth" of the kind assumed by a Newtonian observer. Instead, descriptions of phenomena are organized into logical, unified "systems" (kept as simple as the material to be accounted for will allow). The systems (models or theories) clearly retain a reflexive awareness of being systems to deal with experience of observation rather than direct representations of reality or "truth." We can say that such systems are the cumulative extension of treating reality not as independent but as observed.

In their book on *The Evolution of Physics* (1938), Einstein and Leopold Infeld describe what it means to try to "understand reality" in the post-Newtonian world:

> Physical concepts are the free creations of the human mind, and are not, however it may seem, uniquely determined by the external world. In our endeavor to understand reality we are somewhat like a man trying to understand the mechanism of a closed watch. He sees the face and the moving hands, even hears its ticking, but he has no way of opening the case. If he is ingenious he may form some picture of a mechanism which could be responsible for all the things he observes, but he may never be quite sure his picture is the only one which could

---

3. Paul Arthur Schilpp, *Albert Einstein: Philosopher-Scientist*, I, 53.
4. Ibid., 13.

explain his observations. He will never be able to compare his picture with the real mechanism and he cannot even imagine the possibility or the meaning of such a comparison. But he certainly believes that, as his knowledge increases, his picture of reality will become simpler and simpler and will explain a wider and wider range of his sensuous impressions. He may also believe in the existence of the ideal limit of knowledge and that it is approached by the human mind. He may call this ideal limit the objective truth.[5]

This admirable passage on the nature of modernist physics, so honorably aware of the self-containment and reflexivity of the endeavor and yet so resolute to pursue it, would satisfy Vaclav Havel's appeal for a renunciation of our positive arrogance and the expectation of "a universal solution."[6] And it is no accident that Einstein and Infeld's analogy of the locked watch whose "real mechanism" can never be glimpsed reminds us of Kafka's parables that stress our inescapable ignorance of metaphysical truth.

What Einstein and those of his contemporaries who understood Relativity Theory (such as Lorentz, Minkowski, Eddington, and Russell) emphasized is that the propositions of a theory must not only sustain verification from the experience of observation; they must also conform to the structural principles of the system to which they belong. Certainly a theory like Relativity accounts for observed phenomena. It possesses Einstein's condition (in his epistemological credo) of "a coordination-possibility to the totality of experience." Such a possibility will, of course, include some kind of verification process; observations will yield similar results under similar conditions. But Einstein's other condition for a correct proposition is that it be deduced "according to the accepted logical rules" of the system from which it derives its validity. This is where the reflexivity comes in, and this is what makes the theory modernist. Relativity Theory accounts for a great deal of observational experience, but strictly in terms of its own logical structure and language, its own reflexive, built-in acknowledgment of itself as a theory.

We can see this more clearly by contrasting Relativity with Newton's laws of mechanics, the theory it supplanted. The three laws of motion and the law of gravitation directly refer to certain properties of tangible objects: their masses, their separation in space, the forces acting on them, and their acceleration. The situation of the observer is nowhere explicitly involved in these equations, and the means by which measurements are to be carried out is unimportant. Implicitly Newton's laws of motion do stipulate that the observer is not undergoing any acceleration, or, as a physicist would say, the laws of motion are valid only in "inertial reference frames." In contrast, the Lorentz transformations, the mathematical embodiment of Special Relativity, contain explicit statements about the observer.[7] To perform any calculation with the Special Theory one must specify the observer's position and speed

5. Albert Einstein and Leopold Infeld, *The Evolution of Physics*, p. 31.
6. Havel, "Politics and the World Itself," p. 11.
7. See Mook and Vargish, *Inside Relativity*, pp. 31–45, 96–100.

with respect to the phenomenon under study and (where times of observation are a consideration) the observer's clock reading. But while Newton's equations were about masses with forces acting on them and their consequent accelerations, the Lorentz transformations are about observers making observations. Einstein's equations serve to relate time and distance measurements made by one observer to those of another observer at a different location in space and/or moving at a different speed with respect to the phenomenon under study. This is a crucial point. Relativity Theory is not primarily about nature; it is about physicists making measurements or actually doing physics. In other words the theory is reflexive: it is a theory of physics about doing physics.

The origins of the Special Theory were grounded in observations made by physicists: the empirical connections between electricity and magnetism and the observed properties of light. In his 1905 paper describing Special Relativity, after only three paragraphs summarizing these observations, Einstein launches directly into a detailed and quantitative analysis of time's *measurement*; that is, his analysis turns immediately to an act of doing physics. When he finishes the paper he has resolved the phenomenological questions raised at the outset (including the interrelationship of electricity and magnetism and the expulsion of ether from the canon of physical theory) but he accomplishes this through an analysis of physical measurement embodied in his Special Relativity Theory – a physical theory about doing physics.

This self-referential quality expresses itself everywhere in Relativity. For example, in the Special Theory there are two key postulates that at first appear to make statements about nature. The first is the so-called "principle of relativity" (the laws of physics must appear the same in all inertial reference systems) and the second is the postulate of the invariance of the speed of light (which, one can argue, is really a particular case of the first postulate – if one regards Maxwell's equations as accepted "laws of physics").[8] The first postulate concerns itself not with nature directly (as in Newtonian mechanics) but with model-building in Special Relativity. Einstein's theory deals not directly with the natural world but with the observation of the natural world (the world as perceived from Relativity's railroad car). We are in fact observing a natural world not in itself but contained in a process of observation, "The observ'd of all observers," as Ophelia observes of the deeply reflexive Hamlet.[9]

General Relativity also seems to make a statement about nature: given a certain arrangement of masses, spacetime will become non-Euclidean in a predictable way.[10] But the essence of the theory, embodied in Einstein's field equations, is still a reflexive statement about observers in different reference frames making measurements, the distinction between the General and Special theories being that the former treats measurements made in non-inertial (accelerating) reference frames while the latter does not.

8. A full discussion may be found in ibid., pp. 65–72.
9. William Shakespeare, *The Tragedy of Hamlet, Prince of Denmark*, p. 78 (III.i.155).
10. See Mook and Vargish, *Inside Relativity*, pp. 137–177.

To illustrate this point we can turn to an image used by Einstein himself in a popular or non-specialized account, a book entitled *Relativity*, written in 1916, shortly after he had completed work on the General Theory:

> We imagine a large portion of empty space, so far removed from stars and other appreciable masses that . . . points at rest remain at rest and points in motion continue in uniform rectilinear motion. As reference body let us imagine a spacious chest resembling a room with an observer inside who is equipped with apparatus. Gravitation naturally does not exist for this observer.[11]

Einstein places an observer (a physicist equipped with measuring apparatus) in a "chest," an enclosure with no windows so that reference to anything outside the confines of the chest must be made by measurements of phenomena taking place inside the chest. The physicist can only "know" what he can measure with his apparatus inside the chest. The chest is located so far from any other mass in the universe that there can be no gravitational influence on the chest or its contents from outside.

But now Einstein adds something else: a rope attached to the chest with a hook and what Einstein calls a being, "what kind of being is immaterial to us," who "begins pulling at [the rope] with a constant force. The chest together with the observer then begins to move . . . with a constant acceleration." What, Einstein asks us to imagine, now happens to the physicist? Before the rope began pulling on the chest or room he was floating about freely in space. Once the pulling begins the side of the room opposite to the point at which the rope is hooked begins to approach the physicist at a constant acceleration. Eventually this side of the room makes contact and begins to push him so that he too accelerates. The physicist suddenly finds himself being pulled to one face (now the "floor") of the room. If the surface were hard he would probably stand upright with his feet on the floor. If he now removes his copy of Kafka's short stories from his pocket and releases it, he will find that it falls to the floor of the room. As long as he holds the book, his hand exerts the force necessary to accelerate the book (according to Newton's second law) along with him and the room. As soon as his hand loses contact with the book the requisite force no longer acts on the book, the book ceases its acceleration, and the floor of the accelerating room rushes upon it. This the physicist interprets as the book "falling" to the floor. Indeed anything the physicist may drop will fall to the "floor" with exactly the same acceleration, namely the acceleration that is being imparted to the room via the rope.

Einstein continues:

> The observer will further convince himself *that the acceleration of the body towards the floor of the chest is always of the same magnitude, whatever kind of body he may happen to use for the experiment.*
>
> Relying on his knowledge of the gravitational field . . . the man in the chest will thus come to the conclusion that he and the chest are in a gravitational field

---

11. Albert Einstein, *Relativity*, p. 66.

which is constant with regard to time. Of course he will be puzzled for a moment as to why the chest does not fall in this gravitational field. Just then, however, he discovers the hook in the middle of the lid of the chest and the rope which is attached to it, and he consequently comes to the conclusion that the chest is suspended at rest in the gravitational field.[12]

In an accelerated reference frame, in other words, a physicist in a closed, windowless laboratory can interpret constant acceleration as a gravitational field. Similarly, a physicist truly suspended in a chest (hanging, say, from the limb of a large tree) can interpret the downward pull of gravity as due to the laboratory chest being accelerated upward by the rope. According to the General Theory these two views are physically and mathematically equivalent. In fact this situation illustrates what is called a "principle of equivalence" by Einstein. We can see that it contains a strongly reflexive element: the essence of the principle of equivalence, the basis of General Relativity Theory, is a statement about a physicist making observations or measurements of the behavior of objects around him (Einstein was careful to specify that the man in the room was equipped with apparatus).

If we sought a symbol for the period of Relativity's emergence – the early modernist period of 1905 to 1915 – we could not do better than to contemplate Einstein's image of the sealed laboratory.[13] The laboratory is the place of measurement and an object within the experiment itself, a deeply reflexive location. We can even reverse Einstein and Infeld's earlier simile and say that being in the laboratory is like being *inside* the closed watch and trying to deduce what goes on outside by observing and theorizing upon the phenomena within. We can learn a great deal by this method, but we must also acknowledge the inescapable fact that everything we will ever know must bear the stamp of our limited range of observation, our point of view. We can see as well that in Relativity Theory, as throughout Modernism, the awareness of limitations, the reflexivity, is what makes possible and empowers its discoveries.[14]

---

12. Ibid.
13. See Mook and Vargish, *Inside Relativity*, pp. 141–150.
14. Quantum mechanics too assumes the value of reflexivity by requiring that the measurement protocol be specified in the formulation of the equations governing a quantum-phenomenal measurement. Indeed, all that quantum mechanics ultimately provides in many practical situations is a statement of the probability that a defined sort of measurement technique will yield such and such a value. Quantum theory also sets limits on the accuracy of certain combinations of measurements through the Heisenberg uncertainty principle. Quantum mechanical statements are statements about acts of measurement. As in Special Relativity the statements concern physics itself; they are reflexive. More extensive discussions of quantum mechanics and the role of the observer in the theory may be found in A. S. Eddington, *The Nature of the Physical World*, and in J.C. Polkinghorne, *The Quantum World*. This delightful book on the quantum theory for non-scientists is less than one hundred pages in length and yet communicates both the spirit and the intellectual quandary of quantum theory. This is also an appropriate place to point out that reflexivity in a scientific theory in no way means that the theory is less valuable than "non-reflexive" theories, theories that make explicit statements about nature. In fact, quantum theory, while highly reflexive, makes the most accurate quantitative predictions of any physical theory known at present.

Cubism

In modernist painting, as we have seen, Cubism participated in the important shift of emphasis away from subject matter (the objects painted) and toward treatment (the act of representation). Cubism valorized not the subject itself but the observation and representation of the subject. This was itself a reflexive act. In their book on *Cubism* (1912), Gleizes and Metzinger used this shift of emphasis from reality to observation as part of their program to give the movement an importance that would match the dominance of realistic representation (optical verisimilitude) during the preceding four centuries: "we must regard Cubism as legitimate, for it continues modern methods, and we should see in it the only conception at present possible of the pictorial art. In other words, Cubism is at present painting itself."[15] Given the variety of important artistic activity at the time, it would be naive to accept this claim at its grandiose face value, but there is a modest application of it that works.

The reflexivity of Cubism depended in large part on its relation to the major representational traditions of Western painting, what cubists and their contemporaries called "the Louvre." As Edward Fry puts it: "The new Cubist draftsmanship of Picasso and Braque . . . bore a symmetrical but opposing relationship to the classical, underlying which was an extraordinary intellectual and experiential feat: a Cubist representation from 1909 to 1911 involved the direct visual observation of the world; previous knowledge of the motif, if any; mastery of the classical conventions of representation; and the simultaneous Cubist transformations of those conventions as the motif was being represented."[16] What Fry calls "reflexivity" in this essay seems to mean precisely a knowledge of the tradition and a simultaneous awareness of the possibilities of transforming it in cubist terms.

Fry illustrates what such awareness can mean with a technical analysis of developing cubist technique:

> [We see] that the faceted planes of Analytic Cubism overlap each other, and that therefore some planes must be in front of others. These planar overlays are not consistent, however, for a contiguous group of planes may in one place indicate a given spatial recession but elsewhere contradict that recession; a contradiction that may include the linkage of a figure to its background through so-called *passage*. But this single most conspicuous and imitated formal aspect of Cubism is not just a clever trick that may or may not have been gleaned from Cézanne and that supposedly points towards future abstraction. Rather, it is at once a denial and an affirmation of classical space, effected from within the tradition of perspectival illusionism itself. The affirmation is in the receding steps from plane to plane, comparable to the evenly measurable space of one-point perspective; the denial is the disruption and scrambling of that recession. The

15. Albert Gleizes and Jean Metzinger quoted in Herschel B. Chipp, *Theories of Modern Art*, p. 207.
16. Edward Fry, "Picasso, Cubism, and Reflexivity," p. 298.

reflexivity of self-awareness arises from the juxtaposed presence of both affirmation and denial.[17]

Such a complex relation to the tradition, analogous in its way to Einstein's selective affirmation and denial of the physics that preceded Special Relativity, can be achieved only by artists who combine technical mastery with an intense awareness of their predecessors' work.[18] What we have called Einstein's physics about doing physics has an obvious analogy in Cubism's painting about doing painting – that is, they share the value of reflexivity with reference to their respective traditions.

But what about the relation of cubist representation to the object, to nature? As we have suggested, Cubism – like modernist physics and narrative – focused more and more fully on the act of observation and representation. But – also like the physics and like narrative – Cubism never fully abandons the object, never moves entirely into the abstract or non-objective. Instead, as Cubism developed into what is usually called its "synthetic" phase, the forms on the painting surface began more and more to include what in Realism had been treated as neutral, homogeneous space. The two-dimensional "representation" (the painting) became coincident with the "objects" (nature). Space came to be identified with the picture plane rather than with the realist illusion of depth. The frame of the picture is no longer a "window" on to any other kind of space than the painted plane itself.

This cubist treatment of space alters profoundly the relative status of art and nature. Painting no longer poses as the passive, unmediated receptor (which of course it never was) of the external visual world. Now represented nature on the picture surface is no longer imitated nature; it is itself, painted nature, painting, or as Gleizes and Metzinger call it, "painting itself." We no longer have one object (a painting) pretending to represent another object (nature). Instead, the picture field becomes a kind of final and only certainty and the visual continuum of the painting surface is the effective reality. We have simply the painted surface which offers, in Greenberg's phrase, "space as a total object."[19] Or, as Georges Braque succinctly put it, "One must not imitate what one wants to create." And, he adds, "One does not imitate appearances; the appearance is the result."[20] As we have seen, much of the resistance to Modernism arises from the modernist tendency to collapse distinctions that had supported the realist structure. This too was a self-conscious and reflexive aim of Cubism. In the words of Pierre Reverdy, "A work of art cannot content itself with being a *representation*; it must be a *presentation*. A child that is born is presented, he represents nothing."[21]

17. Ibid., pp. 298–299.
18. It was probably these demands, in addition to lesser individual motives, that limited the full realization of Cubism's power to four painters – to Picasso, Braque, Léger, and Gris.
19. Clement Greenberg, "On the Role of Nature in Modernist Painting," in *Art and Culture*, p. 173.
20. Georges Braque, "Thoughts and Reflections on Art" (1917), in Chipp, *Theories of Modern Art*, p. 260.
21. Pierre Reverdy, "Some Advantages of Being Alone" (1918), in Edward F. Fry, *Cubism*, p. 149.

These claims and generalizations seem less vehement and aloof when they are illustrated by specific works. Picasso's *Still Life with Chair Caning* (1912) (Plate 9), already discussed in our fifth chapter, has acquired legendary value as an explanation piece in the history of Cubism. It has been credited with being the first cubist collage, although this has been disputed in favor of Braque.[22] In any case, Picasso's witty play on problems of reality/representation captures the full implications of the innovation. As we saw earlier, Picasso fixed to his painting surface not a piece of chair caning (as the title suggests) but a piece of oilcloth printed to look like chair caning: not an element from the world of "reality," a tease so often misapprehended in discussions of collage,[23] but a piece of realist representation of reality – that is, a slice of *trompe l'oeil*. Picasso's play here (the familiar pun "JOU" is plainly lettered to the upper left of the imitation caning) seems to be intended to undermine the distinction between reality and representation so that the two collapse into each other – a destruction of distinctions that we have traced throughout Modernism. The acute and wary viewer who understands the game (*jeu*) will be left with the conclusion that the important if not only reality of this ambiguously titled collage is the picture itself. The whole exercise proves the sealed and reflexive nature of the representation/reality dichotomy in modernist art, a kind of epistemological ping-pong in which scoring points (*jouer*) never gets us off the table. The endless mariner's rope which Picasso chose for a frame symbolizes the happily inconclusive process.[24]

This reflexive quality of Cubism, strong from the start and then at the center of the development of collage, continually gains ground as the movement progresses into its later or synthetic phase. From the beginning it was expressed in the technical revolution that we discussed earlier. Edward Fry observes that "one of the most striking ways in which Picasso and the Cubists effected a reflexive transformation of classical draftsmanship was through the negation or inversion of means used for the representation of organic forms: straight lines were substituted for the curved contours of a still-life object or of a human face or body; and organic volumes were replaced by a new set of quasi-geometric volumes, the facets of which became the planar building blocks of Analytic Cubism."[25]

This can be seen in such early analytic works as *Girl with a Mandolin* (1910) (Plate 13), where the transformation into such geometric volumes is

22. About the same time Braque pasted pieces of imitation-woodgrain wallpaper to one of his drawings on paper. See Clement Greenberg, "Collage" (1959), in *Art and Culture*, pp. 74–75.
23. "Confusion on the score of the introduction of the 'real' led no less an authority than Douglas Cooper to insist that Picasso's still-life objects in this picture were set on a chair, and to take issue with Rosalind Krauss, who had described them rightly as resting on a table" (William Rubin, *Picasso and Braque: Pioneering Cubism*, p. 37).
24. It is important to our discussion of reflexivity to understand that these matters were fully understood by the cubists and their contemporaries. Guillaume Apollinaire – poet, critic, and major apologist for the cubists – describes Picasso's collage in *Les Peintres cubistes* (1913) and plays the game with skill. See Fry, *Cubism*, p. 120.
25. Fry, "Picasso, Cubism, and Reflexivity," p. 298.

evidently incomplete. The face of the young model (Fanny Tellier) is disturbingly cubed while her right breast is in the process of becoming a cylinder with a diamond nipple. In fact the well-known painting (Picasso originally considered it unfinished)[26] owes much of its éclat to a kind of troubling mixture of realist techniques that give a sculpted effect to her neck and arms with the "imposition" (as it must originally have appeared) of cubist formal vocabulary. Two years later, as we can see from *Still Life with Chair Caning* (Plate 9) and *The Aficionado* (Plate 5), Picasso had fully colonized the realist techniques and motifs and forced them to subserve cubist aims. We can see this process as emblematic of the progress of modernist reflexivity – as self-referential, as developing meaning by inter-reference among the elements of its own field – at the expense of objectivity, its counter-value in realistic representation.

We can see how far Picasso developed this "reflexive transformation" by looking at two late cubist masterpieces from 1927–28, *The Studio* and *Painter and Model* (Plate 14). Here, in what Alfred Barr calls their "extreme angularity," straight lines and angles are used to represent human faces and figures; and in *Painter and Model* the reflexive transformation points to itself in having the abstracted, angular painter representing the abstracted angular model in realist terms, a curved realist profile on the white canvas. As Harriet Janis put it: "The artist and his model are abstracted to an advanced degree while the concept in the canvas on the easel is in terms of realism. By this reversal in the scheme of reality the extraordinary artist and model are declared ordinary and the natural profile becomes the astonishing product of the artist's invention."[27] The reflexive technical and thematic structures of these two paintings are reconfirmed emblematically by the framed mirrors (or are they paintings?) represented in both of them.

Picasso's choice of a studio and of painter and model as subjects reminds us of Einstein's use of the sealed laboratory to illustrate the principle of equivalence in the General Theory. Studios and laboratories are the locations where observations and measurements become representations. And in modernist painting Picasso, like Einstein in modernist physics, was the most prominent but not the only original contributor to the reflexivity of his movement. As Cubism entered its late phase, the means by which painting is accomplished became more often the subject of painting. Christopher Green observes as well that Gris's *The Painter's Window* (1925) (Plate 15) centers on "an item which had never appeared in Gris' Cubist still lives before 1925: the palette. It is one of a group of pictures made in 1925–26 that dwell on this habitual accessory of the artist: the ubiquitous stage property of so many painters' self-portraits." Green also notes that representations of an open

26. William Rubin, *Pablo Picasso: A Retrospective*, pp. 120–121, and see discussion of *Jeune Fille à la mandoline* in John Golding, *Cubism*, pp. 83–84.
27. Alfred H. Barr, *Cubism and Abstract Art*, p. 96; Janis's analysis of *The Painter and his Model* is on p. 101 of Barr's book.

window developed into one of the most widely used devices of Cubism in the 1920s.[28] In fact, the window in Gris's *The Painter's Window* – that perennial feature serving as an index of depth in so many examples of Renaissance and post-Renaissance Realism, characteristically representing space as receding behind the primary subject to a vanishing point in rows of architectural features or planes of landscape – shows now an objectless grey-green-blue mottled blank. The window image subserves modernist reflexivity by suffering reduction into a light source for the artist.

Such reflexivity was not limited to Cubism.[29] One of the most popular of the experiments in the preternatural Realism to which Picasso himself returned from time to time throughout his career is the *Portrait d'Olga dans un fauteuil* (1917) (Plate 16). Olga appears in emphatically realistic terms, complete with the full realist portrait kit of perspective, shading, shadows, texture, and tint. The *fauteuil* or armchair, however, consists only of a flat fabric chair-shape in extravagant floral pattern; it has no arms or legs and no line distinguishes the back from the seat. The chair belongs suspiciously to the two-dimensional surface (while Olga projects impossibly but vividly forward from it). In addition, Olga rests on this fabric but the fabric rests on nothing. Behind Olga and the fabric (is it behind or is that a *trompe-l'oeil?*) appears to be a wall but it might well be a canvas, even *the* canvas. Faint, apparently irrelevant markings can be seen on it but the unfinished look of the backdrop is qualified by the shadow that something, maybe Olga herself, casts on it. The *jeu* here is not cubist, but it points insistently to the same value of reflexivity.

The discussion could be extended to cover the whole period. In a painting from the same year as Picasso's *Olga*, Matisse took yet another approach to the game: *The Painter and his Model* (1917)[30] has a nude male artist painting a dressed female model. Reflexivity is a strong value throughout all important movements in modernist art, including especially the dark mirror of Dada and continuing on into Postmodernism through Surrealism – but these are beyond the scope of our diagnostic. We turn now to manifestations of reflexivity in modernist narrative.

Narrative

In a 1966 article in *Nature* called "The Logic of the Mind," Jacob Bronowski attempted to trace "the common quality of imagination in science and in literature to the logic of self-reference; and in showing that, within this common quality, the difference of mode between science and literature reflects the different extent to which self-reference enters their languages."[31] His chief

28. Christopher Green, *Cubism and Its Enemies*, pp. 120, 20.
29. We remind our readers that our three selected diagnostics of Modernism – Relativity, Cubism, and modernist narrative – are intended to be suggestive and resonant rather than exclusive.
30. Musée d'Art Moderne, Centre Georges Pompidou.
31. Jacob Bronowski, "The Logic of the Mind," p. 1173.

point was that both science and literature exhibit this quality of self-reference, although in somewhat different degrees; he perceptively linked it to the difference in the "languages" of the two major fields and he dwelt on certain developments in twentieth-century physics and mathematics. We, in turn, have shown that Relativity Theory contains strong structural elements of self-reference, of reflexivity, and these elements are reflected in the media (mathematics, words, diagrams) employed in its modeling of the cosmos.

Modernist narrative, as critics and scholars have stressed throughout the period, has reflexivity or self-reference as a major characteristic. This phenomenon is so well established that it needs no further proof; and such monuments of late Modernism as Woolf's *The Waves*, Joyce's *Finnegans Wake* (1939), and Faulkner's *Absalom, Absalom!* have sometimes seemed to be composed entirely of a kind of sealed self-reference. We begin, however, with Conrad's "The Secret Sharer" (1910) in which self-reference is a prominent theme as well as an inescapable characteristic of the language.

The narrator-captain in this brief masterpiece helps the fugitive Leggatt naked from the sea and clothes him: "The shadowy, dark head, like mine, seemed to nod imperceptibly above the ghostly gray of my sleeping suit. It was, in the night, as though I had been faced by my own reflection in the depths of a somber and immense mirror." The reflexive metaphor of the mirror initiates for the narrator-captain an adventure in which the experience of reflexivity, of an intensely compounding self-referentiality, will lead him to full maturity as a leader. He is talking with his "double,"[32] a young ship's officer like himself – except that unlike the narrator, Leggatt has already in his own eyes failed a test in leadership by killing an insubordinate seaman during a storm. Leggatt (legate, envoy) escapes from the *Sephora* (self-bearer, self-producer) and swims to the ship where the narrator faces his first trial as captain. It is clearly the narrator's public duty in accordance with the law and his own professional self-interest, to return the fugitive to his captivity, but this he declines to do. Instantly, without thought or even consciousness of deliberate choice, he recognizes that Leggatt must be saved. The new captain's efforts to protect his secret sharer have all the immediacy of self-preservation. The story shows a young officer finding his authority not in the external world of public reputation and of moral and legal systems but in the inner world of identification, affection, and integrity.

By means of its theme of self-reference "The Secret Sharer" deals with an apparent paradox in the exercise of authority: that in order to be a success in the external world of affairs, in order to lead his crew and to captain his ship, a leader requires an internal source of significance, an internal reflexive moral center. While the captain develops this value he becomes for a time "double," at once public and private:

I was constantly watching myself, my secret self, as dependent on my actions as

32. Joseph Conrad, "The Secret Sharer," pp. 374, 373.

my own personality, sleeping in that bed, behind that door which faced me as I sat at the head of the table. It was very much like being mad, only it was worse because one was aware of it.

What his "other self" teaches the young captain is in fact the existence of a selfhood unvalorized by external rules and expectations. Rejecting the option of turning himself in and going to trial for killing his subordinate, Leggatt declares:

> You don't suppose I am afraid of what can be done to me? Prison or gallows or whatever they may please. But you don't see me coming back to explain such things to an old fellow in a wig and twelve respectable tradesmen, do you? What can they know whether I am guilty or not – of *what* I am guilty, either? That's my affair.[33]

In Leggatt's radical independence of external forms of judgment the narrator-captain sees what he himself lacks: an internal margin of reference for his own conduct, his own decisions. His complete achievement of the quality he admires in Leggatt, "that something unyielding in his character which was carrying him through so finely,"[34] occurs just at the story's end when he arranges for Leggatt to swim off and brings his ship close to land in a virtuoso demonstration of seamanship. This exhibition puts the ship, the crew, and his command at risk in a way that cannot be justified by commercial or moral systems. It has almost no practical utility; it is not necessary to save Leggatt, who is an expert swimmer. It does not "make sense." It refers only to that reflexive system of inner need that the narrator's contact with his secret sharer has clarified. The calculated brush with disaster justifies his command from within. At the moment of his success the narrator ceases to be "double" and becomes single, integral, in a superb celebration of authoritative integrity.

"The Secret Sharer" has received much critical attention precisely because it deals so powerfully with the value of reflexivity. It provides a clear and brief example of the ways in which meaning develops in modernist narrative. Constant attention to the situation of his "double" forces the narrator to create his authority as captain – the lack of which he felt acutely before Leggatt turned up. The metaphor of being "double" enables Conrad to explore dramatically the source of value that will underpin the new captain's command. Unlike earlier accounts of leadership the source of authority here is not external, not in the winning of social approbation and the realization of prescribed ideals. The source of authority, like the source of other meanings in Modernism, is reflexive: it lies in the inner power of reference to one's own contained values and strengths. The fact that Conrad represents it as being exercised in defiance of utilitarian, legal, and religious rationales makes the point that

33. Ibid., pp. 383, 396.
34. Ibid., pp. 395–396.

the true springs of authority can never be objective, never realist. They exist in an internal dynamic, a reflexive exchange, or not at all.

The conception of language as itself a reflexive system is treated variously and at length by early modernist fiction.[35] James Joyce in *A Portrait of the Artist as a Young Man* made language an explicit theme of his novel, introducing a narrative reflexively preoccupied with its own medium in much the same way that Cubism makes the production of paintings and the agents of representation – studios, artists, and their paraphernalia – one of the subjects of painting. But in the broader terms of our present cultural diagnostic, that of modernist narrative, Henry James had dealt with the problem earlier and in greater epistemological and psychological depth in *The Golden Bowl* (1904).

James's last novel deals from its opening with the question of what the various characters *know* about each other and about themselves, and what they know depends in turn on what they are able to *see*. *The Golden Bowl* continues James's lifelong exploration of the nature of aesthetic and social perception, its power to command the resources of life and enlist them in the causes of beauty and happiness. The theme appears at the very beginning when the Prince engages in a superficially frivolous dialogue with Maggie Verver, his fiancée who will become the "Princess." He wonders about the "romantic" way Americans view what he takes to be the more complex and shaded world of Europe: "'You see too much – that's what may sometimes make you difficulties. When you don't, at least,' he had amended with a further thought, 'see too little.'" It will be the Prince's fate to discover that Maggie and her father can learn to see just about everything, that they are not limited by what he and his lover Charlotte Stant want them to see. He will in fact go on to see what Maggie wants *him* to see so that her version of their world comprehends and subdues the scripted system of illusion that he and Charlotte have – with self-interested and self-congratulatory subtlety – devised for her. Close to triumph at the novel's end, Maggie thinks of the Prince: "Only *see*, see that *I* see, and make up your mind on this new basis."[36]

The central symbol of the novel, the golden bowl itself, is crystal covered in gold. The hidden crystal, however, is flawed; the flawless golden surface hides a crack. The epistemological question raised tacitly but insistently by

35. The modernist conception of language as a contained system of internal references was most influentially developed by Ferdinand de Saussure in his *Course in General Linguistics* (1906–11). As a work on the nature of language, though not necessarily language as narrative, the *Cours de linguistique générale* is based on student notes from Saussure's courses in general linguistics given at the University of Geneva between 1906 and 1911 and on certain personal notes found after his death. Those familiar with the study of semiology (semiotics) will see strong affinities with Saussure's theories and the reflexivity of modernist narrative, perhaps especially in the following discussion of Henry James's *The Golden Bowl*. In the interest of coherence and in order to contain our discussion within tolerable bounds we have limited our chief areas of discussion to three cultural diagnostics. Semiology, of course, would be relevant as would other major branches of Structuralism, as in anthropology and psychology. So would quantum theory, phenomenology, Expressionism; in short, if our description of Modernism is accurate, most advanced thinking in *all* fields from the 1890s to World War II can be related to it. See Chapter 1, pp. 8–10.

36. Henry James, *The Golden Bowl*, pp. 48, 452.

the text is whether or not the integrity of the bowl has importance given that the crack cannot be perceived under the perfect gold covering. Or – to put the philosophical question in psychological terms – can it matter to Maggie Verver and her father that Charlotte and the Prince have been lovers before and again engage in a liaison if father and daughter remain ignorant of that history and that relationship? If the system which constitutes the relationship between Charlotte and the Prince can be perfectly and beautifully covered (sealed, perfectly reflexive) and Maggie and her father remain happy in their imperturbable relation to each other, does it matter that one is cleverly secret and the other innocently public? Maggie's answer to this – when she penetrates the secret liaison by exercising a superior subtlety of intuition – is that it does matter. She sets herself the task of retrieving her husband from his secret connection.

The novel represents this struggle in a luxuriance of metaphors and tropes, images and patterns. For our present purpose of showing the sophisticated reflexivity of the narrative, the theme of narrative itself is most pertinent. In the same sense that a cubist painting is about painting or that Relativity Theory is about doing physics, *The Golden Bowl* is a narrative about narratives. The struggle between Maggie and her antagonist Charlotte Stant Verver (Mr Verver has married his daughter's husband's secret lover) can be seen as a battle of scripts or texts.

First of all there are allusions, always at least gently ironic, to romantic fairy-tale archetypes. The arrangement of characters alludes to a familiar grand fairy-tale script in which Maggie the Princess is married to the most charming Prince under the benevolent eye of her father-king. Charlotte fits the role of wicked stepmother who must be overcome (with the somewhat uneven help of a fairy godmother in the form of Fanny Assingham). This fairy-tale pattern holds together throughout the novel, but in an adult version with the stepmother entrapping the husband-prince who must be rescued by the wife-princess. As in all fairy tales the princess succeeds but as in no fairy tale at the cost of an indefinite loss, the loss of that daily contact with her father that has been the sustaining element throughout her life. The structural allusion to and departure from an archetypical fairy tale or romance supports the novel's strong reflexive elements in much the same way that analytic cubist paintings assert at once their origins in and departure from the great tradition of significant subjects on view in, for example, the Louvre.

Within the general structural reflexivity of *The Golden Bowl* are many individual scripts which characters write for each other, the most obvious and notable of these being the fiction of benevolent family arrangements that Charlotte and the Prince try to sell to Maggie and her father. This mendacious version of their relationship is offered to the reader in one of the most striking images in modernist narrative, projected from Maggie's point of view:

> This situation had been occupying for months and months the very centre of the garden of her life, but it had reared itself there like some strange tower of ivory, or perhaps rather some wonderful beautiful but outlandish pagoda, a structure

plated with hard bright porcelain, colored and figured and adorned at the overhanging eaves with silver bells that tinkled ever so charmingly when stirred by chance airs. She had walked round and round it – that was what she felt; she had carried on her existence in the space left her for circulation, a space that sometimes seemed ample and sometimes narrow: looking up all the while at the fair structure that spread itself so amply and rose so high, but never quite making out as yet where she might have entered had she wished . . . though her raised eyes seemed to distinguish places that must serve from within, and especially far aloft, as apertures and outlooks, no door appeared to give access from her convenient garden level.[37]

The image of the enclosed tower or pagoda, sealed in its beauty and strangeness from penetration, embodies the closed system of meaning, the narrative, belonging exclusively to Charlotte and the Prince. Maggie must build a counter-structure, *her* narrative, that will contain and ultimately render transparent the opaque pagoda-tower she needs to decode. It is a battle of competing texts, and her opening move is to show her husband that she has penetrated his structure: "Only *see*, see that *I* see."

These narratives are fictions that the characters have made up, and power derives from the credibility of one's script. In this novel, in order to maintain the credibility of one's narrative, it is necessary to lie. Maggie counters the lie of the lovers' narrative with a powerful lie of her own. Once she has made the Prince see that she sees, she needs to make Charlotte believe that she does not. In this narrative of hers she succeeds in enlisting her husband, in leading him to lie to Charlotte on behalf of her own counter-fiction. She explains it to her fairy godmother:

> Mrs Assingham's face lighted. "He'll simply, he'll insistently have lied?"
> Maggie brought it out roundly. "He'll simply, he'll insistently have lied."

As Maggie feels her narrative gain in power she begins to see her family almost as "figures rehearsing some play of which she herself was the author." Near the end we arrive at a scene of appalling tension in which Maggie and Charlotte trade lies that Maggie pledges with "Upon my honour," and that Charlotte seals with a kiss.[38]

The lies in *The Golden Bowl* are not condemned outright, simply because they are lies. The lies seem justified or unjustified depending on the rightness of the cause, of the virtue of the entire fiction or system or narrative that each character tries to impose. Maggie's system appears justified because she is the wife, mother, daughter, friend with the most generous aims and –

---

37. Ibid., p. 330.
38. Ibid., pp. 476, 488, 498–499. The reader has been prepared for acts of lying by several dialogues between Fanny Assingham and her husband in which she instructs him to lie to preserve Maggie's safety and in which the business of creating versions of reality by means of scripts is treated in some detail, especially as the slow-witted but experienced Colonel Assingham requires a good deal of explanation to get Fanny's point that it is necessary "to lie 'for' her," and "to lie *to* her, up and down, and in and out" (p. 410).

ultimately and above all – the widest comprehension. Charlotte's system, her narrative, seems false and hollow because it lacks these larger justifications and is merely selfish. As the novel develops, Charlotte's narrative seems narrower and narrower and uglier and uglier while Maggie's expands. At the end it is possible to pity Charlotte (as Maggie does pity her) but it is no longer possible to admire her. The reader's initial pity for Maggie, however, is lost in admiration. It does not matter that she has lied, any more than it matters that the narrator-captain in "The Secret Sharer" has taken unacceptable risks with his command of the ship. External, objective systems of judgment – ethical or aesthetic – count for little. What counts is the integrity of one's reflexive order, or what in Einstein's physics might be seen as the logical consistency of the theory.

At a particularly telling moment in *The Golden Bowl*, Charlotte in her torment escapes from the country house to seek solace alone in the garden. As a kind of cover for her flight she takes with her a volume of a novel Maggie has lent her. Maggie follows her, ostensibly out of simple helpfulness, and offers her another volume: "I saw you come out – saw you from my window and couldn't bear to think you should find yourself here without the beginning of your book. *This* is the beginning; you've got the wrong volume and I've brought you out the right."[39] In a novel like *The Golden Bowl* there could hardly be a more reflexive image of power: Maggie is reordering the text for Charlotte. Her structure – her narrative – will triumph. She has won.

Maggie's answer to the epistemological problem posed by the golden bowl – does it matter if our world is sound or cracked if we are innocent of the crack – is that there can be no such thing as such innocence. Simply to decide that nothing evil is happening, to try to "know nothing on earth" as Fanny Assingham does for a spell, is to fail. Maggie must learn evil because she lives "on earth," in the world. She must learn to "*see*." We are so constituted that ignorance is not bliss, that it ultimately undermines our happiness. Innocence in the modernist world is psychologically and aesthetically ephemeral. Not even Maggie can afford it; even Maggie can be pillaged. Charlotte Stant, by continuing her love affair with the Prince after his marriage, does manage to steal from Maggie and Maggie misses her husband, the husband she should have possessed entirely upon her marriage and whom she does possess entirely at the end of the novel. The battle of reflexive systems is a battle to the death because all our happiness depends upon it; and since the Prince is a key element in Maggie's system he cannot be a key element in Charlotte's. The idea that he entertains with Charlotte for a time, that such a double life and double system will work benevolently for everybody, presupposes that the systems are not mutually exclusive. But they are, and this Mr Verver knows and acts on when he separates from his daughter in an act of final sacrifice and takes Charlotte with him to the America she dreads. As

39. Ibid., p. 540.

he and Maggie agree, "It's success."[40] Their system has won. And they, as collectors, have always known that one must pay a price for everything; so from now on Maggie and her father will live apart. It's a large price, a princely sum, for a magnificent acquisition.

We have been looking at *The Golden Bowl* as a battle of narratives or fictions – a battle of texts, with at least one inescapable book metaphor in the "right" volume of the novel that Maggie hands to Charlotte. In Franz Kafka's *The Castle* (written 1922; published unfinished as *Das Schloss* in 1926) literal texts abound in the forms of letters, memoranda, files, internal narratives, and other documents; and the interpretation of these makes up much of the novel itself. In its preoccupation with texts and textuality, *The Castle* may be viewed as a masterwork of modernist reflexivity, approximately contemporary with Picasso's last cubist paintings like *The Studio* and *The Painter and his Model*, and like them gaining its meaning and strength from its supreme reflexivity. In *The Castle* the endless interpretation of documents parallels and parodies the reader's struggle to understand the novel itself. In the first chapter K. labors to make sense of the messages from the Castle relayed to him by Schwarzer and in the second he tries to analyze the note from the "Chief of Department X." K. goes on to interpret the mayor's interpretation of Castle procedure and its dealings with him as a putative land-surveyor; he interprets the landlady's interpretation of his interpretation of his relation to the Castle and Frieda's interpretation of the landlady's interpretation of K.'s intentions. He tries to interpret the Amalia story which is largely itself composed of Olga's interpretations of her family's interpretations of their relation to the Castle and Amalia's attitude toward it. He interprets Pepi's interpretation of Frieda and Pepi's speculations on Frieda's interpretation of his usefulness to her.

K.'s interpretation of all these interpretations gives the novel a profoundly reflexive quality and establishes the texture of knowledge and even of life as a process of unending, literally *inconclusive*, interpretation – so that ultimately the inescapably reflexive act of interpretation becomes not an activity secondary to experience (as it is regarded in realistic fiction) but an activity equal in primacy to all other human experience in the novel, deeply implicated even in sexual passion and central to professional ambition. It is as if any human act or even perception can give rise to unlimited speculation, as if the resonance of being alive is such that each moment may be inexhaustible in its implications, implications inseparable from the moment itself. Or, indeed, as if the implications and thus the potential for reflexive interpretation constitute – for human beings – the moment itself. In *The Castle* life is text.

To exhaust life in an interpretation of it, to equate life with its own interpretation, contains a fundamental absurdity in the fullest existential sense. It violates logic and common sense but not common experience. Kafka's presentation of the absurd is in fact what gave him a crucial influence on

40. Ibid., pp. 320, 578.

succeeding modernist writers. In *The Stranger* (*L'Etranger*, 1942) Albert Camus, who admired Kafka and who was influenced by him, has his imprisoned protagonist remark, "I learned that even after a single day's experience of the outside world a man could live a hundred years in prison."[41] Meursault is speaking of the denseness and richness of the world, the earthly world that (as he makes clear to the priest who tries to prepare him to leave it) is all he has and all he wants. As distinguished from Camus's (and Sartre's) secular representation of the absurd, Kafka's presentation of the absurd is inescapably religious, the expression of a complete and original integration of sensibilities, marked everywhere with the influence of Kierkegaard. Kafka's K., in contrast to Meursault, engages in a relentless, fevered attempt to approach the Castle, to approach, that is, Truth or Divinity and to receive some kind of acknowledgment from it.

This endless searching without ever finding, implying an inalterable but eternally unverified conviction of the absolute logic and order of the world, is what gives rise to the seamless reflexivity of K.'s experience. At the beginning of the novel, he tries to approach the Castle directly on foot: "So he resumed his walk, but the way proved long. For the street he was in, the main street of the village, did not lead up to the Castle hill; it only made toward it and then, as if deliberately, turned aside, and though it did not lead away from the Castle, it led no nearer to it either."[42] The main street is a metaphor for the narrative itself, which of course never leads to the Castle because in Kafka as in Kierkegaard there is no *way* to the absolute. As one of Kafka's "Reflections" puts it, "There is a goal, but no way; what we call the way is only wavering."[43] In *The Castle*, all roads lead back to K. himself, as landladies and landlords, secretaries and servants, officials and assistants, chambermaids and lovers all point out to him by interpreting his misguided actions and his own misinterpretations as the causes of his perplexity.

At one point K. stumbles in upon Bürgel, who calls himself a "liaison secretary." Bürgel playfully describes a miraculous occurrence in which a putatively hypothetical supplicant might come upon precisely the putatively hypothetical official who might intercede for him with the Castle:

"And now, Land-Surveyor, consider the possibility that through some circumstance or other, in spite of the obstacles already described to you, which are in general quite sufficient, an applicant does nevertheless, in the middle of the night, surprise a secretary who has a certain degree of competence with regard to the given case. I dare say you have never thought of such a possibility? That I will gladly believe. Nor is it at all necessary to think of it, for it does, after all, practically never occur. What sort of oddly and quite specially constituted, small, skillful grain would such an applicant have to be in order to slip through the incomparable sieve? You think it cannot happen at all. But some night – for who

41. Albert Camus, *The Stranger*, p. 98.
42. Franz Kafka, *The Castle*, p. 14.
43. Franz Kafka, *The Great Wall of China*, pp. 166.

can vouch for everything? – it *does* happen. Admittedly, I don't know anyone among my acquaintances to whom it has ever happened . . ."

It becomes obvious that Bürgel, in a virtuoso improvisation on the event, is describing the immediate situation between himself and K. The hypothetical narrative the "liaison secretary" is spinning actually reflects the present scene between K. and himself; and through some intensely reflexive miracle of Providence or chance K. is being offered the single, supreme opportunity, the one opening in many lifetimes, to make his request to a true official of the Castle. But K. is exhausted and goes to sleep. He loses his chance and is aware of having lost it, though as Bürgel says, "there are, of course, opportunities that are, in a manner of speaking, too great to be made use of, there are things that are wrecked on nothing but themselves."[44]

Our final example of reflexive patterning in *The Castle* occurs as K. watches the hectic distribution of files to the officials in their rooms at the Herrenhof, thinking that he is learning something of the workings of the Castle from his unannounced observation of these strange proceedings. It turns out, however, that the bizarre stratagems for distributing the files have been improvised solely on his account, that it is his presence in the passage that has produced the strangeness in the system. Far from being the neutral, objective observer K. assumed himself to be, he is the primary influence on the phenomena he imagines he merely observes. As the landlord interprets it for him:

> it was on his account, solely and exclusively on his account, that the gentlemen had not been able to come forth out of their rooms, since in the morning, so soon after having been asleep, they were too bashful, too vulnerable, to be able to expose themselves to the gaze of strangers; they literally felt, however completely dressed they might be, too naked to show themselves.

What we have here is a Kafkaesque version of the dilemma posed in theories of quantum measurement. It could be used to illustrate Heisenberg's uncertainty principle (first published in 1927): one cannot observe an event without influencing it. There is no such thing as an objective, non-reflexive observation in *The Castle* any more than there is in quantum theory. And K.'s efforts to gain admission to the Castle, to achieve recognition from it, gain a supreme irony from this. He is already inside the system; he already belongs to the Castle. As Schwarzer tells him at the beginning of the first chapter: "This village belongs to the Castle, and whoever lives here or passes the night here does so, in a manner of speaking, in the Castle itself."[45] In Kafka's masterpiece, the profoundly religious metaphysic joins with a radically avant-garde aesthetic in a celebration of reflexivity, helping to stamp it as a central value of Modernism.

The reflexive devices of modernist fiction – hermetic moral and psychological systems, scripts and other fictional improvisations by characters or voices,

---

44. Kafka, *The Castle*, pp. 335, 346–347, 351.
45. Ibid., pp. 369, 4.

documents and their interpretations – receive their most advanced integration in William Faulkner's *Absalom, Absalom!* The central narrative, upon which all the characters agree, chronicles the rise of Thomas Sutpen and the creation of Sutpen's Hundred, a one hundred square mile property with a vast hastily constructed mansion intended to serve as the setting for the origin of a dynasty. The central narrative also records the rapid destruction of this mushroom estate and of Sutpen's incipient dynasty by the Civil War and by the associated evil of fratricide. What the central, realist consensus does not provide are the *motives* that produce the events and that give the events, however bizarre, coherence and significance. As in Faulkner's earlier *The Sound and the Fury* (and as in classical tragedy), the meaning of the narrative is achieved primarily by the recognition of meaning on the part of the characters.[46] But unlike *The Sound and the Fury* (and unlike classical tragedy), *Absalom, Absalom!* generates meaning not from a recognition of the significance of external events, but by means of the actual creation of a number of narratives by characters who figure in the narratives themselves and who lend these narratives significance by means of their own recognition of significance in their own and others' narratives.

Certainly such binding and complicated reflexivity is not easy for readers to grasp. Faulkner enables us to appreciate it by means of a progressive development of and detachment from the central structural curve, the consensus concerning the "historical" facts of Sutpen's rise and fall, bound up as they are with a history (the Old South and the American Civil War) already itself approaching mythic status. He begins very gently by showing Rosa Coldfield, in her attempt to understand what happened between her nephew Henry and his half-brother Charles Bon, forced to create an image of Bon: "Miss Rosa . . . had never seen (and was never to see alive) Charles Bon at all. . . . Miss Rosa never saw him; this was a picture, an image." Of course characters in realist novels have images of other characters and such images may be true or false (confirmed or denied by the descriptive or dramatic "facts" of the realist narration), but such objectification is lacking here. Miss Rosa's image of Charles Bon is never *corrected* by the narrative; on the contrary, Miss Rosa's image becomes a significant part of the reader's image of Charles Bon, "a man with an ease of manner and a swaggering gallant air in comparison with which Sutpen's pompous arrogance was clumsy bluff and Henry actually a hobble-de-hoy."[47]

Quentin's father, Mr Compson, presents himself as a more detached observer-narrator of the Sutpen saga: "I can imagine them as they rode, Henry still in the fierce repercussive flush of vindicated loyalty, and Bon, the wiser, the shrewder. . . ." Mr Compson goes on to speculate on the fatal shooting. He hypothesizes first that Henry objects to the fact that Bon went through a ceremony of marriage with his mistress and therefore cannot be completely

46. See our discussion of *The Sound and the Fury* in Chapter 4, pp. 99–103.
47. William Faulkner, *Absalom, Absalom!*, p. 58.

free to marry his sister Judith. From this thought he goes on to imagine that Henry objects to Bon's engagement to his sister because Henry has learned from his father that Charles is their half-brother and marriage to Judith would be incest. And in fact these hypotheses and scripts do generate narrative, narrative speculation on Henry's *motive* for killing Bon. But Mr Compson's imagination is not strong enough or not complete enough to reach the conclusion that Quentin and Shreve arrive at in their joint tacit scripting of Henry's motive, revealed in an imagined dialogue with his father:

> – He must not marry her, Henry
>   – Yes. I said Yes at first, but I was not decided then. I didn't let him. But now I have had four years to decide in. I will. I am going to.
>   – He must not marry her, Henry. His mother's father told me that her mother had been a Spanish woman. I believed him; it was not until after he was born that I found out that his mother was part negro.[48]

What makes Shreve and Quentin's script superior to Mr Compson's is not confirmation by any kind of objective narration or plotting, but its psychological and aesthetic strength. In creating the racist motive for fratricide they enlist not only the entire sequence of event and motive that preceded it but the mythic force of historical and national calamity. The motives that drive such calamity can never be stated objectively; they must be *imagined*.

Absalom, Absalom! gives primacy to what Keats called the truth of the imagination. Quentin listens to his father's account of a visit Sutpen pays to his daughters during the Civil War: "and (the demon) drank the parched corn coffee and ate the hoe cake which Judith and Clytie prepared for him and kissed Judith on the forehead and said, 'Well, Clytie' and returned to the war, all in twenty-four hours; he [Quentin] could see it; he might even have been there. Then he thought *No. If I had been there I could not have seen it this plain.*" In other words, imagined reality is more vivid, more real, than simply observed historical reality (realist reality). Similarly, Shreve shrewdly invents Bon's mother's lawyer, his character, his schemes, even his servile and flattering letters. So that the final story is a fiction imagined by Quentin and Shreve in their rooms at Harvard:

> both thinking as one, the voice which happened to be speaking the thought only the thinking become audible, vocal; the two of them creating between them, out of the rag-tag and bob-ends of old tales and talking, people who perhaps had never existed at all anywhere, who, shadows, were shadows not of flesh and blood which had lived and died but shadows in turn of what were (to one of them at least, to Shreve) shades too, quiet as the visible murmur of their vaporizing breath.[49]

It is the moral function of *Absalom, Absalom!* to establish the aesthetic

48. Ibid., pp. 85, 283. Italics, as throughout this book, are the original author's, not ours.
49. Ibid., pp. 155, 251–252, 243.

and psychological primacy of imagined over historical reality. What makes the ruthless, barbarous, racist, sexist Sutpen significant is his fidelity to his visionary ambition; and Sutpen's Hundred, his mushroom estate, becomes representative of the power and vanity – vanity in its deepest sense, as evanescence – of human aspiration, of the illusory nature of its fulfillment, as embodied in the myth of The Old South, the Plantation, the hallucination of a momentary American aristocracy. The novel deals with dreams of self-fulfillment through possession, love, or honor. It also deals with the ultimate destruction of these reflexive systems, these aspirations, by history – by the Civil War. But the history presented here is not a history that denies the power of reflexivity. On the contrary, the history represented is a history imagined by character-narrators, by Rosa Coldfield, Mr Compson, Shreve, and Quentin. It is a history itself contained reflexively within narrative, in which the imagined event has primacy over the observed event. As Shreve puts it, "Because why not? Because listen. What was it the old dame, the Aunt Rosa, told you about how there are some things that just have to be whether they are or not, have to be a damn sight more than some other things that maybe are and it dont matter a damn whether they are or not?"[50]

What creates significance in *Absalom, Absalom!* is the extraordinary intensity of imagination and the binding reflexivity of the narrators' engagement with the events and characters they describe. Even the ironic nihilist posturing of Mr Compson does not prevent him from having an obsessive commitment to the story, in part because it is through the story that he tries to reach his son Quentin. And the two final narrators actually become the characters they are describing so that the narrators and the characters merge and become four riders, "Charles-Shreve and Quentin-Henry":

> They were both in Carolina and the time was forty-six years ago, and it was not even four now but compounded still further, since now both of them were Henry Sutpen and both of them were Bon, compounded each of both yet either neither, smelling the very smoke which had blown and faded away forty-six years ago from the *bivouac fires burning in a pine grove, the gaunt and ragged men sitting or lying about them, talking not about the war yet all curiously enough (or perhaps not curiously at all) facing the South where further on in the darkness the pickets stood – the pickets who, watching to the South, could see the flicker and gleam of the Federal bivouac fires myriad and faint and encircling half the horizon . . . .*[51]

The scene is vivid, and it is complete. The absence of confirmation from a

---

50. Ibid., p. 258. It is possible at points to distinguish between Shreve's brilliant, cruel analysis of these "Southern" events and Quentin's more complex, conflicted engagement with them as a Southerner. Shreve constantly shows his distance from and lack of close sympathy with the sensibilities he relentlessly ridicules. He thinks it doesn't matter whether Rosa Coldfield is called "Miss Rosa" or "Aunt Rosa" for the purposes of their narrative, whereas to Quentin the implied difference in respect and intimacy separates white from black. We see, however, that these merely personal limitations (reasserted on the last page of the novel) do not limit the validity of the joint narrative.

51. Ibid., pp. 267, 280–281.

realist observer is neither a felt nor a philosophical absence. This scene of civil warfare, an explicitly, even assertively imagined reality, born of sympathy and honor and imagination, transcends the power of mere realistic history, of the pretense of merely recorded actuality. *Absalom, Absalom!* confirms the value of reflexivity as the way meaning develops in Modernism.

Chapter 7 Conclusion

> History, *mother* of truth; the idea is astounding. Menard,
> a contemporary of William James, does not define
> history as an investigation of reality, but as its origin.
>
> Borges, "Pierre Menard, Author of Don Quixote"

In the preceding chapters we have identified a set of values that we believe
defines Modernism, considered as an historical period of advanced intellectual
activity from approximately the late nineteenth century through to World
War II. We have extracted these values from an analysis of three cultural
diagnostics: Relativity Theory, Cubism, and selected modernist narrative. As
we acknowledged at the outset, analysis of other intellectual territory – such
as the momentous changes in linguistics, or in anthropology, or in psychology,
or in mathematics, or in philosophy – might yield additional values of equal
or almost equal breadth of application. We limited our discussion because
we knew that in order for our radically interdisciplinary study to be persuasive
our analysis would have to be authoritative and specific as well as general.
The values we abstracted from our cultural diagnostics would not only have
to be values operating in similar ways but also values formulated in such a
way as to be recognizable across traditional disciplinary boundaries. Finally,
we limited our range of inquiry so that we could move more fully into the
events we examined, so that we could hope to take our readers *inside* them,
inside Modernism.

We believe that the values in question do in fact characterize in a high
degree other advanced intellectual activity during this period, including linguistics, anthropology, psychology, mathematics, and philosophy. Saussure's
linguistics bears strong affinities with our value of contextualization; it occupies
a middle ground between individual subjectivity and positivist "objectivity";
and it shifts attention from "reality" to the observation, measurement, and
representation of reality. His idea that language is primarily a self-referential
system that generates meaning within itself may be seen as a masterful embodiment of modernist reflexivity. Like most manifestations of Structuralism,
structural anthropology as expounded by Lévi-Strauss is also driven by these
values and explicitly acknowledges its debt to Saussure's linguistics.
Psychoanalysis operates precisely in that middle ground between positivist

objectivity and the entirely inner life, and it also directly relates to our modernist values of epistemic trauma and contextualization (in this case the integration of experience with personal history). The work of Gödel in mathematics brought even the most abstract of sciences in from the ideal of any ultimate and comprehensive set of axioms to a recognition of its own unstable reflexivity. And those readers who have a knowledge of modernist philosophy, especially of phenomenology and Existentialism, must have been wondering why we have not appealed to such names as Husserl, Heidegger, and Sartre in support of the values we see as constituting Modernism. But excursions into these fields might very well have led us into another volume without materially advancing our definition – into another volume, that is, of the same book.

Probably the single most important methodological contribution that such a study as this can make to the work of cultural history lies in a creative act of identification. In the final analysis – literally in the final analysis – Modernism is a definition, a construction, a product of present awareness focusing on past value. Of course other studies and other scholars have arrived and will arrive at other definitions, but for them as well Modernism will be a collection of values that define it, even when such studies and scholars lay claim to some version of historical objectivity. An historical period as we can know it is not an object, or a collection of objects, or a museum of historical remains (no matter how complex, intense, or alive such remains may seem).

Modernism does not exist beyond or outside or above a definition of it. Our definition *is* our Modernism. It is true that we extracted the values that constitute our Modernism from historical remains, specifically our three cultural diagnostics. But as soon as the work of extraction began, in fact as soon as the remains were themselves identified, the work of construction began. It was never finished. As long as we keep the identity of Modernism before us it continues to develop. Historical definitions that contain meaning never rest inert or static but, like memory itself, continue their creative growth.

Much of what we have had to say about Modernism arises from its emergence from the preceding culture of Realism. And much of the process of self-definition within Modernism has to do with its self-conscious relation to that preceding culture (an aspect of its historical reflexivity). Having taken our own analyses of the major characteristics of the period as far as we wish to go, we turn briefly to the question of how our definition of Modernism can help us to grasp what happened next, how it can help us understand its successor; and also, remarkably, conversely, how the developing definition of Postmodernism contains ideas that clarify the preceding ethos of Modernism. What follows here amounts to a methodological suggestion concerning how our Modernism and the unfolding identification of Postmodernism might assist each other.

The polymorphous reflection of Modernism in Postmodernism has produced much analysis and argument. Cultural historians and theorists of cultural history tend to view what is now called Postmodernism in one of two general ways:

1. as a late and distinguishable development within the modernist revolution

(sometimes called "late Modernism"); or

2. as a new ethos and a new aesthetic (new collection of "values").

Preference for one view or the other depends largely on the size of the observer's historical canvas (with highly focused studies of events from the last forty years tending to see Postmodernism as a dissociation from and even a rejection of modernist values), but both positions prove helpful in defining Modernism itself. This is because in the emerging definition of Postmodernism we can identify changes in or departures from the values that constituted Modernism; and this process of identification assists our understanding of the earlier period.[1]

It is possible to look at the various modernist values discussed in this book and see how each one is developed, altered, or rejected in what most commentators see as the postmodern ethos and aesthetic. In the place of modernist epistemic trauma as identified in our second chapter, Postmodernism affirms a denial of prescriptive norms. In physics, postmodern models of the cosmos – such as the unified quantum field theory involving ten-dimensional super-strings[2] – tend not so much to refute or discredit earlier constructs as to emerge almost as free creations, with vastly different relations to the criteria of internal consistency and external verification. In painting, developments such as Pop or Super Realism do not so much attack modernist art as Cubism attacked Realism but persuasively demonstrate that we must now admit the techniques of the comics, arrangements of soup cans, or meticulous representations of the rear end of a station wagon as seamless entries into our high aesthetic culture. In postmodern narrative we are asked to accept the fact that we will never know what "really" happened in Robbe-Grillet's *Last Year at Marienbad* because what happened depends not contingently but entirely on how persuasive a version of events can be; we are asked to accept in García Márquez's *One Hundred Years of Solitude* that Ramedios the Beauty simply floated up to the sky one day out of a simultaneously magic and realistic Macondo; that in Cortázar's "Letter to a Young Lady in Paris" the narrator apologizes for his melancholy propensity to vomit up rabbits as agents of disorder and creativity.

Certainly such phenomena should and do serve as what we have called "cultural diagnostics" for the postmodern period (approximately since World War II as we would date it) and certainly it is difficult to imagine them taking place without Modernism, without Einstein or Picasso or Kafka. But are they developments of modernist values or are they discrete departures from such values? The answer is that this is a question of definition and

---

1 Ihab Hassan has an interesting but confusing table of developments from Modernism to Postmodernism in "Toward a Concept of Postmodernism," *The Dismemberment of Orpheus: Toward a Postmodern Literature.* Elizabeth Ermarth has an informed summary of the most important attempts to distinguish Postmodernism in *Sequel to History,* pp. 4–7, including the notes. So, more fully, does Astradur Eysteinsson in his chapter on "Reading Modernism through Postmodernism," in *The Concept of Modernism,* pp. 103–142. Danuta Fjellestad's *Eros, Logos, and (Fictional) Masculinity* provides a current, lucid account of modernist and postmodernist thinking on her central theme.

2 See, for example, Murray Gell-Mann, *The Quark and the Jaguar,* pp. 126–129.

categorization and that therefore such cultural events are both developments and departures. Where Modernism wrestled with the difficulties caused by the absence of universal temporal, spatial, and ethical coordinates – what we have described as a value shift from normative to contextual – Postmodernism adopts without traumatic struggle the surreal, bizarre, and metanatural. Where Modernism negotiated the difficult transition from examination of reality to examination of observation, Postmodernism accepts the premiss that all values are "constructions" on the model of language – local, contained, self-referential. Where Modernism sought depth and abstraction, Postmodernism turns toward surface and eccentric particularity. For what was in Modernism a dominant value of order, Postmodernism substitutes design and pattern. And finally the reflexivity of Modernism, its self-awareness, becomes in Postmodernism a more radical and complete self-referentiality moving toward visions of total (and so completely free) self-containment.

Viewed through most of the many lenses of Postmodernism, Modernism can look discouragingly anxious, serious, portentous, heavy. But without the trauma, the contextualization, the observation, the abstraction, the reflexivity of Modernism none of our current buoyancy, urbanity, unmoored hilarity, our agency and currency and radical constructivity would be imaginable. This realization leaves us with a *growing* concept of Modernism, not because its ethos and aesthetics have not been supplanted (they have) but because the wave of our current culture washes back over the unheroic but supremely courageous achievement of the recent past, revealing as far as we can see its volatile integrity.

List of Works Consulted

Abel, Richard M. "Scientific Imagination and the American Novel". *Dissertation Abstracts International* 39 (1979): 7400A.

Abrash, Merritt. "The Hubris of Science: Wells's Time Traveler." In *Patterns of the Fantastic II* (Starmont Studies in Literary Criticism 3), ed. Donald M. Hassler. Mercer Island, WA: Starmont House, 1985, pp. 5–11.

Ackerman, James S. "Art History and the Problem of Criticism." *Daedalus*, 89 (Winter 1960): 253–263.

Ackerman, James S. "The Demise of the *Avant Garde*: Notes on the Sociology of Recent American Art." *Comparative Studies in Society and History*, 11, no. 4 (October 1969): 371–384.

Ackroyd, Peter. *Notes for a New Culture: An Essay on Modernism.* New York: Barnes & Noble, 1976.

Aichelburg, Peter C. and Roman U. Sexl (eds). *Albert Einstein: His Influence on Physics, Philosophy and Politics.* Braunschweig/Wiesbaden: Fried. Vieweg & Sohn, 1979.

Albergotti, J. Clifton. *Mighty is the Charm: Lectures on Science, Literature, and the Arts.* Washington, DC: University Press of America, 1982.

Aldridge, Alexandra B. "Scientising Society: The Dystopian Novel and the Scientific World View." *Dissertation Abstracts International* 39 (1978): 3560A–3561A.

Aldridge, Alexandra B. *The Scientific World View in Dystopia.* (Studies in Speculative Fiction, 3). Ann Arbor, MI: UMI Research Press, 1984.

Alter, Robert. *Partial Magic: The Novel as Self-Conscious Genre.* Berkeley: University of California Press, 1975.

Altieri, Charles. *Painterly Abstraction in Modernist American Poetry: The Contemporaneity of Modernism.* Cambridge: Cambridge University Press, 1989.

Amsler, Mark (ed.) *The Language of Creativity: Models, Problem-Solving, Discourse* (Studies in Science and Culture, 2). Newark: University of Delaware Press; London: Associated University Presses, 1986.

Angus, Douglas. "Modern Art and the New Physics." *Western Humanities Review*, 16 (1962): 103–112.

Appleman, Philip. "The Dread Factor: Eliot, Tennyson, and the Shaping of Science." *Columbia Forum*, n.s. 3, no. 4 (1974): 32–38.

Arbur, Rosemarie. "Ars Scientia = Ars Poetica." In *Patterns of the Fantastic II* (Starmont Studies in Literary Criticism, 3), ed. Donald M. Hassler. Mercer Island, WA: Starmont House, 1985, pp. 13–27.

Arnason, H.H. *History of Modern Art*, 2nd edn. Englewood Cliffs, NJ: Prentice-Hall; New York: Harry N. Abrams, 1985.

Ashton, Dore (ed.) *Twentieth-Century Artists on Art*. New York: Pantheon Books, 1985.

Auerbach, Eric. *Mimesis*, trans. Willard Trask. New York: Doubleday Anchor, 1957.

Baker, Beulah P. "Energy and Event as Motive, Motif and Design in the Poetry of William Carlos Williams." *Dissertation Abstracts International* 37 (1977): 7747A–7748A.

Banville, John. "Physics and Fiction: Order from Chaos." *New York Times Book Review*, April 21, 1985: 1, 41–42.

Barr, Alfred H. *Cubism and Abstract Art*. New York: Museum of Modern Art, 1936.

Barthes, Roland. *The Pleasure of the Text*, trans. Richard Miller. New York: Hill & Wang, 1975.

Battistini, Andrea. "Letteratura e Scienza." In *Letteratura Italiana Contemporanis*, ed. Gaetano Mariani and Mario Petrucciani. Rome: Lucarini, 1982, pp. 761–788.

Bay-Peterson, Ole. "T.S. Eliot and Einstein: The Fourth Dimension in *The Four Quartets*." *English Studies*, 66 (1985): 143–155.

Beebe, Maurice. "*Ulysses* and the Age of Modernism." In *Ulysses: Fifty Years*, ed. Thomas F. Staley. Bloomington, IN: Indiana University Press, 1974, pp. 172–188.

Beer, Gillian. "The Language of Discovery." *Times Literary Supplement*, November 2, 1984: 1255–1256.

Belsey, Catherine. "Constructing the Subject: Deconstructing the Text" (1985) in *Contemporary Literary Criticism*, 3rd edn, ed. Robert Con Davis and Ronald Schleifer. New York and London: Longman, 1994.

Bender, Todd K. "Scientific Models of Reality and Literary Impressionism in Joseph Conrad." *STTH: Science, Technology and the Humanities*, 1 (1978): 229–239.

Berger, Harold L. "Anti-Utopian Fiction of the Mid-Twentieth Century." *Dissertation Abstracts International* 32 (1971): 420A.

Bergonzi, Bernard. "The Advent of Modernism." In *The Twentieth Century* (History of Literature in the English Language, Vol. VII), ed. Bernard Bergonzi. London: Barrie & Jenkins, 1970, pp. 17–45.

Bernstein, Jeremy. "Personal History (Physics – Part I)." *The New Yorker*, January 26, 1987: 35–68.

Bernstein, Jeremy. *Einstein*. New York: Fontana Press, 1991.

Beznos, Maurice J. "Aspects of Time according to the Theories of Relativity in Marcel Proust's *A la recherche du temps perdu*: A Study of the Similitudes in Conceptual Limits." *Ohio University Review*, 10 (1968): 74–102.

Bishop, Neil B. "Energie textuelle et production de sens: images de l'energie dans *Les fous de Bassan* d'Anne Herbert." *University of Toronto Quarterly*, 54 (1984–85): 178–199.

Blatt, Sidney J. *Continuity and Change in Art: The Development of Modes of Representation*. (In collaboration with Ethel S. Blatt.) Hillsdale, NJ: Erlbaum, 1984.

Boas, Mary D. *Mathematical Methods in the Physical Sciences*, 2nd edn. New York: John Wiley, 1983.

Borges, Jorge Luis. *Ficciones*, ed. Anthony Kerrigan. New York: Grove Press, 1962. Part I, "The Garden of Forking Paths," is dated 1941; Part II, "Artifices," 1944.

Bork, Alfred B. "Durrell and Relativity." *Centennial Review*, 7(1963): 191–203.

Bradbury, Malcolm and James McFarlane (eds) *Modernism: 1890–1930*. London: Penguin Books, 1987.

Breton, André. *Manifestos of Surrealism*, trans. Richard Seaver and Helen R. Lane. Ann Arbor, MI: University of Michigan Press, 1972.

Breton, André and Philippe Soupault. *The Magnetic Fields*. Paris: 1921.

Brogen, Howard O. "Science and Narrative Structure in Austen, Hardy and Woolf." *Nineteenth Century Fiction*, 11 (1956–57): 276–287. *To the Lighthouse* and relativity.

Bronowski, Jacob. "A Retrospective." *Leonardo*, 18 (1985): 215–282.

Bronowski, Jacob. "The Logic of the Mind." *Nature*, 209, no. 5029 (March 19, 1966): 1171–1173.

Bronowski, Jacob. *The Visionary Eye: Essays in the Arts, Literature and Science*, selected and edited by Piero E. Ceriotti in collaboration with Rita Bronowski. Cambridge, MA: MIT Press, 1978.

Brook, Donald. "On Order in Art and in Science." *Leonardo*, 14, no. 3 (1981): 231–232.

Brown, Hanbury. *The Wisdom of Science: Its Relevance to Culture and Religion*. Cambridge: Cambridge University Press, 1986.

Brown, Sharon L. "Lawrence Durrell and Relativity." *Dissertation Abstracts* 26 (1966): 7310.

Brush, Stephen G. "Scientific Revolutionaries of 1905: Einstein, Rutherford, Chamberlin, Wilson, Stevens, Binet, Freud." In *Rutherford and Physics at the Turn of the Century*, ed. Mario Bunge and William R. Shea. New York: Science History Publications, 1979, pp. 140–171.

Brush, Stephen G. "The Second Scientific Revolution, 1800–1950." Unpublished typescript.

Buck, Philo M., Jr. "Science, Literature, and the Hunting of the Snark." *College English*, 4 (1942–43): 1–11.

Bunge, Mario. "Borges y Einstein, o la fantasia en arte y en cincia." *Revista de Occidente*, 73 (1987): 45–62.

Bürger, Peter. "The Significance of the Avant-Garde for Contemporary Aesthetics: A Reply to Jürgen Habermas." *New German Critique*, 23 (Winter 1981): 19–22.

Bürger, Peter. *The Decline of Modernism*, trans. Nicholas Walker. Cambridge: Polity Press, 1992.

Cameron, J. M. *The Night Battle*. London: Burns & Oates, 1962.

Camus, Albert. *The Myth of Sisyphus*, trans. Justin O'Brien. New York: Vintage Books, 1955. First published as *Le Mythe de Sisyphe* in 1942.

Camus, Albert. *The Stranger*, trans. Stuart Gilbert. New York: Vintage Books, 1957. First published as *L'Étranger* in 1942.

Carlisle, E. Fred. "Metaphoric Reference in Science and Literature: The Examples of Watson and Crich and Roethke." *Centennial Review*, 29 (1985): 281–301.

Carter, Steven Michael. "Epistemological Models Shared by American Projectivist Poetry and Quantum Physics." *Dissertation Abstracts International* 46 (1985): 980A.

Carter, William C. "Proust, Einstein et le sentiment religieux cosmique." *Bulletin de la Société des Amis de Marcel Proust et des Amis de Combray*, 37 (1987): 126A.

Cartwright, Michael P. "*The Alexandria Quartet*: A Comedy for the Twentieth Century: Or, Lawrence Durrell, the Pardoner and His Miraculous Pig's Knuckle." *Dissertation Abstracts* 31 (1970–71): 5391A.

Cassirer, Ernst. *Substance and Function* and *Einstein's Theory of Relativity* (bound together). New York: Dover Publications, 1953, 1923.

Cézanne, Paul. *Correspondence*. Paris: Bernard Grasset, 1978.

Chapple, J.A.V. "Conrad's Brooding over Scientific Opinion." *Conradian*, 10 (1985): 59–67.

Chefdor, Monique, Ricardo Quinones, and Albert Wachtel (eds). *Modernism: Challenges and Perspectives*. Urbana: University of Illinois Press, 1986.

Chiari, Joseph. *The Aesthetics of Modernism*. London: Vision, 1970.

Chipp, Herschel B. *Theories of Modern Art: A Source Book by Artists and Critics*. Berkeley: University of California Press, 1968.

Clark, Ronald W. *Einstein: The Life and Times*. New York: World Publishing, 1971.

Clignet, Remi. "The Variability of Paradigms in the Production of Culture: A Comparison of the Arts and Sciences." *American Sociological Review*, 44 (1979): 392–409.

Coen, Ester. *Umberto Boccioni*. New York: Metropolitan Museum of Art (distributed by Harry N. Abrams, Inc.), 1989.

Cohen, I. Bernard. *Revolutions in Science*. Cambridge, MA: Belknap Press of Harvard University Press, 1985.

Cohen, I. Bernard. *The Birth of a New Physics*. Harmondsworth: Penguin, 1987.

Conrad, Joseph. *The Secret Agent*, ed. Martin Seymour-Smith. Harmondsworth: Penguin Books, 1986. First published in serial form in 1906; revised book form in 1907.

Conrad, Joseph. "The Secret Sharer" (1910). In *Great Short Works of Joseph Conrad*. New York: Harper & Row, 1967.

Conrad, Joseph. *Victory*. New York: Anchor Books, 1957. First published in 1915.

Conroy, Mark. *Modernism and Authority: Strategies of Legitimation in Flaubert and Conrad*. Baltimore, MD: Johns Hopkins University Press, 1985.

Constein, Carl F. "Relativity in the Novels of Virginia Woolf." *Dissertation Abstracts International* 17 (1957): 851.

Cooper, Douglas. *The Cubist Epoch*. London: Phaidon, 1994.

Craven, Thomas Jewell. "Art and Relativity." *The Dial*, vol. 70 (May 1921), 535–39.

Cullis, Tara E. "Literature of Rupture: Science and Literature in the Twentieth Century." *Dissertation Abstracts International* 44 (1983): 1782A.

Curtin, Deane W. (ed.). *The Aesthetic Dimension of Science: Proceedings of the 1980 Nobel Conference at Gustavus Adolphus College, St. Peter, Minnesota*. New York: Philosophical Library, 1980.

Darst, D. H. "Renaissance Symmetry, Baroque Symmetry and the Sciences." *Diogenes*, 123: 69–90.

Davenport, Edward A. "Scientific Method as Literary Criticism." *ETC: A Review of General Semantics*, 42 (1985): 331–350.

Davies, Alistair. *An Annotated Critical Bibliography of Modernism*. Totowa, NJ: Barnes & Noble, 1982.

Davis, Robert Con and Ronald Schleifer (eds). *Contemporary Literary Criticism*, 2nd edn. New York and London: Longman, 1989.

Dawson, Carl. "From Einstein to Keats: A New Look at *The Alexandria Quartets*." *Far-Western Forum: A Review of Ancient and Modern Letters*, 1 (1974): 109–128.

Derrida, Jacques. "Structure, Sign and Play in the Discourse of the Human Sciences" (1966). In *Writing and Difference*, trans. Alan Bass. Chicago: University of Chicago Press, 1978.

Dickens, Charles. *The Posthumous Papers of the Pickwick Club*. London: Oxford University Press, 1971. First published in 1836–37.

Digby, Joan and Robert Brier (eds). *Permutations: Readings in Science and Literature*. New York: Morrow, 1985.

Donley, Carol C. "Modern Literature and Physics: A Study of Interrelationships." *Dissertation Abstracts International* 36 (1975–76): 3684A.

Donley, Carol. C. "A Little Touch of / Einstein in the Night – : Williams' Early Exposure to the Theories of Relativity." *William Carlos Williams Newsletter*, 4 no. 1 (1978): 10–13.

Donley, Carol C. "Relativity and Radioactivity in William Carlos Williams's *Paterson*." *William Carlos Williams Newsletter*, 5, no. 1 (1979): 6–11.

Duggan, Brother I. Pius. "Relativity, Quantum Theory, and the Novels of Samuel Beckett." *Dissertation Abstracts International* 32 (1971): 2637A.

Durrell, Lawrence. "Space-Time and Poetry." In *A Key to Modern British Poetry*. Norman: University of Oklahoma Press; London: Nevill, 1952, pp. 24–48.

Dyck, Martin. "Relativity in Physics and in Fiction". In *Studies in German Literature of the 19th and 20th Centuries*. Festschrift for Frederic E. Coenen, ed. Siegfried Mews. (University of North Carolina Studies in the Germanic Languages and Literatures, 67). Chapel Hill: University of North Carolina Press, 1970, pp. 174–185.

Dyson, Freeman. *Infinite in all Directions*. Harmondsworth: Penguin Books, 1989.

Eddington, A. S. *The Mathematical Theory of Relativity*. Cambridge: Cambridge University Press, 1965. First published in 1922.

Eddington, A. S. *The Nature of the Physical World*. New York: Macmillan, 1930.

Eddington, A. S. *Report on the Relativity Theory of Gravitation*. London: Fleetway Press, 1920.

Eddington, A. S. *The Theory of Relativity and Its Influence on Scientific Thought*. Oxford: Clarendon Press, 1922.

Edgerton, Samuel Y., Jr. *The Renaissance Discovery of Linear Perspective*. New York: Basic Books, 1975.

Ehrenfeld, David W. *The Arrogance of Humanism*. New York: Oxford University Press, 1978.

Einstein, Albert. "Clerk Maxwell's Influence on the Evolution of the Idea of Physical Reality." In *Essays in Science*. New York: Philosophical Library, 1934.

Einstein, Albert. "On the Method of Theoretical Physics." In *Essays in Science*. New York: Philosophical Library, 1934.

Einstein, Albert. *The Meaning of Relativity*, trans. E.P. Adams. Princeton, NJ: Princeton University Press, 1945. First published 1922.

Einstein, Albert. *Relativity*. New York: Crown Publishers, Inc., 1961.

Einstein, Albert and Leopold Infeld. *The Evolution of Physics*. New York: Simon & Schuster, 1966. First published in 1938.

Einstein, Albert, et al. *The Principle of Relativity: A Collection of Original Memoirs on the Special and General Theory of Relativity*. New York: Dover Publications, 1952.

Elderfield, John. *Henri Matisse: A Retrospective*. New York: Museum of Modern Art, 1992.

Elgar, Frank. *Picasso*. Paris: Fernand Hazen, 1987.

Ellmann, Richard and Charles Feidelson (eds) *The Modern Tradition*. New York: Oxford University Press, 1965.

Eoff, Sherman H. *The Modern Spanish Novel: Comparative Essays Examining the Philosophical Impact of Science on Fiction*. New York: New York University Press, 1961; London: Owen, 1962.

Erickson, John D. "The Proust–Einstein Relation: A Study in Relative Points of View." In *Marcel Proust: A Critical Panorama*, ed. Larkin B. Price. Urbana: University of Illinois Press, 1973, pp. 247–276.

Ermarth, Elizabeth Deeds. *Realism and Consensus in the English Novel*. Princeton, NJ: Princeton University Press, 1983.

Ermarth, Elizabeth Deeds. *Sequel to History: Postmodernism and the Crisis of Representational Time*. Princeton, NJ: Princeton University Press, 1992.

Eysteinsson, Astradur. *The Concept of Modernism*. Ithaca, NY: Cornell University Press, 1990.

Faraday, Michael. *Faraday's Diary*, Vol. IV. London: G. Bell & Sons, 1933.

Fasel, Ida. "Spatial Form and Spatial Time." *Western Humanities Review*, 16 (1962): 223–234.

Faulkner, Peter. *Modernism*. London: Methuen, 1977.

Faulkner, Peter. *The English Modernist Reader*. Iowa City: University of Iowa Press, 1986.

Faulkner, William. *Absalom, Absalom!* New York: Vintage International, 1990. First published in 1936.

Faulkner, William. "Delta Autumn." In *Go Down Moses*. New York: Vintage Books, 1973, pp. 335–365. First published in 1942.

Faulkner, William. *The Sound and the Fury*. New York: Vintage Books, 1954. First published in 1929.

Fjellestad, Danuta. *Eros, Logos, and (Fictional) Masculinity*. Uppsala: Acta Universitatis Upsaliensis, 1998.

Fleischman, Avrom. "Science in Ithaca." *Wisconsin Studies in Contemporary Literature*, 8 (1967): 377–391. Reprinted in *Fiction and the Ways of Knowing: Essays on British Novels*. Austin: University of Texas Press, 1978.

Fokkema, Douwe W. *Literary History, Modernism and Postmodernism*. Amsterdam: Benjamins, 1984.

Fokkema, Douwe W. and Ibsch Elrud. *Modernist Conjectures*. London: St Martin's Press, 1988.

Forster, E. M. *A Passage to India*. New York: Harcourt Brace Jovanovich, 1952. First published in 1924.

Foster, Steven M. "Ambiguous Gifts: The Impress of Science on Contemporary Anglo-American Poetry." *Dissertation Abstracts*, 26 (1965–66): 2749.

Foster, Steven M. "Relativity and *The Waste Land*: A Postulate." *Texas Studies in Literature and Language*, 7 (1965): 77–95.

Frank, Philipp G. *Einstein: His Life and Times*. London: Jonathan Cape, 1948.

Franklin, Steve. "Space-Time and Creativity in Lawrence Durrell's *Alexandria Quartet*." *Perspectives on Contemporary Literature*, 5 (1979): 55–61.

Freud, Sigmund. *The Future of an Illusion*, trans. W.D. Robson-Scott; ed. James Strachey. London: Hogarth Press, 1962. First published in 1927.

Freud, Sigmund. *Early Psychoanalytic Writings*, ed. Philip Rieff. New York: Collier Books, 1963.

Friedman, Alan J. and Carol C. Donley. *Einstein as Myth and Muse*. Cambridge: Cambridge University Press, 1985.

Friedman, Alan Warren. "A Key' to Lawrence Durrell." *Wisconsin Studies in Contemporary Literature*, 8 (1967): 31–42.

Friedrich, Antal. "Remarks on the Method of Art History, I." *Burlington Magazine*, 91 (February 1949): 49–52.

Fry, Edward F. *Cubism*. New York: Oxford University Press, 1978.

Fry, Edward F. "Picasso, Cubism, and Reflexivity," *Art Journal*, 47, no. 4 (Winter 1988): 296–310.

Fullner, J.Z. "Contemporary Science and the Poets." *Science*, 119 (1954): 855–859. Eliot, MacLeish, Frost.

Gabo, Naum. "The Constructive Idea in Art." In *Modern Artists On Art*, ed. Robert L. Herbert. Englewood Cliffs, NJ: Prentice-Hall, 1964.

Gaggi, Silvio. *Modern/Postmodern: A Study in Twentieth-Century Arts and Ideas*. Philadelphia: University of Pennsylvania Press, 1989.

Garte, Edna J. "Kandinsky's Ideas on Changes in Modern Physics and Their Implications for His Development." *Gazettes des Beaux-Arts*, October 1987: 137.

Gauguin, Paul. *Noa Noa*. Paris: Jean-Jaques Pauvert , 1988.

Gavin, Harry R. and James M. Heath (eds). *Science and Literature* (Bucknell Review, 27, no. 2). Lewisburg, PA: Bucknell University Press; London: Associated University Presses, 1983.

Gell-Mann, Murray. *The Quark and the Jaguar*. New York: W. H. Freeman, 1994.

Gibson, James J. "Pictures, Perspective, and Perception." *Daedalus*, 89 (Winter 1960): 216–228.

Glicksberg, Charles I. "Depersonalization in the Modern Drama." *Person*, 39 (1958): 158–169.

Goldberg, Stanley. *Understanding Relativity: Origin and Impact of a Scientific Revolution*. Boston: Birkhauser, 1984.

Golding, John. *Cubism: A History and an Analysis, 1907–1914*. London: Faber & Faber, 1969.

Gombrich, E.H. *Art and Illusion*. New York: Bollingen Foundation; Princeton, NJ: Princeton University Press, 1961.

Gordon, Bonnie Bilyeu (ed.). *Songs from Unsung Worlds: Science in Poetry*. Boston: Birkhauser, 1985.

Gould, Stephen Jay. *Wonderful Life: The Burgess Shale and the Nature of History*. London: Hutchinson Radius, 1990.

Gray, Ronald. *Franz Kafka*. Cambridge: Cambridge University Press, 1973.

Green, Christopher. *Cubism and Its Enemies: Modern Movements and Reaction in French Art, 1916–1928*. New Haven and London: Yale University Press, 1987.

Green, Kevin Xavier. "Herbert, H.G. Wells, and J.S. Huxley: Unexpected British Connections." *Australian Literary Studies*, 12 (1985): 47–64.

Greenberg, Clement. *Art and Culture: Critical Essays*. Boston: Beacon Press, 1965. First published in 1961.

Grof, Stanislav (ed.) *Ancient Wisdom and Modern Science*. Albany: State University of New York Press, 1984.

Hafner, E.M. "The New Reality in Art and Science." With comments by George Kubler and Thomas Kuhn. *Comparative Studies in Society and History*, 11, no. 4 (October 1969): 385–412.

Haftmann, Werner. *Painting in the Twentieth Century*, 2 vols. London: Lund Humphries, 1965.

Hamilton, George Heard. "Cézanne, Bergson, and the Image of Time." *College Art Journal*, 16, no. 1 (Fall 1956): pp. 2–12.

Hampshire, Stuart. *Modern Writing and Other Essays*. New York: Knopf, 1971.

Harris, Kathryn G. "Robert Frost and Science: The Shaping Metaphor of Motion in the Poems." *Dissertation Abstracts International* 37 (1976): 967a.

Harris, Paul André. "Time Spaced Out in Words: From Physics to Faulkner." *Dissertation Abstracts International*. 1991 May; 51(11): 3743A–3744A.

Hassan, Ihab. *The Dismemberment of Orpheus: Toward a Postmodern Literature*, 2nd edn, revised. Madison: University of Wisconsin Press, 1982.

Hassan, Ihab. *The Right Promethean Fire: Imagination, Science, and Cultural Change*. Urbana: University of Illinois Press, 1980.

Havel, Vaclav. "Politics and the World Itself." *Kettering Review*, Summer 1992: 8–13.

Hawking, Stephen W. *A Brief History of Time: From the Big Bang to Black Holes*. London: Bantam, 1988.

Hayles, N. Katherine. *The Cosmic Web: Scientific Field Models and Literary Strategies in the Twentieth Century*. Ithaca, NY and London: Cornell University Press, 1984.

Haynes, Roslynn D. *H.G. Wells, Discoverer of the Future: The Influence of Science on His Thought*. New York: New York University Press; London: Macmillan, 1980.

Heath-Stubbs, John and Phillips Salman (eds). *Poems of Science*. Harmondsworth: Penguin, 1984.

Heath-Stubbs, John and Phillips Salman (eds). "Poems of Science." *Interdisciplinary Science Review*, 8 (1983): 379–385.

Heisenberg, Werner. *The Physicist's Conception of Nature*. Westport, CT: Greenwood Press, 1970.

Helmholtz, Herman. "On the Interactions of Natural Forces." In *The Correlation and Conservation of Forces*, ed. Edward L. Youmans. New York: D. Appleton, 1865.

Hemingway, Ernest. "A Clean, Well-Lighted Place," in *The Short Stories of Ernest Hemingway*. New York: Scribners, 1953.

Henderson, Linda Dalrymple. "A New Facet of Cubism: 'The Fourth Dimension' and 'Non-Euclidean Geometry' Reinterpreted." *The Art Quarterly*, 34, no. 4 (1971): 410–433.

Henderson, Linda Dalrymple. "Modern Art and the Invisible Waves and Dimensions of Occultism and Science." In *Okkultismus und Avant-Garde 1900–1915*. Schirn Kunsthalle Frankfurt, 1995.

Henderson, Linda Dalrymple. *The Fourth Dimension and Non-Euclidean Geometry in Modern Art*. Princeton, NJ: Princeton University Press, 1983.

Henning, Edward B. *Creativity in Art and Science, 1860–1960*. Cleveland: Cleveland Museum of Art in cooperation with Indiana University Press, 1987.

Herbert, Robert L. (ed.). *Modern Artists on Art*. New Jersey: Englewood Cliffs, 1965.

Hilscher, Eberhard. "Thomas Manns Beziehungen zur Philosophie und Naturwissenschaft." *Neue deutsche Hefte*, 23 (1976): 40–58.

Hodin, J.P. *Modern Art and the Modern Mind*. Cleveland: Case Western Reserve University Press, 1972.

Holton, Gerald and Yehuda Elkana (eds). *Albert Einstein: Historical and Cultural Perspectives*. Princeton, NJ: Princeton University Press, 1982.

Hughes, Robert. *Shock of the New*. New York: Alfred A. Knopf, 1980.

Huyssen, Andreas. *After the Great Divide: Modernism, Mass Culture, Postmodernism*. Bloomington: Indiana University Press, 1986.

Hye, Allen E. "Bertolt Brecht and Atomic Physics." *STTH: Science, Technology and the Humanities*, 1 (1978): 157–168.

Ivins, William, Jr. *Art and Geometry: A Study in Space Intuitions*. New York: Dover Publications, 1964. First published in 1946.

Ivins, William, Jr. *On the Rationalization of Sight, with an Examination of Three Renaissance Texts on Perspective*. (Paper no. 8). Da Capo, New York, 1973. First published in 1938.

Jacobus, John. *Matisse*. New York: Harry N. Abrams, 1983.

Jaffe, Hans L.C. *Picasso*. New York: Harry N. Abrams, 1983.

James, Henry. *The Golden Bowl*. Harmondsworth and New York: Penguin Books, 1987. First published in 1904.

James, Henry. *The Turn of the Screw*, ed. Robert Kimbrough. New York: Norton, 1966. First published in 1898.

Johnson, Julie M. "The Theory of Relativity in Modern Literature: An Overview and *The Sound and the Fury*." *Journal of Modern Literature*, 10, no. 2 (June 1983): 217–230.

Jordan, Jim M. *Paul Klee and Cubism*. Princeton, NJ: Princeton University Press, 1984.

Jordanova, L. J. (ed.) *Languages of Nature: Critical Essays on Science and Literature*. Foreword by Raymond Williams. New Brunswick, NJ: Rutgers University Press, 1986.

Joyce, James. *Dubliners*. Harmondsworth: Penguin Books, 1981. First published in 1914 but Joyce had tried to publish it as early as 1912.

Joyce, James. *A Portrait of the Artist as a Young Man*. New York: Viking, 1975. First published in 1916.

Kafka, Franz. *The Castle*, trans. Willa and Edwin Muir. New York: Schocken Books, 1974.

Kafka, Franz. *The Great Wall of China: Stories and Reflections*, trans. Willa and Edwin Muir. New York: Schocken Books, 1974.

Kafka, Franz. *The Penal Colony: Stories and Short Pieces*, trans. Willa and Edwin Muir. New York: Schocken Books, 1976.

Kafka, Franz. *The Trial*, trans. Willa and Edwin Muir. New York: Schocken Books, 1968.

Kahnweiler, Daniel-Henry. *Juan Gris: His Life and Work*, trans. Douglas Cooper. New York: Henry N. Abrams, 1946.

Keller, Alex. "Continuity and Discontinuity in Early Twentieth-Century Physics and Early Twentieth-Century Painting." In Pollock, *Common Denominators in Art and Science*.

Kepes, Gyorgy. "Introduction to the Issue 'The Visual Arts Today'." *Daedalus*, 89 (Winter 1960): 3–13.

Kern, Stephen. *The Culture of Time and Space 1880–1918*. Cambridge, MA: Harvard University Press, 1983.

Kiely, Robert (ed.) *Modernism Reconsidered*. Cambridge, MA: Harvard University Press, 1983.

Klee, Paul. *The Notebooks of Paul Klee*, ed. Jurg Spiller. New York: G. Wittenborn, 1961.

Klee, Paul. *On Modern Art*. London: Faber & Faber, 1984.

Klee, Paul. *Pedagogical Sketchbook*. London: Faber & Faber, 1984.

Knapp, James F. *Literary Modernism and the Transformation of Work*. Evanston, IL: Northwestern University Press, 1988.

Knust, Herbert. "Brechts Galileo-Evangelium." *Euphorion*, 79 (1985): 207–225.

Kostelanetz, Richard (ed.) *The Avant-Garde Tradition in Literature*. Buffalo, NY: Prometheus Books, 1982.

Kozloff, Max. *Cubism and Futurism*. New York: Harper and Row, 1973.

Kubler, George. "Comment." *Comparative Studies in Society and History*, 11 (1969) 398–402.

Kuhn, Thomas S. "Comment." *Comparative Studies in Society and History*, 11 (1969): 403–412, 426–430.

Kuhn, Thomas. *The Copernican Revolution*. Cambridge, MA: Harvard University Press, 1957.

Kuhn, Thomas S. *The Structure of Scientific Revolutions*. Chicago: University of Chicago Press, 1962.

Kumar, Shiv K. "Space-Time Polarity in *Finnegans Wake*." *Modern Philology*, 54 (1956–57): 320–333.

Kuznetsov, Boris. "Einstein and Dostoevski." *Diogenes*, 53 (1966): 1–16.

Langdon, M. "Some Reflections of Physics in *Finnegans Wake.*" *James Joyce Quarterly*, 17 (1979–80): 359–377.

Langer, Susanne K. "Abstraction in Science and Abstraction in Art" In *Problems of Art*. New York: Charles Scribner's Sons, 1957.

Langer, Suzanne K. "On Artistic Sensibility." *Daedalus*, 89 (Winter 1960): 242–245.

Langer, Susanne K. *Philosophical Sketches*. Baltimore, MD: Johns Hopkins University Press, 1962.

Laporte, Paul M. "Cubism and Relativity with a Letter of Albert Einstein." *Art Journal*, 25, no. 3 (Spring 1966): 246–248.

Laporte, Paul M. "Cubism and Science." *The Journal of Aesthetics and Art Criticism*, 7, no. 3 (March 1949): 243–256.

Laporte, Paul M. Letter to the Editor. *The Magazine of Art*, April 1948: 156.

Laporte, Paul M. "The Space-Time Concept in the Work of Picasso." *The Magazine of Art*, January 1948: 26–32.

Lawder, Standish D. *The Cubist Cinema*. New York: New York University Press, 1975.

Lawson, Hilary. *Reflexivity: The Post-Modern Predicament*. La Salle, IL: Open Court Paperbacks, 1985.

Leatherbarrow, W. J. "Einstein and the Art of Yevgeny Zamyatin." *Modern Language Review*, 82 (1987): 142–151.

Lebas, Gerard. "The Mechanisms of Space-Time in *The Alexandria Quartet.*" *Caliban*, 6, no. 1 (1970): 79–97.

Lentricchia, Frank. *Ariel and the Police: Michel Foucault, William James, Wallace Stevens*. Madison: University of Wisconsin Press, 1989.

Levin, Harry. "What Was Modernism?" In *Varieties of Literary Experience*, ed. Stanley Burnshaw. New York: New York University Press, 1962.

Levine, George. "Literary Science – Scientific Literature." *Raritan*, 6, no. 3 (1987): 24–41.

Levine, George. *The Realistic Imagination: English Fiction from Frankenstein to Lady Chatterley*. Chicago: University of Chicago Press, 1981.

Levine, George and Alan Rauch (eds) *One Culture: Essays in Science and Literature*. Madison: University of Wisconsin Press, 1987.

Lewis, Nancy W. "Lawrence Durrell's *Alexandria Quartet* and the Rendering of Post-Einsteinian Space." *Dissertation Abstracts International* 37 (1977).

Leymarie, Jean. *Georges Braque*. Munich: Prestel-Verlag, 1988. Published in conjunction with the exhibition *Georges Braque* held at the Solomon R. Guggenheim Museum, New York, June–September 1988.

Lista, Giovanni. *Le Futurisme*. Paris: Fernand Hazen, 1985.

Livingston, Paisley. *Literary Knowledge: Humanistic Inquiry and the Philosophy of Science*. Ithaca, NY: Cornell University Press, 1988.

Lovejoy, Arthur O. *The Great Chain of Being*. Cambridge, MA: Harvard University Press, 1936.

Lukács, Georg. *Studies in European Realism*. London: Merlin Press, 1972.

Lukács, Georg. *The Theory of the Novel*, trans. Anna Bostock. Cambridge, MA.: MIT Press, 1971.

Lyotard. Jean-François. *The Postmodern Condition: A Report on Knowledge*, trans. Geoff Bennington and Brian Massumi. Foreword by Fredric Jameson. Minneapolis: University of Minnesota Press, 1984.

McCloskey, Donald N. *The Rhetoric of Economics*. Madison: University of Wisconsin Press, 1985.

McCormmach, Russell. *Night Thoughts of a Classical Physicist*. New York: Avon Books, 1983.

McCully, Marilyn (ed.). *A Picasso Anthology: Documents, Criticism, Reminiscences*. Princeton, NJ: Princeton University Press, 1982.

McDaniel, Judith. "Wallace Stevens and the Scientific Imagination." *Contemporary Literature*, 15 (1974): 221-237.

Mach, Ernst. *The Science of Mechanics: A Critical and Historical Account of its Development*, trans. Thomas J. McCormack. LaSalle, IL: Open Court, 1960. First published in 1883.

McMorris, M.N. "Time and Reality in Eliot and Einstein." *Main Currents in Modern Thought*, 29 (1972–73): 91–99.

Magie, William F. "The Primary Concepts of Physics." *Science*, 35 (1912).

Mann, Thomas. "Death in Venice" (1911) in *Death in Venice and Seven Other Stories*, trans. H. T. Lowe-Porter. New York: Vintage Books, 1954.

Mann, Thomas. *Doctor Faustus: The Life of the German Composer Adrian Leverkühn as Told by a Friend*, trans. H. T. Lowe-Porter. New York: Vintage Books, 1971. First published in 1948.

Martin, Marianne W. *Futurist Art and Theory, 1919–1925*. Oxford: Clarendon Press, 1968.

Martin, Ronald E. *American Literature and the Universe of Force*. Durham, NC: Duke University Press, 1981.

Matisse, Henri. *Écrits et propos sur l'art*. Paris: Hermann, 1972.

Matisse, Henri. "Matisse Speaks." *Art News Annual*, 21 (1952).

Mellor, Anne K. "*Frankenstein*: A Feminist Critique of Science." In *One Culture: Essays in Science and Literature*, ed. George Levine and Alan Rauch. Madison: University of Wisconsin Press, 1987, pp. 287–312.

Melville, Herman. "Bartleby." In *Billy Budd, Sailor and Other Stories*. New York: Penguin, 1986.

Mermoz, Gérard. "On the Syncronism between Artistic and Scientific Ideas and Practices: An Exploration of Hypotheses, 1900–1930s," in Pollock, *Common Denominators in Art and Science*.

Meyerhoff, Hans. *Time in Literature*. Berkeley: University of California Press, 1955.

Michelson, Bruce. "The Tragic Scientists." In *Elizabethan and Modern Studies*, ed. J.P. Vander Motten. Ghent: Seminarie voor English and American Literature, Rijksuniversiteit Gent, 1985, pp. 173–180.

Miller, Arthur I. *Imagery in Scientific Thought: Creating 20th-Century Physics*. Boston: Birkhäuser, 1984.

Mook, Delo and Thomas Vargish. *Inside Relativity*. Princeton, NJ: Princeton University Press, 1987.

Moraze, Charles. *Les Origines sacrées des sciences modernes*. Paris: Fayard, 1986.

More, Louis. "The Theory of Relativity." *The Nation*, 94 (1912): 379, 371.

Moser, Walter. "The Factual in Fiction: The Case of Robert Musil." *Poetics Today*, 5 (1984): 411–428.

Muller, Herbert J. *Science and Criticism: The Humanistic Tradition in Contemporary Thought*. New Haven, CT: Yale University Press, 1943.

Muller, Joseph-Emile. *Cézanne*. Paris: Fernand Hazen, 1982.

Musil, Robert. *The Man without Qualities*, trans. Eithne Wilkins and Ernst Kaiser. New York: G. P. Putnam's Sons (Perigee Books), 1980.

Nabokov, Vladimir. *Ada*. New York: McGraw Hill, 1969.

Nabokov, Vladimir. *Pale Fire*. New York: Berkeley Medallion Books, no date but copyright 1962 by G. P. Putnam's Sons.

Nabokov, Vladimir. *Transparent Things*. New York: McGraw-Hill, 1972.

Nash, J. M. "The Nature of Cubism: A Study of Conflicting Explanations." *Art History*, 3, no. 4 (1980) 435.

Nelson, Norman E. "Science and the Irresponsible Imagination." *Yale Review*, 43 (1953–54): 71–88.

Newton, Sir Isaac. *Philosophiae Naturalis Principia Mathematica*, trans. Florian Cajori as *Sir Isaac Newton's Mathematical Principles of Natural Philosophy and His System of the World*. Berkeley: University of California Press, 1966. First published in 1687. Newton prepared three editions of the work, the last in 1726.

Nicholson, Marjorie Hope. *Newton Demands the Muse: Newton's Opticks and the Eighteenth Century Poets*. Princeton, NJ: Princeton University Press, 1946.

Opper, Jacob. *Science and the Arts: A Study in Relationships from 1600–1900*. Rutherford, NJ: Fairleigh Dickenson University Press, 1983.

Ortega y Gasset, José. *The Dehumanization of Art and Other Writings on Art and Culture*, trans. Helen Weyl et al. Princeton, NJ: Princeton University Press, 1968. First published in 1948.

Ortega y Gasset, José. *The Modern Theme*, trans. James Clough. New York: W. W. Norton, 1933. First published in 1923.

Panofsky, Irwin. *Meaning in the Visual Arts*. New York: Doubleday; Chicago: University of Chicago Press, 1955.

Park, David. *The Image of Eternity: Roots of Time in the Physical World*. Amherst, MA: University of Massachusetts Press, 1980.

Pawel, Ernst. *The Nightmare of Reason: A Life of Franz Kafka*. New York: Vintage Books, 1984.

Peacock, Ronald. "Abstraction and Reality in Modern Science, Art and Poetry." In *Literature and Science*. Proceedings of the 6th Triennial Congress of the International Federation for Modern Languages and Literatures, Oxford, 1954. Oxford: Blackwell, 1955, pp. 324–330.

Penrose, Roland. *Picasso: His Life and Work*. Berkeley: University of California Press, 1981. First published in 1958.

Perez-Gomez, Alberto. *Architecture and the Crisis of Modern Science*. Cambridge, MA: MIT Press, 1983.

Perloff, Marjorie. *The Futurist Moment: Avant-Garde, Avant Guerre, and the Language of Rupture*. Chicago and London: University of Chicago Press, 1986.

Philosophy of Science and Literary Theory. Special issue on "New Literary History", 17 (1985): 1–171.

Planck, Max. *Where is Science Going?* trans. and ed. James Murphy. London: G. Allen & Unwin, 1933.

Polkinghorne, J. C. *The Quantum World*. Princeton, NJ: Princeton University Press, 1984.

Pollock, Martin (ed.). *Common Denominators in Art and Science*. Proceedings of a discussion conference held under the auspices of the School of Epistemics, University of Edinburgh, November 1981. Aberdeen, Scotland: Aberdeen University Press, 1983.

Pope, Alexander. *The Complete Poetical Works of Pope*, ed. H.W. Boynton. Boston, MA: Houghton Mifflin, 1931.

Popper, Karl R. *The Logic of Scientific Discovery*. New York: Basic Books, 1959.

Prousok, Rudi. "Science in Mann's *Zauberberg*" *Publications of the Modern Language Association of America*, 88 (1973): 52–61.

Proust, Marcel. *Swann's Way*, trans. C. K. Scott Moncrieff. New York: Modern Library, 1956. First published in 1913.

Purdy, Strother B. *The Hole in the Fabric: Science, Contemporary Literature, and Henry James*. Pittsburgh: University of Pittsburgh Press, 1977.

Quinones, Ricardo. *Mapping Literary Modernism: Time and Development*. Princeton, NJ: Princeton University Press, 1977.

Rabinovitz, Robin. "Time, Space, and Verisimilitude in Samuel Beckett's Fiction." *Journal of Beckett Studies*, 2 (1977): 40–46.

Read, Herbert. *A Concise History of Modern Painting*. New York: Thames & Hudson, 1985.

Reiss, Timothy. *The Discourse of Modernism*. Ithaca, NY and London: Cornell University Press, 1982.

Rewald, John. *Post-impressionism from Van Gogh to Gauguin*. New York: Museum of Modern Art, 1956.

Richardson, J. A. *Modern Art and Scientific Thought*. Urbana: University of Illinois Press, 1971.

Ringhold, Francine. "The Metaphysics of Yoknapatawpha County: 'Airy Space and Scope for Your Delirium.'" *Hartford Studies in Literature*, 8 (1975–76): 223–240.

Root-Bernstein, Robert Scott. "On Paradigms and Revolutions in Science and Art: The Challenge of Interpretation." *Art Journal*, 44 (1984): 109–118.

Rorty, Richard. *Philosophy and the Mirror of Nature*. Princeton, NJ: Princeton University Press, 1979.

Rosenthal-Schneider, Ilse. *Reality and Scientific Truth*, ed. Thomas Brun. Detroit: Wayne State University Press, 1980.

Rothenberg, Albert. *The Emerging Goddess: The Creative Process in Art, Science, and Other Fields*. Chicago: University of Chicago Press, 1979.

Rubin, William (ed.) *Pablo Picasso: A Retrospective*. New York: Museum of Modern Art, 1980.

Rubin, William. *Picasso and Braque: Pioneering Cubism*. New York: Museum of Modern Art, 1989. Catalogue of the exhibition.

Rubin, William. *Picasso in the Collection of the Museum of Modern Art*. New York: Museum of Modern Art, 1980.

Russell, Bertrand. *The ABC of Relativity*, 3rd edn. New York: New American Library, 1969.

Ryan, Judith. *The Vanishing Subject: Early Psychology and Literary Modernism*. Chicago: University of Chicago Press, 1991.

Ryan, Steven T. "Faulkner and Quantum Mechanics." *Western Humanities Review*, 33 (1979): 329–339.

Saussure, Ferdinand de. *Course in General Linguistics*, trans. Wade Baskin. New York: McGraw-Hill, 1966. First published as *Cours de linguistique générale* in 1915.

Schapiro, Meyer. *Cézanne*. New York: Harry N. Abrams, 1988.

Schapiro, Meyer. "The Nature of Abstract Art." *Marxist Quarterly*, 1 no. 1 (January–March 1937), p. 83.

Schapiro, Meyer. "Style." In *Anthropology Today*, ed. Sol Tax. Chicago: University of Chicago Press, 1982, pp. 287–312.

Schapiro, Meyer. *Van Gogh*. New York: Harry N. Abrams, 1983.

Schatzberg, Walter, Ronald E. Waite, and Jonathan K. Johnson (eds) *The Relations of Literature and Science: An Annotated Bibliography of Scholarship, 1880–1980*. New York: Modern Language Association of America, 1987.

Scheick, William J. "The Fourth Dimension in Wells's Novels of the 1920s." *Criticism*, 20 (1978): 167–190.

Schilpp, Paul Arthur, ed. *Albert Einstein: Philosopher-Scientist*. La Salle, Illinois: Open Court Publishing, 1969.

Schlant, Ernestine. "Hermann Broch and Modern Physics." *Germanic Review*, 53 (1978): 69–75.

Schwartz, Sanford. *The Matrix of Modernism: Pound, Eliot, and Early Twentieth-Century Thought*. Princeton, NJ: Princeton University Press, 1985.

Schweber, Silvan. "Darwin and the Political Economists: Divergence of Character." *Journal of the History of Biology*, 13 (1980): 195.

Shakespeare, William. *Macbeth* in *The Complete Works*, ed. G. B. Harrison. New York: Harcourt Brace, 1952.

Shakespeare, William. *Hamlet*, ed. T.J.B. Spencer. Harmondsworth: Penguin, 1980.

Shlain, Leonard. *Art and Physics: Parallel Visions in Space, Time, and Light*. New York: Morrow, 1991.

Siegle, Robert. *The Politics of Reflexivity: Narrative and the Constitutive Poetics of Culture*. Baltimore, MD: Johns Hopkins University Press, 1986.

Spanos, William. *Repetitions: The Postmodern Occasion in Literature and Culture*. Baton Rouge: Louisiana State University Press, 1987.

Spencer, Sharon. *Space, Time and Structure in the Modern Novel*. New York: New York University Press, 1971; Chicago: Swallow, 1974.

Sperry, Roger. *Science and Moral Priority: Merging Mind, Brain and Human Values*. New York: Columbia University Press, 1983.

Sporn, Paul. "Physique moderne et critique contemporaine." *Poétique*, 17 (1986): 315–333.

Springer, Michael. "Wissenschaft und Phantastik: Am Beispiel von Albert Einstein und Stanislaw Lem." *Kurbiskern*, 1 (1980): 71–88.

Stein, Gertrude. *Picasso*. New York: Dover Publications, 1984. First published in 1938.

Steinberg, Leo. "The Eye Is a Part of the Mind." *Partisan Review*, vol. 20, no. 2 (1953), pp. 194–212.

Steiner, George. *On Difficulty and Other Essays*. New York: Oxford University Press, 1978.

Stendhal, *Scarlet and Black*, trans. Margaret R. B. Shaw. Harmondsworth: Penguin, 1965. First published as *Le Rouge et le noir* in 1830.

Stent, Gunther S. "Creation in Art and Science." *Interdisciplinary Science Review*, 8 (1983): 371–378.

Stern, J. P. *On Realism*. London and Boston: Routledge & Kegan Paul, 1973.

Stevenson, Randall. *Modernist Fiction: An Introduction*. Hemel Hempstead, Herts: Harvester Wheatsheaf, 1992.

Stone, Edward. "From Henry James to John Balderston: Relativity and the '20s." *Modern Fiction Studies*, 1, no. 2 (1955): 2–11.

Suppe, Frederick (ed.) *The Structure of Scientific Theories*. Urbana: University of Illinois Press, 1977.

Sypher, Wylie. *Rococo to Cubism in Art and Literature*. New York: Random House, 1960.

Terrel, Denise. "Science et esthétique: La Science-fiction et l'espace einsteinien." *Caliban*, 22 (1985): 67–85.

Thiher, Allen. "The Nachlass: Metaphors of *Gehen* and Ways toward Science." In *Kafka and the Contemporary Critical Performance: Centenary Readings*, ed. Alan Udoff. Bloomington: Indiana University Press, 1987, pp. 256–265.

Topper, David R. and John H. Holloway. "Interrelationships between the Visual Arts, Science, and Technology: A Bibliography." *Leonardo*, 13 (1980): 29–33.

Torgovnick, Marianna. *The Visual Arts, Pictorialism, and the Novel: James, Lawrence, and Woolf*. Princeton, NJ: Princeton University Press, 1985.

Tribe, Laurence H. "The Curvature of Constitutional Space: What Lawyers Can Learn from Modern Physics." *Harvard Law Review*, 103, no. 1 (November 1989): 1–39.

Tyler, Stephen. *The Unspeakable: Discourse, Dialogue, and Rhetoric in the Modern World*. Madison: University of Wisconsin Press, 1987.

Tyrrell, H.J.V. "Science, Art and History: Where the Cultures Meet." *Proceedings of the Royal Institution of Great Britain*, 51 (1979): 45–67.

Vargish, Thomas. *The Providential Aesthetic in Victorian Fiction*. Charlottesville: University Press of Virginia, 1985.

Venturelli, Aldo. "Kunst und Wissenschaften in den Kapiteln 71 und 72 des *Mann ohne Eigenschaften*." *Musil-Forum*, 10 (1984–85): 159–169.

Virtanen, Reino. "Proust's Metaphors from the Natural and the Exact Sciences." *Publications of the Modern Language Association*, 69 (1954): 1038–1059.

Vitz, Paul C. and Arnold B. Glimcher. *Modern Art and Modern Science: The Parallel Analysis of Vision*. New York: Praeger, 1983.

Waddington, Conrad H. *Behind Appearance: A Study of the Relations between Painting and the Natural Sciences in This Century*. Cambridge, MA: MIT Press, 1969.

Waggoner, Hyall A. "Archibald MacLeish and the Aspect of Eternity." *College English*, 4 (1942–43): 402–412.

Walter-Echols, Elizabeth. "Science as Metaphor in Hermann Broch's *Die Schuldlosen*." *Kentucky Philological Association Bulletin*, 1979: 27–36.

Watt, Ian. *The Rise of the Novel: Studies in Defoe, Richardson, and Fielding*, 3 vols. London: Chatto & Windus, 1960.

Weaver, Jefferson Hane. *The World of Physics*. New York: Simon & Schuster, 1987.

Weinberg, Stephen. *Dreams of a Final Theory*. New York: Vintage Books, 1993.

Weisskopf, Victor. "Art and Science." *Leonardo*, 14, no. 3 (1981): 238–242.

Weisskopf, Victor. "Science and Art: Complementary Views of Human Experience." *Ernanos-Jahrbuch*, 53 (1984; pub. 1986): 311–323.

Wetzels, Walter. "Relativitätstheorie gemeinverstandich: techniken popularwissen- schaftlicher Didaktik am Beispiel Albert Einsteins." *Zeitschrift für Literaturwissenschaft und Linguistik* 10 (1980): 14–24.

Whitehead, A.N. *An Enquiry Concerning the Principles of Natural Knowledge.* Cambridge: Cambridge University Press, 1919.

Whitehead, A.N. *Science and the Modern World.* New York: The Free Press, 1967. First published in 1925.

Whittaker, Sir Edmund. *A History of the Theories of Aether and Electricity,* 2 vols. New York: Harper Torchbooks, 1953. First published in 1910.

Wilde, Alan. *Horizons of Assent: Modernism, Postmodernism, and the Ironic Imagination.* Baltimore, MD: Johns Hopkins University Press, 1981.

Will, Clifford M. *Was Einstein Right: Putting General Relativity to the Test.* New York: Basic Books, 1986.

Williams, L. Pearce. *Relativity Theory: Its Origins and Impact on Scientific Thought.* Malabar, FL: Robert E. Krieger, 1968.

Woolf, Virginia. *The Waves.* New York: Harcourt, Brace, Jovanovich, 1959. First published in 1931.

Yourgrau, Wolfgang. "On the New Physics and Modern Literature." *Denver Quarterly,* 1 (1966–67): 29–41.

Zadworna-Fjellestad, Danuta and Lennart Björk (eds). *Criticism in the Twilight Zone.* Stockholm: Almqvist & Wiksell International, 1990.

Zayes, Marius de. "Picasso Speaks." *The Arts,* 1923: 319.

Ziolkowski, Theodore. "Hermann Broch and Relativity in Fiction." *Wisconsin Studies in Contemporary Literature,* 8 (1967): 365–376.

Index